Modello

A Story of Hope for the Inner City and Beyond

An Inside-Out Model
of Prevention and Resiliency in Action
through Health Realization

Jack Pransky

NEHRI PUBLICATIONS

NorthEast Health Realization Institute
RR 2 Box 2340
Cabot VT 05647
802.563.2730 FAX 802.563.3351

Modello: A Story of Hope for the Inner-City and Beyond: An Inside-Out Model of Prevention and Resiliency in Action through Health Realization. © 1998 by Jack B. Pransky. All rights reserved. Printed in the United States of America

No part of this book may be used or reproduced in any manner without written permission from NEHRI Publications or the author except for brief, credited quotations embedded in articles and reviews. For information, address NEHRI Publications, NorthEast Health Realization Institute, RR 2 Pransky Rd, Cabot, VT 05647.

Typesetting and design by Russell Smith
Editing by Ronnie Wood

Library of Congress Cataloging-in-Publication Date
Pransky, Jack B.
    Modello: A Story of Hope for the Inner-City and Beyond: An
    Inside-Out Model of Prevention and Resiliency in Action
    through Health Realization / Jack Pransky — 1st ed.
    p. cm.
ISBN 0-9659057-1-3   (PBK): $23.00
1. Sociology 2. Prevention 3. Health Realization 4. Psychology of
Mind 5. Resiliency   I. Title
Library of Congress Catalog Card Number: 98-091465
                                        1998 CIP

Hope is one of the greatest things in the world, so this is why you talk stories.

— Sydney Banks

People's lives become what they think is possible.

— Roger Mills

Acknowledgements

From the bottom of my heart I thank Roger Mills, George Pransky, and Syd Banks for bringing this new understanding into our consciousness.

In memoriam to Robert Thomas, a wonderful human being.

Thank you Wendy Soliday, for inviting me to that conference in Burlington.

Thanks to Janis Solek-Tefft for early editorial suggestions and to Judy Sedgeman for her support and liaison work.

Special thanks goes to Ronnie Wood for her editing and to John Wood for their wondrous generosity.

Very special thanks goes to all the people who graciously allowed me to interview them, and especially to Lloyd Fields and Cynthia Stennis for helping me so much with this book.

No words can begin to describe the gratitude I have for Pam Gibson for all her work in helping this book come to fruition.

Most special of all are the women from these housing projects who opened their lives to new possibilities and who, through their receptivity and openness with me during our interviews, are living proof of a better way and that it's there for the taking—for all. These lovely ladies have shown us the way.

Foreword

> *Stories remind us of our grand nature and our infinite*
> *possibilities. They awaken us from our habitual day-to-day*
> *lives, invite us to dream, and inspire us to do more and be*
> *more than we might have originally thought possible.*
>
>

—Canfield and Hansen
> ***A 3rd Serving of Chicken Soup***
> ***for the Soul***
>

What you are about to read is a remarkable story.

This story, indeed, shows us the "grand nature and infinite possibilities" living within every person—even those society would rather forget, blame or write off: low-income mothers and their children in urban America. The story of Modello, however, is a story of hope, a story of what can happen when people—no matter their race, class, ethnicity, gender—realize their innate resilience—the power they possess to transform and change their lives.

The lives chronicled so faithfully here create a tapestry and give a texture and richness to the powerful long term studies of human resilience. This body of research has scientifically established that, among other things, human beings have an innate "self-righting mechanism" propelling them to healthy development and learning (Werner and Smith, *Overcoming the Odds*, 1992). Furthermore, the stories of these changed lives put faces on the statistics identified in earlier evaluations of the Health Realization approach applied in Modello/Homestead Gardens—significant reductions in child abuse, delinquency, dropping out, drug trafficking, teen pregnancy, and significant improvements in parent-child relationships.

Ultimately, the story of Modello and Homestead Gardens demonstrates that Health Realization offers the prevention, education, and intervention fields the best examples for how resilience operates—what I call the "Black Box" in resilience research. It shows us that resilience is there at all times for all people—if we understand we have it, and if we choose to access it by letting go of our conditioned thinking. Health Realization also offers an explanation for why the "protective factors" of caring relationships, positive beliefs, and opportunities for participation and contribution emerge in study after study as the critical variables promoting successful development and learning. It is in the presence of this rapport, respect, and engagement that individuals more easily relax, let go of their conditioned thoughts, and access their innate common sense, wisdom, and well-being.

The story told so eloquently here shows us how simple and commonsensical are solutions to even seemingly intractable social problems like poverty and racism. In these times when many people are feeling a growing sense of powerlessness to change society, *Modello* demonstrates that social change is an inside-out process. It starts with each of our hearts and minds, with our thoughts about ourselves and others.

Finally, it is up to us to spread this compelling story, a story that connects us at a deep level with stories of all our lives, that binds us together in our shared humanity.

Bonnie Benard
Resiliency Associates
Berkeley, California

Author's Note~Preface

As the two women spoke I sat mesmerized, transfixed, deeply moved. Nowhere in all my years in the field of prevention of social problem behaviors had I seen such a level of change in people. Clearly, something had happened to them of such magnitude that their lives would never be the same. They would never turn back. My book, *Prevention: The Critical Need* was about to go to press. I had just spent three years of my life researching what worked in prevention, but I had never seen results like this.

It did something for my hope.

Serendipity. In late 1990 a guidance counselor in my children's school named Wendy Soliday had invited me to attend that conference in Burlington, Vermont. She had been looking for parent representatives and knew of my interest in prevention. I did not expect to hear anything new. A Dr. Roger Mills was the keynote speaker and brought the two housing project residents with him. Mills had introduced a completely new approach to prevention and community change, and the results he achieved in two drug and violence-infested low-income, inner-city housing projects were nothing short of astonishing.

Instead of working to change unhealthy, destructive conditions that kept people immersed in problems, this approach, called "Psychology of Mind" (or, later, "Health Realization" when applied to prevention), attempted to change people and communities from the inside-out. Dr. Mills spoke of how "innate mental health" was present in everyone and could be drawn out; it was obscured only by the way people held and used their thinking. I had no idea what

Mills was talking about—but I couldn't run away from what I witnessed in the two women.

After the talk I introduced myself to Dr. Mills.

"Are you related to George Pransky?" he asked.

Apparently, unbeknownst to me, my second cousin had co-founded Psychology of Mind with Roger Mills.

I stopped the presses of my *Prevention* book and managed to squeeze in a brief description of the Modello project.

A few months later, while reading the book, *Teacher*, about how principal Dennis "Doc" Littky turned around a terrible school in Southern New Hampshire, the thought popped into my head, "I wonder if I could write a similar book about what happened in Modello—the true story as it unfolded, and how it changed people's lives."

Roger Mills approved my idea. We arranged interviews, and I was about to fly to south Florida when I saw Hurricane Andrew bearing down on my destination. I decided to wait.

When I arrived a month later, everything had changed. The area was devastated. Everyone had been moved out of the Modello Housing Project.

Thanks to Lloyd Fields and Cynthia Stennis, two of Dr. Mills's former staff on the project, I was able to track down and interview many of the people whose lives had most improved. I was even more deeply touched by the powerful and lasting changes that had occurred in these women's lives. If I could only find out how this change had occurred and get the story out I believed it could be immensely helpful to humanity. What had made so much difference in their lives? I had to investigate. I needed to understand it for myself. So I began to study the principles and concepts embodied in Psychology of Mind.

To my utter amazement, after a while I found my own life changing. Before I knew it, I was seeing through different eyes. My life had been going along fine; suddenly it was even better. I was more peaceful, more content. I took things more in stride, less personally. I was less stressed at work. My relationship with my wife and kids had been going pretty well; suddenly it was wonderful. And the change was effortless; I only realized it when I looked back and saw it.

What was happening to me? I was only supposed to be an investigative reporter!

I can only hope that this book is as helpful to humanity as learning about these principles has been to me, as it has been to so many people whose lives have changed as a result—from some of the worst situations to some of the healthiest and happiest.

Important note: Many people contributed to the success of this story. The real heroes, however, are the housing project residents who opened themselves up to the new, who put themselves on the line, who took the risks, who took a chance to let go enough of what they believed to allow their innate health to rise to the surface and change their lives. For their bravery the rest of us benefit immeasurably. For this we are forever grateful, for these ladies (as they like to be called) proved that such change is possible.

In the process of writing this book the ladies took it upon themselves to remind me in no uncertain terms how important it was for me to respect the story exactly as it happened—with no embellishment—and to respect their privacy and desire to not be used or exploited. To that end, as much as humanly possible, I have endeavored to portray the story exactly as conveyed to me by the residents, the staff, and others who witnessed it. Within the text the tone is as they expressed it. The quotes are exact except where I changed words or phrases in the interest of understandability.

At their request their names have been changed to protect their privacy.

Jack Pransky
Cabot, VT
May, 1998

I. Modello

This is a book about hope, about the triumph of the human spirit, about how all people have something inside them so powerful, so beautiful, so resilient that once tapped even some of the most terrible living conditions can be overcome.

It is a story of discovery, of profound yet simple truths, of how a "new" understanding of the human mind changed lives in one of the most violent and dangerous low-income, inner city housing projects in South Florida.

What is this understanding? Put simply, it is that everyone has an innate capacity for health and well-being, for wisdom and common sense, and this health, when brought to light, when truly realized, once unleashed, can create the "miracle" of change.

Only one's thinking keeps it hidden, buried, obscured from view—overriding it by making other things appear so "real."

At first nearly everyone thought Dr. Roger Mills crazy. How could he bring such ideas into this kind of environment? How could he expect anyone to listen? How could he expect anyone to care? He would be laughed right out of the projects—or worse!

Yet, two and a half years later, many lives and destructive conditions had changed.

This book is not the place for statistics. Statistics are boring and statistics can mislead. But most all who knew would agree that in the Modello and Homestead Gardens housing projects violence, delinquency, child abuse and neglect, alcohol and drug abuse, truancy, teenage pregnancy, and welfare dependency decreased markedly. Many residents improved their education and secured jobs.

In a nation seeking answers to violence, to crime and drugs, to abuse and poverty, to welfare dependency, to the hopelessness of the inner-city and beyond, what took place in the Modello and Homestead Gardens public housing projects cannot be ignored. What happened there has implications for humankind.

It all began in a place called Modello . . .

* * *

The Modello Housing Project was someone's idea of "model" living quarters for poor people. They stuck it out of the way on the outskirts of Miami, a city that seems to extend forever south down U.S. 1, spilling over its borders into Perrine, Goulds, Naranja, Leisure City, Homestead, into areas not considered part of any official "city" or "town."

Modello's dreary beige buildings foretold the mess, the roughness, the tragedy within. Residents feared leaving their units, for shootings had become a way of life, as had the crack, the dealers, the gangs, robberies, beatings, prostitution—the utter despair of it all.

We begin with what it was like to live there, in the words of the people who lived it.

Lisa: There was lots and lots of crime, a lot of mothers, mostly, feeling like they were trapped in the situation they were in, including myself—a lot of feelings about your children growing up in this type of environment. Because there were drugs galore, people breaking into your houses, fights—women fighting each other like animals out in the street—no one wanting to talk about anything, a lot of problems dealing with the kids.

Cicely: Drugs were real bad. Gangs were on every corner. There were shootouts every day. All the kids were running around like there was no school. That's how bad Modello was, for about three or four years.

Lisa: It started getting real bad around '78, then by '83 it was really rough out there.

Cicely: People wouldn't even walk out their door.

Lisa: When I'd get home I'd have to run people off my front porch because they were shooting dice right on my front door. Then they'd start complaining because you'd ask them to leave. I mean, it was bold! It was nothing to be sitting on your front porch with your children and have people drive by with random shootings—and you'd throw the kids in the house because the cops were chasing them or the drug dealers were shooting at each other. It was rough. There was a lot of falling on your knees during that time, dodging bullets. When they started, there wasn't any looking around trying to be nosy. It was—hit the ground!

Cicely: There were a lot of people that wouldn't come in there, like for pizza [delivery]. No way would they come in there any more.

Lisa: You couldn't even get a taxi. They said that they were told not to go in there. It had gotten so bad that I actually called the police one time for a friend, and they asked me to meet them out on the street because they didn't even want to come in there. It was so bad that the police didn't even want to come in, and they wanted me to go out of my house! And I'm, like, "Are you crazy!? You've got the guns and the car, and I'm going to walk out there!? It's 10:00 at night. I'm not going to walk down on U.S. 1 and flag down a cop." That was how bad it was.

Cicely: Two or three times a week at night people would just go in there robbing, and some got shot in there. I mean, it was really rough.

Lisa: Everyone felt such hopelessness. It was depressing. It felt like we were in this world, and everyone else was in another world. It was, like, this is what my life is going to be.

Cicely: Everybody felt like there was nothing we could do. We were just tired.

Lisa: We couldn't even dream of things we wanted to do.

Cicely: Our lives were at a standstill like.

Patty: I had moved in from across town. It was very bad. My kids, they used to hear gun shots at all times at night, and people talking loud and all kinds of noises going on outside the window. People would come looking in the windows!

Thelma: We couldn't even go out to the clothesline to hang our clothes, because they'd be shooting. We couldn't go to the store. And sitting on the porch was a no-no. You couldn't even get on no porch, there were so many dealers on your front and back porch.

People were getting killed, robbed. Ooooh, it was so bad! Little children walking around with no one looking after them. Police running after other children with crack. It was bad. It was so rough.

Sam MacKinnon [Perrine Optimists]: Young men were selling drugs right out in the street, just like it was a normal transaction—no problem. Robberies were occurring at night where you would see guys brandishing guns right in front of the children. Kids were going around playing "crackman." You know, they'd pick up leaves and they'd pick up rocks, and they'd be selling the leaves for the rocks.

Pam Gibson [Housing and Urban Development]: When we first went in there it was not unusual to have helicopters flying overhead looking for people. Obviously the drugs were hot and heavy, and it was during the time that crack was really hitting a high pitch and fever. So we had a lot of women that were selling their daughters as prostitutes so that they would have drug money. It was a horrible place. It really was.

Sam: You had prostitution being done in the open where children were able to see it. They could walk around one corner and see one guy having oral sex. And there were times at night where in the middle of the basketball court there was a spectacle of having sex.

Pam: We had a guy they call S.M., who had been shot by the police a few years earlier and had been in prison, and when he came out he was never quite the same. He would come out every once in a while, cock his shotgun and tell everybody, "It's time to do roll call!" So kids grew up around that. Actually, he kind of kept order because he also had this big fan-back chair that he would sit on at his corner, and he would give the guys so many sells, and then he'd send them home. He'd say, "You don't have to make that much money. You just make a certain amount." So he kind of kept them from fighting each other. Rather than twenty people running to your car, he'd send them out one at a time. "Okay, you've made enough money today. Come on!" There were some real characters in Modello.

Dr. Roger Mills: There were six entrances into the Modello project, and there was a different gang at every entrance. It was like the Burger King of drug dealing. People would drive through and get their crack and drive away. There were shootouts every night between these gangs, turf battles. It was just like the wild west, literally.

Sam: There were a lot of robberies committed by people who didn't live here, and a lot of inter-violence for those who did live here—one family against another family.

Pam: So many times in Modello when we first started working there people would not even communicate with each other. I mean, they were mortal enemies. "You don't cross my area!" "You don't come into my territory." "You don't touch my kids or talk to them."

Sam: The dropout rate was ridiculous. I think there were only three kids in the high school at that time. Junior high was the break point. Once they got to junior high that was the farthest they would pretty much go. I think there had only been like a few graduates before that. It was just heading nowhere. It was a dead-end street.

Pam: I remember we had one kid who would sleep out on the slide at night, and even when his parents left the area he would come into Modello and sleep out on the slide. I'm talking about an eight or nine year old kid. There was also a pedophile in the neighborhood. It was really kind of odd because nobody really did anything about it, and so you'd have your young kids subjected to that. He was a kid himself—18 or 19, so legally he's not a kid, but mentally he wasn't there—and he was sexually molesting kids. The kids had to look at everything. You'd come home and find crack on your doorstep. You saw people getting high. You saw people doing things that wouldn't happen in your or my neighborhood. You saw people get shot and killed. You saw people die a lot. We had babies die—from neglect—a lot of that. The kids there were exposed to all that. It was chaos initially. It was hard to believe that people lived the way that they did. I mean, you don't live in your neighborhood and have helicopters fly overhead searching for people. You don't have people living in vacant units and doing whatever they want. You don't have people fondling one another in the middle of the project—a woman doing a blow job so she can get a little bit of money for crack. You don't have that everywhere. Everything that's normal to us was abnormal to them.

Major Tom Lamont (Metro-Dade Police): We staked out drug deals [at Modello] and got attacked. People threw bottles and rocks at us. Officers and citizens got hurt.

Florida Magazine (10/87): Modello is not some fine wine. It's the ugliest welfare project in Dade County, a county with 60 ugly welfare projects, 12,000 ugly welfare apartments. Modello is near Homestead, 25 miles from Miami, a million miles from the flashiness and big money of downtown Brickell Avenue. It is home to 100 women, virtually all of them black welfare mothers. It is also home to 100 teenagers and 300 children who squat on asphalt, play with cartons, crawl under pilfered shopping carts. Mary lives at Modello. She fought with all her strength against moving there because she had heard stories of its crime and desolation. But she has four children and no job. It was Modello or nothing.

Dr. William Stokes (United Way Task Force, 3/87): You name it, and it's a problem in Modello.

Rosie (*Miami Herald*, 6/87): The image of this place has always been so bad. But it's not that the residents here are lazy. It's just that Modello has been neglected for so long.

II. The Idea~1985-1987

Dade County State Attorney Janet Reno knew she had to take action.

The July, 1984 Grand Jury report had issued a stark challenge: Black youths from inner-city housing projects in Dade County were dropping out of school at alarming rates, followed by "unemployment and a self-perpetuating cycle of alienation and failure." They entered kindergarten at a significant disadvantage that multiplied as they moved through school. Black males from these neighborhoods were far more likely to be in jail by the age of twenty-five and become involved with drugs and crime than any other group. Black females from these neighborhoods were more likely to become pregnant as teenagers. The school, the neighborhood and family all had to assume equal responsibility. Serious action needed to be taken—now!

Reno assigned the task to her able Chief Assistant State Attorney, Tom Petersen, who had staffed the Grand Jury report. "Tom is the only one who would be able to pull this off," she said. He hated the blight of public housing. He hated to see all those wasted lives. He was a passionate, intense person—a doer. Besides, his heart yearned to be working out in the field.

Reno pulled together the Dade County Superintendent and the County Manager to form an intergovernmental consortium to tackle the problems in low-income, inner-city neighborhoods. She offered Tom Petersen an official leave of absence from state attorney office duties to head the consortium. Reno's office would pay one-third of his salary, Metro-Dade County and Dade County Public Schools the other two-thirds.

Tom was thrilled. He had been a VISTA volunteer in the early war-on-poverty days, organizing Dade County's first pre-trial release program where people charged with minor crimes could work out an arrangement with the state attorney's office to perform community service in lieu of a trial. He would now have the opportunity to prevent problems up front; of crime, school failure, drug abuse, welfare dependency and more.

On April 5, 1985 Janet Reno proposed "an experiment" to deal with the problems described in the Grand Jury report.

The studies uniformly reveal that inner city students enter kindergarten testing significantly below their non inner city counterparts and that the gap between the two groups widens as the student progresses from elementary school to junior high school to high school. The problem is a complex one that can only be dealt with in the context of the inner city child's family and neighborhood . . . No one agency is responsible for these problems. Their solution must involve a joint effort of the schools, social service agencies and the criminal justice system.

Reno proposed a five point interagency effort: 1) academic intervention; 2) parent involvement; 3) coordinated efforts against crime and delinquency, substandard housing and neighborhood environmental problems; 4) organized activities and services; 5) economic development to enhance welfare recipients' self-sufficiency.

She told Tom to let her know in which neighborhoods he wanted to start. They'd select a few, then he could pull people together and move in.

With unbounded enthusiasm Petersen set about his task. With Tom's talents he could have been a wealthy, successful corporate lawyer, but his interests lay elsewhere. Money didn't matter to him— a good thing because this project paid little. What did matter were victories such as when he'd gotten 300 women who'd been arrested for welfare fraud out of jail and into community service. They'd been moonlighting, flipping hamburgers at minimum wage to pull in a few extra bucks to support their children. They hadn't told the welfare office and were nabbed. It didn't seem fair. It started Tom thinking about what living in welfare housing does to people. Now his boss afforded him the chance to do what he'd always wanted. Tom felt grateful for Janet Reno. Few state or district attorneys acted preventively. Most were too busy reacting after the fact while poverty and resulting problems worsened.

Reno and Petersen knew that only in collaboration with other agencies and professionals could they make a real difference. Tom would develop programs at the neighborhood level with full participation from residents. This was Tom's signature talent: to pull together all manner of people toward a common end, to bring together all types of agencies to coordinate services.

To begin they selected three of the toughest communities in Miami. Two were public housing projects: Larchmont Gardens in Overtown, and Liberty Square. The Department of Housing and Urban Development (HUD) had to be involved, for they essentially served as landlords.

Petersen worked simultaneously on two fronts: drawing together local and county agencies into action, and hanging out in the projects to meet residents, identify natural leaders, understand their problems and gently bring folks along at their own pace. Tom felt quite comfortable in this role. Never intimidated, naturally friendly and helpful, Tom would hang out with anyone, anywhere. People from all walks of life usually responded in kind.

In early 1986 the "experiment" began with a grocery store in Larchmont Gardens, operated by the residents. Not only would it provide on-premise groceries, but it would serve also as a training opportunity for mothers on welfare, offering them a chance to make it into the job market and stand on their own feet. It was so successful that six months later a similar store opened in Liberty Square, then a day care center. Larchmont Gardens added a preschool, a Medical Clinic, and Little League baseball. Service providers were deployed to the projects. It all provided a ray of hope and a new sense of spirit among at least some residents.

As usual, the south end of the county felt neglected. Liberty City and Overtown always got the attention and money. South Dade County had the same problems, yet it seemed no one cared. Pressure mounted from a South Dade Task Force formed recently by the United Way. Its chairperson, William Stokes, President of Miami Dade Community College Kendall Campus, pushed Tom to select a site in the south. Robert Thomas, "a terrific guy" from United Way who staffed the Task Force had recently written a report suggesting a possible site, a place called Modello.

The Modello Housing Project was not only one of the worst housing projects around, it also had space for agencies to move into and work.

Tom Petersen: When I first came down to Modello I did what I did in Liberty Square and Larchmont Gardens—go down and hang out, after a while try to find two or three women who seem to be recognized as leaders, then do a survey. I put together a questionnaire, and they would go door-to-door to everybody in the project. I would pay them, and the people they interviewed also got $5.00 for participating in the questionnaire. Then we had a meeting to discuss the results. Then we started talking about the store. That was a long process. We were in our third housing project, and I went back to the consortium and said, "I really need an assistant, somebody else to do this, especially because of the geographic distance between Modello and the other places."

Tom proved a whiz at securing grant money and in April, 1986 hired Pam Gibson, an attractive, tough, caring, blonde-haired woman to assist him. Pam had been a seasoned community organizer since 1983 and now worked for HUD. Pam offered what Tom lacked: experience with the players in South Dade. She had worked in other South Dade housing projects and knew some folks in Modello.

Pam: They were always shocked by Tom a little bit. If they didn't know him through his association with Janet Reno, he was very personable and always going to people's houses. Most people come in and say, "I have a program for you." He had a survey, and he sat down with people. There was a year of planning and pulling together before there was any structure.

They set their sights on opening a Modello store. This brought almost immediate trust. They were offering something tangible: easy access to groceries, economic development, a few jobs.

Modello had no conveniences, not even a soda machine—not that one would have remained in working order had it been there. Residents had to "walk a half-mile through the weeds along U.S. Highway 1, past whizzing cars and through dust, to buy groceries at Winn Dixie." To buy candy at Circle K.A. store, their children had to cross the four lane highway and "would be robbed blind in five minutes."

Tom found the perfect spot for the store, a trashed out community center near one of Modello's other centers of commerce, a prime crack-dealing corner. From the Miami business community Tom secured seed funding, and the store opened in the spring of 1987.

Tom and Pam hired two residents, Carrie Mae and Mary, and trained them to work the store counter. Both were fairly typical Modello residents. Mary, for example, was a 24 year old who had grown up in Homestead yet had never been to Miami. She "had fought with all her strength against moving there because she had heard stories of its crime and desolation. But she has four children and no job. It was Modello or nothing . . . She was a smart girl, a spelling bee champ. But she had to pick beans for a week each month. So she fell behind. In high school, she dropped out, ran off, and at 16, had her first baby. At 24 Mary's life had run out . . ."

With Tom's connection to the state attorney's office providing instant clout, he and the United Way Task Force drew in over twenty agencies. The Department of Human Resources assigned a drug counselor. Youth and Family Development assigned another counselor. The schools became involved. Tom brought in the Private Industry Council (PIC) to provide job training. The Perrine Optimists opened a base of operations to help with crime prevention and hired Sam MacKinnon. The YWCA opened a child care center in the building adjacent to the store in the center of the projects. All bases were covered.

Service providers descended on the projects like a swarm of bees. Pam had the task of coordinating all. This quickly became overwhelming. Modello was not a large site, and all services were supposed to operate out of a "pathetic, dimly lit" set of offices behind the store—so tiny not everyone could fit at once. Fortunately the workers were only assigned there part time. Pam arranged office hours but occasionally they still tripped over each other.

Frustration began to mount. Tom put Pam in charge of the store which was not an instant success. It began to eat away at her time. Worse, Pam watched the programs come in with their set packages without bothering to adjust to Modello's special needs. Pam heard many service providers complain, "This client doesn't want to cooperate." "These people just don't want to help themselves!" When a "client" didn't fit the mold the service providers blamed the clients. As a trained community organizer always trying to meet people's needs as they defined them, Pam could not abide this mentality. She didn't see a lot of stretching to find out what about their agency programs may not fit this community. Many providers became disgruntled. They'd offer short-term programs and, eventually, one-by-one, drop out.

One agency provided a jobs package and fired up residents to take courses at the skills center. When completed they were supposed to end up with decent jobs. Once their training ended, however, they wouldn't get hired. They still had no degree nor any real credentials. Expectations raised, nothing delivered, hopes dashed once again. The residents became disgusted and angry, and walked.

Another agency sent in a young female social worker who was afraid to come into Modello. She insisted on being escorted in and out. She was terrified of her clients—not overly conducive to establishing productive working relationships. It didn't last.

Reno, Peterson, and the United Way had only the best of intentions, sincerely wanting to make a real difference and believing they could. They came in with cameras rolling and speeches, and they did make some difference. But expectations proved unrealistic. Residents became disappointed. Some were downright angry. Pam complained to Tom. It concerned him. Besides, a grant he'd secured was about to end. He needed to find some way of continuing funds for Rosie, the powerful resident leader he had hired.

Maybe he should give a shot to this strange man he couldn't figure out who seemed to latch on to the goings-on at Modello, who was always hanging around wanting to start some kind of program: Dr. Roger Mills.

Tom Peterson had met Roger Mills through a colleague at the University of Miami where, in Tom's spare time, he was involved in a study of delinquency. His co-researcher, Dr. Nancy Peck, had met Dr. Mills who had recently begun to teach a class there. Through her Roger had learned of Tom's efforts and persuaded her to take him to a community meeting that Tom was holding in Larchmont Gardens.

Mills became intrigued with Tom's approach. Trained as a community organizer himself Roger loved the idea of bringing together the university and all major agencies to solve the seemingly unsolvable problems of the inner city. Plus, he saw an opportunity to test out some of his new ideas. He and a few colleagues had been developing a new approach to psychology, and he wondered whether it could be applied preventively in neighborhoods such as these. Robert Thomas, whose wife Ann was a colleague of Roger's at an institute developed to promulgate these ideas, suggested that he look into what was happening in Modello.

* * *

Dr. Roger Mills got out of his car and walked into the Modello Housing Project looking like the man in the moon—unlike anything that would have been moving in the projects—seemingly oblivious to all the danger and turmoil around him. With his round face, toothy grin, straight blonde-slightly-graying hair that hung over his forehead, a barrel-chested football player body looking a bit worn by father time, wearing suspenders to hold up his pants, the man simply looked out of place.

A few moments before he'd nonchalantly waved hello and smiled at the drug gang hanging out at the project entrance as he drove in.

"How are you doing?" he said cheerfully.

It had taken them by surprise. From a White man these Black men were used to fear, or a deal, or the cops. Who the hell was this? They harassed him a bit to let him know who was boss but let him pass.

On his way to the building where the meeting would be held, Roger said a friendly hello to everyone he passed. They turned and looked at him strangely as he walked on by. What White man would come in here alone? Everyone else came in groups. Initially Roger had entered with Tom or anyone he could find. After being introduced to a few folks, before long he was walking around by himself.

Yet Roger's eyes were opened wide. He had never seen such a distressing community, with so much drug dealing out in the open, where the neighborhood culture supported it so much that nobody wanted to mess with the drug dealers. The police didn't even want to go in. The drug dealers boldly stood on every corner, harassing or confronting anyone who drove in who they didn't know or who wasn't there to deal.

Roger heeded the rundown buildings, the doors falling off hinges, the broken windows, the paint peeling off walls, the broken cars, the piles of garbage littered all over the yards. Little kids ran around, badly clothed, dirty, as if their health was not cared for. It was a school day, yet more than two hundred kids roamed the grounds unsupervised. It looked like the middle of summer or a holiday. Nobody seemed to care. He watched some kids play a game that looked like "drug dealer vs. the cops." The drug dealers were the good guys.

The project was struggling. Another woman they'd hired at the store was causing great problems, squabbling with everyone and sometimes not coming to work. Tom's intent to have the store owned and run by the resident's council seemed thwarted by craziness. Tom needed to do something.

These difficulties did not surprise Roger. He understood this was the way these folks were used to coping with life. He knew it would not be easy at first to get them to function in a healthy way—beyond their own ego and personal survival needs—so they would contribute to the community and help each other.

Roger saw another problem. He labeled it the "salad bar approach." Many services had been brought in, such as primary health care, job training, food stamps, G.E.D. courses, and day care, in hopes that residents would come by and sample them. The residents weren't necessarily of the mind to take advantage of those services. Roger observed that the project lacked any leadership training for the residents. He saw no attempt to raise residents' self-esteem to bring them to a level where they would have the wherewithal and the means to productively use those services.

Dr. Mills asked Tom and the consortium if he could write a grant to bring this missing component into Modello.

When he first entered Modello Roger wanted to be careful not to cause a stir. He didn't want to be seen as another agency coming in with a flurry of media and speeches about what would be accomplished. He wanted only to get to know the folks, hear their stories, learn about their lives. He wanted them get to know him as a human being so they could begin to trust him.

Roger showed up at a meeting in Modello called by Tom and the Task Force. Many women scurried about preparing for the event. Roger grabbed some chairs and moved them into place. He spoke to anyone near him. His was the only White face in the audience and one of the only male faces.

He had come an hour early on purpose. While helping to set up Roger carefully observed who came around and looked most interested. In the kitchen he hung out and chatted and helped the women with the food. Afterwards he stayed to help with the dishes, put away the chairs and shoo out the kids. Standing outside the building with some residents after the meeting he chatted some more, eyes attuned to those who came most often and seemed most concerned, to those who seemed to be natural leaders.

It was all part of building rapport. Dr. Mills asked about their families, their kids, how long they'd been there. He asked whether they were working, if they wanted to work. He asked how their kids were doing in school, and what they thought about the school. He tried to find out what they liked, and what they were like. What were their hobbies? How many years of school had they attended? What did they think about living in Modello? What paths had brought them here? After each meeting he asked what they thought about it and the entire effort.

He listened. He could hear their skepticism.

"We've heard all this before," they said. "As soon as the press is gone the agencies will be gone. As soon as the TV cameras aren't here anymore we won't see the director of PIC or the director of the county social service agency or United Way down here."

At best they adopted a "wait and see" attitude. At worst, "We've seen all this before. Nothing's ever going to change here." Among the most vocal was a heavyset, powerful looking woman named Rosie.

* * *

From the beginning of Tom's arrival months earlier Rosie had already made her position clear to Tom Petersen. When she first met him she had faced him with her arms crossed, eyes narrowed. Suspicious.

"Lots of people come in here and say they want to do things, but they don't come through."

Not that the residents had ever made it easy. They went out of their way to give service providers a hard time. The providers would get frustrated and depart. The residents were testing them, and they didn't pass the test. It was the same story every time. Every time they'd be left as always, with more unfulfilled promises and more dashed hope. Why should this man be any different?

In spite of herself Rosie found herself taking a liking to Tom. He seemed different. He showed genuine concern. He didn't have an office downtown; he worked out of his car. He gave her his home phone number. Nobody had ever done that before. Besides, he was creating jobs and talking about hiring her!

It took Tom only a few minutes to realize that without Rosie's support he wouldn't get to first base in Modello. She was the unofficial mayor, head of the Modello Tenant's Council. Everyone knew her. She was a tough cookie with a bellowing voice. She never hesitated to stand up and bellow for what she believed best for the residents, and for herself.

So Tom put her to work conducting surveys to find out what the residents needed. "What does Modello need?" she would call to the residents in a voice that demanded attention.

Tom had won her over. Now, months after Tom had come in, who was this other White man hanging around? Dr. Who? Why didn't he go away when everybody else did?

* * *

When Dr. Mills wasn't hanging out in Modello he wrote a grant and submitted it to Tom who gave it to his contacts.

The Task Force considered giving Dr. Mills support. They had experienced only marginal success. Yes, they'd opened the store and a day care center and brought in all those services. These had clearly made some difference, but they were not seeing much impact on the residents' lives. Plus, Modello always seemed fraught with difficulties.

Tom had tried to place control of the store in the hands of the Tenants Council, but the council didn't seem to really exist. It had a name and Rosie was apparently its leader, but it hadn't met for years. The by-laws had been lost, and they kept saying they couldn't have an election because they couldn't find the by-laws. Tom and Pam offered, "Why don't you have an election of a new Tenant Council and get a group you can work with that really does represent the residents." They replied that they had to get their act together first and find the by-laws or rewrite them. They then found all kinds of reasons why they couldn't have an election. It symbolized how things ran in Modello. Something else needed to happen.

Even though they couldn't figure him out, the Task Force appreciated that Mills wanted the residents involved. He wanted to listen to their ideas. He considered the residents equals and treated them that way. He believed that they could work together equally to help solve their and the community's problems. They were behind whatever he wanted to do—until some members read the specifics of his grant proposal and saw the language of "Psychology of Mind."

"Dr. Mills," they said, "with all due respect, what does self-esteem or people's thoughts have to do with the fact that their roofs are falling in, that they're dodging bullets on the way home, that their kids are involved with drugs, that their old man is beating on them and sleeping with their daughter. All these terrible things are going on in their lives. What does this have to do with 'thought', or anything you're talking about?"

Dr. Mills replied, "It has everything to do with it. The reason things are the way they are down there is that people who live there don't think they can do any better. They've been conditioned, because of their upbringing or their experience with society or whatever they've learned in their lives, to think that that's the best they can do. The best they can do is be dependent and hustle and manipulate and steal and cheat and lie to get ahead and not trust anybody and be suspicious and think that the world's against them. I'm not saying that's right or wrong—people have reasons for thinking that way— but as long as somebody is caught up in that kind of thinking, they can't change their life."

"But they think that way because of the conditions they're in."

"Look at that adult skills center sitting a block from Modello," Roger responded, "it's been there for as long as Modello has. It offers G.E.D. and nursing assistant training and day care provider training, and it offers day care while people are in class—and extremely few residents from Modello have ever gone there. In fact, the residents have been asking us to provide some of the same services that are already offered right there! When you look at how people are responding so far to what we've done, what do you see? We've sent in a ton of services, but people aren't taking advantage of them. No matter what their reasons for thinking that way, the way they're thinking is not allowing them to take advantage of those services."

Despite their protests, Roger knew they were pretty much at the end of their rope and close to being willing to try almost anything. Few residents had become involved. If they held a parenting class, two parents might show up for the first session, then none for the second. The staff brought in to run G.E.D. classes or vocational training or promote job development would be sitting there twiddling their thumbs. The few residents who did come around almost never completed the programs. Their surveys showed that there were extremely high levels of apathy, anomie, depression, and hostility. Residents were feeling, "What's the use?" It wasn't hard for the Task Force to admit that apathy was a psychological state; it was apparently another leap to admit that they had to work to try to change that psychological state.

"It can only change by giving people jobs, getting them more income," Task Force members argued. "It will only change by having HUD come in and fix up the buildings and paint them, so they can live decently."

Roger persisted, "It's in people's heads. You've got to change how people think, and in order to do that you've got to understand that it has something to do with their thinking."

"No! We've got to change the conditions first!"

"There's two sides to the coin," Roger continued. "Of course you have to have jobs and vocational opportunities and day care and all those things available. But the other side of the coin has to be there too. People have to be motivated to take advantage of it and see it and want it, and see that its going to help them—to have that feeling of hopefulness."

"It's too simple. You're a White Ph.D. You come in there and talk psychology to these people and they'll just write you off—because you're not one of them. They'll say, 'It's easy for you. This might work for upper middle class White people who are intellectual and have gone to college...!' It's too cognitive. It's too abstract to work with these kinds of people, most of whom have even dropped out of high school."

Tom Petersen said to him, "Look, Roger, I really don't agree philosophically with your approach. It just seems to me that community organizing and sociological realities, and changing people's economic status, and inspiring them through some kind of political process, has always seemed to be more germane to alleviating some of the problems in a place like Modello than counseling, no matter what kind of counseling that is."

Tom: I guess the crux of my difference with Mills was that I've always believed in a very pragmatic, eclectic approach to the problem. That's just my bias, that there is no one way to solving these problems. There's no one doctrine, there's no one philosophy, there's no one approach to solve such a range of problems in a community of people. You have to be very eclectic and very pragmatic and bring in whatever seems to work. The store was a good idea. It wasn't a panacea. "Nothing's a panacea," was my philosophy, and that's why I really objected to Mills's claim that he had a panacea in a field where I don't believe there is any panacea. About the most you can do is bring together whatever loosely knit groups of people and approaches, and try to keep them all working together. That's what you do. You can't try to impose any doctrine or any view on the group as a whole. That's what really bothered me. Roger really does believe he had a panacea.

The Task Force barraged Roger with angry criticism. It began seeping into his home life. Some officials began phoning him late at night, yelling that his approach would never work with uneducated people. "What they really need is jobs, not counseling. Self-esteem is a waste of time with low-income people!" Newly married, Roger's wife Clytee began pleading with him not to answer the phone. Roger wondered if he should give it up. He came within an inch of saying, "The hell with it!" But something in the back of his mind told him if he persevered it would be worth it. Throughout history when anyone tried something radically different it was met with resistance. Perseverance had led to enormous breakthroughs in understanding and improved quality of life.

"Look, let's give it a shot," Mills said. "The grant's been written. It looks like it's going to get funded. I'm down there. I've already developed relationships with some people. I've gotten the Community College to offer college credit for a leadership class, and we've got about twenty people that want to take part. Let's give it a shot."

Roger was learning an important lesson. He couldn't come on too strong with this stuff. He softened a bit and said, "Look, what I'm talking about is just one piece of a bigger picture. We'll work with all the people you've brought in. We're not saying that we know more than anyone else, we're just going to add another piece that will make your job easier."

Roger learned that he needed to back off and start approaching the agencies the same way he did the residents. He had to show more respect for what they'd been trying and not come across as if he knew more than they did or had something totally new that they didn't have a part in.

After seemingly endless meetings over a four or five month period, Youth and Family Development received a juvenile justice and delinquency prevention grant for Roger's effort to begin officially in October, 1987. Mills had been hanging around in Modello for a few months and now, before the grant money arrived, he had a Leadership Training Class to run for the residents.

III. The Discovery~1976-1987

In 1976 Roger Mills's life changed. He met Sydney Banks.

For three years since receiving his Ph.D. from the University of Michigan Dr. Mills had been Executive Director of the Lane County Community Mental Health Center and an adjunct professor at the University of Oregon in Eugene. He was a single parent, turning the corner of thirty, living in a communal household.

Roger hated to be alone. He worked a twelve hour day at the office, then went drinking with his friends until 2:00 a.m. He believed that If he didn't have friends around, maybe nobody wanted to be with him, so he'd have to call somebody else and go drinking.

At work he was a hard driver who got an awful lot done. His colleagues called him arrogant, pushy, aggressive. They knew he was intelligent and knew what he was talking about, but they didn't like to see him coming because he'd "get in their face" and pull rank. Mills threw himself into University politics. Who favored whom? Who would be department head? Who got the best ratings from students? Roger took things very personally. His professional life was in high gear.

> **Dr. Mills:** Before I gained this understanding and started to find more peace of mind and unconditional self-esteem I thought that the way to prove myself to other people, or get people to accept me and like me, was to prove how intelligent I was. I always had to get the last word in. I was argumentative. They thought I was obnoxious and arrogant. Then I wondered why I didn't have many friends, except other people who were intellectual snobs like me [laughs]. I didn't know it then, but it's a self-confirming reality. It's a trap. You do it to yourself.

It troubled Dr. Mills that the mental health system didn't seem to be helping people. He watched clients become chronically dependent on the system, sometimes for twenty years. He watched every day as they arrived at the halfway house to see their counselor. He watched as they were released. He watched them relapse. He observed many mental health staff barely able to cope, burned out, having problems with their families, going through divorces, not being able to handle their kids, drinking too much. It struck him that the mental health of the professionals was not much different than the clients—the blind leading the blind. Roger wanted to do something about it, to find out what really worked.

With a Dean at the University of Oregon Dr. Mills worked to secure a research grant for primary prevention. Its intent was to test any program that might be able to show improved mental health results. Under the grant, funded in 1976, Roger and colleagues were eager to try any approach that might hold promise: assertiveness training, Parent Effectiveness Training, community development programs to bring together citizens to solve their community problems. They tried programs in the schools, encounter groups, grief counseling for widowed women who were depressed. They tested over twenty different approaches. One seemed to stand out.

A psychiatrist friend on Roger's mental health Board had returned from San Francisco raving about a seminar he'd attended called ARC (Awareness, Responsibility, and Communication). He'd been especially impressed with its trainers, George Pransky, who doubled as a family therapist, and John Enright, a Gestalt psychologist and former student of Fritz Perls. They were teaching people how to take responsibility for their own lives. Intrigued, Roger hired them through the grant as adjunct research faculty to come to Oregon and put together an ARC-based program called, "The Good Neighbor Project."

The Good Neighbor Project offered public seminars, followed by support groups and home visiting. Through talks, confrontation and other gimmicks they taught people about their belief systems, about how people really weren't victims, they just believed they were and acted that way. They talked about how beliefs become self-confirming: if you believe something, you act that way, it turns out that way, and then reinforces the belief that things won't change. The Good Neighbor Project seemed to yield somewhat better results than the other pilot programs. According to Mills, follow-up interviews revealed that those who came to understand how their belief systems colored the way they saw things began to do better in their lives. They became more accepting of themselves and others, were less judgmental, less reactive, and less stressed in their jobs. They got along better with their friends and families. They felt better about themselves. The key factor seemed to be helping people to understand their belief systems.

Roger Mills and George Pransky became friends. Periodically they would visit. One day in the winter of 1976 George phoned Roger and told him he would be stopping by. Someone had told John Enright about a fellow named Sydney Banks out on Saltspring Island across the bay from Vancouver, British Columbia who was having impressive effects on people. Apparently Banks was talking to groups of people, and their lives were changing. George didn't understand how that could happen and decided to check it out.

George Pransky appeared at Roger's door, shaken.

This was completely unlike George. He always seemed so cocksure of himself and his work. Whatever he'd heard had apparently shaken his foundations. He was at a complete loss to explain it.

"When I first walked in, I felt it," said George. "I saw more happy couples in that room than I'd ever seen before in my life. I'll tell you, Roger, it did something to my hope. It made me feel hope again. And that was before this guy Syd Banks even entered the room."

Later Banks had called into question everything George did as a therapist.

"Let me understand this," Syd had said when he learned of George's profession, "people come to you in pain, so you try to get them deeper into the pain to make them feel better? Very interesting."

George was a family therapist who had problems with his own primary relationship. Banks questioned how he could help others when he didn't have the answers for himself.

George left feeling extremely irritated. Yet its truth kept gnawing at him and wouldn't let go.

"I never heard anything that rang as true in my life," he said to Roger, "but I don't understand what it was. All I can say is that I know he knows what he's talking about." George explained that it was like listening to an expert mechanic talk about fixing cars. Even though you can't follow everything he says, you have complete confidence of his knowledge. That's what this felt like.

Roger became intensely curious. He would have to find out for himself. On a lark, with the woman he was seeing at the time, Roger drove north to ferry over to Saltspring Island, all the while saying, "This is crazy! What am I doing this for? It's the middle of winter. It's cold. It's raining. We missed the ferry! I should be home sitting in front of my fireplace or drinking with my friends."

Soon Roger would experience the same reaction as George.

* * *

Sydney Banks was an ordinary laborer turned philosopher as the result of an apparently powerful, enlightening experience he'd had a couple of years earlier. A soft-spoken, shy, bearded man with a combined Scottish brogue and Western Canadian accent, he had come to realize something about "thought" and the human experience that had changed his life. The story went that then a very troubled woman appeared at his door to ask for his help. He told her she must have the wrong person. She insisted. So he talked with her about what he had seen, and she heard something in what he said that changed her life. Syd hadn't asked for this experience; it had just happened to him. Now he realized that he'd been given a gift that could help humanity. So he began to talk with people on Saltspring Island about what he'd come to understand. To some who listened, what he said made indelible sense. It touched a chord. Many people's lives improved. The word gradually spread and people began coming over to the island to hear him speak.

Roger sat in a room full of people waiting for Syd Banks to arrive. A low-key, unassuming man quietly walked in, sat down, and began to speak in a soft voice. Roger was unimpressed, but like George he was struck by the people who had been listening for a while to Syd Banks. They seemed super healthy, the epitome of all that his own research was trying to discover. In his extensive professional search to find what worked Roger had never seen this level of mental health in people. These people were at ease, confident, assertive, calm, sure of themselves, genuinely loving, caring, considerate, respectful, unassuming. The couples seemed truly in love but not clingy or phony. They were great with their kids who were well behaved and respectful. Roger marveled at the ease with which everyone interacted.

Dr. Mills tried to impress them with his credentials. They were not interested. All that mattered to them was Roger, the person. They accepted him right away as if they'd known him all their lives. It made him immediately suspicious.

Like George, what struck Roger about Syd Banks was his absolute, calm certainty, yet seemingly without arrogance. Syd would even say, "Don't listen to me. The feeling inside you is all that matters."

In his soft voice Syd Banks spoke: "You can't find the answers to happiness in unhappiness. Delving into painful memories just agitates those memories and makes them seem real, as if they still exist in the moment. If you want people to be happy, teach them happiness. Everybody has that capacity. If they've ever been happy even once in their lives they obviously know how to be that way in the present. Inside each person is a recognition of their birthright for happiness and the feelings that will create it. This is the untouched potential in human beings that the spiritual masters talk about when they say, 'Look within.' It is so powerful and beautiful. And you find it by looking in silence, and by looking now—not in the past."

It was a wrench—it went against everything Roger had learned in psychology—but it made sense. Roger came to learn that Syd Banks shunned having a following. It seemed that all he wanted was to help people discover what had helped him, to find their way out of perceived problems by helping them see those problems for what they were: creations of their own thoughts. He wanted to help people realize their inherent, natural state of health within that was only being obscured by those thoughts. He spoke of "Mind," "Consciousness," and "Thought," and said that these, in combination, created and explained all human experience. As intelligent as Roger was, like George, he couldn't completely grasp what Syd was saying, but the feeling was indescribable. It played tug of war with his suspicions.

Roger had always prided himself on eclecticism. One approach works in one situation, another works in another, different approaches work at different times with different people. When Syd Banks talked about a deeper, more universal understanding of life, Roger's mind didn't want to accept it. He was deeply struck, however, by Syd's notion that people had something inside them so beautiful—a deeper level of wisdom and understanding, of beauty and love and compassion—far more beautiful than what people showed or what they learned to think about themselves. And, it was the same for everyone. All they had to do was uncover it. Roger too was struck by the hopefulness.

Roger drove back to Eugene thinking it had to be a sham. Those people must be only pretending to be happy and peaceful to put on a show for the psychologist from the states. Determined to get to the bottom of it, before long Roger drove back to Saltspring and rented a cabin on the lake. From there he would sneak up on people, drop in on them when they least expected it, convinced he would find them fighting or unhappy. No one could be that content all the time.

The reverse happened. By sticking his nose in their business Roger not only found that this wasn't a cult and nothing was lurking under the surface, he inadvertently became caught up in their feeling. Roger began to feel silly talking about his career accomplishments. He realized that he only felt the need to do it out of his own insecurity. It was just what Syd was talking about. Roger had thoughts of insecurity that made him feel insecure. Then he had thoughts that if he talked about his accomplishments he would somehow look impressive in other's eyes, so he talked that way. But it was all controlled by his thinking. It was his own thinking! He had inadvertently made it all up. It was an illusion. He only thought he needed to do it!

Roger returned to Eugene feeling happier, lighter, and more relaxed than he had ever felt. He found himself so at ease he couldn't understand why the intrigues of University politics had ever appealed to him. He felt tranquil and content. For the first time in his life he loved being alone, to return from work earlier, to light a fire in the fireplace, unplug the phone and simply enjoy the evening without a lot of distractions. He began to turn down his friends when they called with, "Some stewardesses are in town. Let's go out drinking and party." Without really being aware of it he began to restructure his life to be quiet by himself and have more time to enjoy his daughter.

People at the university began to say, "What's wrong with Mills? Is he sick?" He'd dropped out of all the wheeling and dealing. Roger found himself getting more done with less effort, making better decisions, saying things at meetings that people saw as sound, common sense. People seemed to respect him more.

Syd Banks began to invite Roger for weekends to his house on Saltspring. They would relax or work on his house or in the yard. Roger kept looking for the rituals and techniques in Syd's approach. Syd said there were none. It was all in the understanding. Reliance on techniques or rituals actually took people away from that understanding because they thought that the answer lay in the techniques, in something outside of themselves. So Roger stopped looking and simply relaxed. Sometimes they would spend hours barely talking. It felt wonderful to be with Syd, as it did with all his new friends on Saltspring. Roger would go back to Eugene to find that everyone suddenly looked so serious, stressed out, tired.

"Geez," thought Roger, "I was like this!"

Meanwhile, George was experiencing problems. He had left Saltspring thinking it was a fascinating experience but had gone back to his life, such as it was, and found it very unsatisfying. He tried to return to his therapy practice and found it no longer made sense. ARC had grown, and the organization now conducted trainings all across the country, but George no longer felt into it. As a trainer he became less and less effective. His life no longer felt right. He was off-kilter.

George checked in with Roger and discovered that Roger was changing. It amazed him. George began to wonder whether there really was something to what Sydney Banks was saying. After all, if Mills could change, anyone could!

George asked Roger to speak at a large training ARC was setting up in Santa Cruz.

George's partner, John Enright, seeing George at a loss and becoming ineffective, sent him back to Saltspring Island with his family for the summer to rejuvenate. Before long George's life also began to change. His marriage vastly improved. None of the self-help books he had read or any marriage counseling theories had ever helped them. Now he and his wife, Linda, found themselves truly happy in their relationship. Why? It was hard to pin down. They seemed to simply start enjoying and appreciating each other more, paying less attention to what they had thought were problems, and soon their so-called problems dissipated.

Roger and George began to teach what they'd been learning on Saltspring, though they found it difficult to put into words. They simply tried to help people find the same warm feeling inside them that they had found for themselves.

They decided to try to apply what they'd learned to the Good Neighbor Project. Previously they believed, much as cognitive psychologists, that people could change their beliefs by using willpower, or by reprogramming their beliefs or reconditioning their thoughts, or by positive thinking. They believed that through techniques or activities they could help people change their beliefs from the outside. Now it all seemed unnecessary. Change had to be realized from within—as it had for them. They now saw that everyone had within them a higher state of mental clarity that they could move to, no matter how dysfunctional their behavior, that people could learn to see their functional and nonfunctional thinking for themselves—and in seeing it, they would change themselves.

Dr. Mills: I had been going from one thing to another. One year it would be encounter groups, the next year it would be T.A. [Transactional Analysis], the next year it would be Gestalt, the next year it would be ARC, and I started to see that it was a fad, whatever was "in." But I now saw people on Saltspring change permanently in a very visible, dramatic way to a level of mental health way beyond what I expected was possible. It wasn't that they were coping a little better with the stress in their marriage, or fighting a little less or handling their disagreements with a little more dignity—they stopped fighting altogether. They saw the ridiculousness of fighting, period. And they fell in love again. The quality of the feelings in those marriages and families was a hundred times nicer and positive than from any form of therapy or approach that I'd seen. The results were light years beyond anything I'd seen before. And I'd seen people that had been involved in *est*, Lifespring, encounter, ashrams and all kinds of trips, and I didn't see that their level of happiness or contentment, and wisdom in terms of how to live a beautiful, rewarding life, was much better than it had been, except maybe they'd learned to cope a little bit better. So the changes that I had seen with anything in the past were marginal. This was a whole different ball game. It wasn't even close. And that's what happened to me. All of a sudden it seemed silly to go running around trying to find the right technique, or the right ritual, or the right movement to join.

By 1979, the third year of their five year university grant, Mills began to see that Good Neighbor Project participants were functioning in a less stressful way than participants in the other projects funded under his grant. They had more self-esteem, felt better about themselves and were more accepting of others. The reason appeared to be that these people took more responsibility for their lives. They began to see that everybody looks at things differently so they didn't have to take others' viewpoints as personally or get caught up in people's "separate realities." They saw themselves and others with more objectivity.

Dr. Mills: What we started to see was that people who were learning about their own thinking, how their habits of thought led to a cycle of negative behavior and negative outcomes which reinforced their negative thinking—when people got caught up in that spiral they didn't see the light at the end of the tunnel, or see any way out, it just got worse. But when people saw that it had something to do with their thinking, they got better and improved dramatically compared to people in other parts of the grant.

* * *

"Don't you see," Syd Banks said one day to Roger and George, "this means a whole new way of thinking about psychology and what you're teaching people in therapy, and how you help people. This is how people can learn about themselves."

For some reason Syd knew that what he was saying could best go out through psychology. George and Roger were the psychologists that caught on. Together they had fascinating discussions and gradually began to understand the implications. They began to spend a lot of time at Syd's house.

"You know I just have a ninth grade education," Syd would say. "I don't know any psychological terms. Could you teach me how to say this in psychological terms?"

Roger and George would throw out terms such as, "You could call that a 'frame of reference'."

"Yeah, that makes sense, write that down," said Syd.

They thought they were teaching Syd, but Syd was slyly teaching them to express his philosophy in psychological terms. They had to invent a whole new glossary of terms. Thus developed the earliest depiction of a new psychology that later came to be known as "Psychology of Mind."

George began to apply the new concepts to his therapy practice; meaning, he had to completely alter the way he conducted therapy. He no longer took people back into the past. He no longer had them get deeper into their painful feelings. He wanted them to go in the opposite direction—toward their health, to realize that they had this healthy state in them, to see how their patterns of thinking were getting in the way so they could access this healthy state through their insight. Though George felt unsure of what he was doing, his results with clients improved. Results occurred sooner and were longer-lasting. It amazed him.

It soon became clear that George and ARC had to part. John Enright didn't really understand what George was talking about. Yet George had intrigued fellow ARC staff member Dr. Keith Blevens about the new concepts. In 1978 Dr. Blevens assisted Drs. Mills and Pransky in writing the first brief laying out the early interpretation of the concepts. They self-published it and disseminated it around the country through the ARC network. George and Roger formed a new company called "New Psychology Associates" to begin putting out this new approach.

In turn, Blevens called an old graduate school colleague and friend, Dr. Enrique Suarez in Florida and excited him about these new ideas. By 1979 Suarez persuaded Roger to move to Miami and start the "Advanced Human Studies Institute." Ric Suarez helped formulate the early concepts (calling it "Neocognitive Therapy"), and they began to write a book about this new approach. By 1980, *Sanity, Insanity and Common Sense* was released by a small publisher. In 1987 it was revised and picked up by a larger publisher, this time co-written with Darlene Stewart, who had also moved from Oregon to Florida after becoming involved through the schools in the Good Neighbor Project. She had taken it home, applied it to her marriage, and her marriage dramatically improved.

Darlene's husband Chuck Stewart began applying the concepts to the alcoholics he counseled and found it helped them as well. A few other psychologists became involved and joined the Advanced

Human Studies Institute. In 1986 Dr. Jane Nelsen wrote a book called *Understanding*, based on the early concepts. Joe Bailey began to work on *The Serenity Principle*, applying this understanding to alcohol abuse. Meanwhile, George Pransky was working on a book applying these concepts to improving relationships titled, *Divorce is Not the Answer* (now called *The Relationship Handbook*) and moved his practice to La Conner, Washington. Although Suarez and Mills went different ways because of divergent views, Psychology of Mind had begun to spread.*

* * *

Thus, in the midst of their research at the University of Oregon Roger Mills and George Pransky had stumbled upon something on Saltspring Island that was achieving results far beyond anything they had studied. It was not unlike what happened to British scientist Sir Alexander Fleming in 1928 when he accidentally discovered something in his petri dish that he wasn't looking for, something killing the bacteria he was trying to work on, something that later came to be known as penicillin. It had finally dawned on him, "Hey, this is the answer I've been looking for!"

Meanwhile, Roger Mills had shifted what he thought worked to change people. Change had to come from within. His eclectic self began to dissipate; he saw everything in a new light. Everything that appeared to work he now saw as a placebo—if people believed something would work it sometimes did. But the real vehicle for change had to be people's thoughts. Thoughts are always the intermediary between people and their lives. If people gain

---

*Note update: As of this publication date, in 1998 George Pransky wrote the most definitive work to date on Psychology of Mind, *Renaissance of Psychology*, Syd Banks wrote a long-awaited a book on the philosophy behind it, *The Missing Link*, Roger Mills wrote *Realizing Mental Health*, and Dr. Richard Carlson wrote the hugely popular New York Times best seller, *Don't Sweat the Small Stuff* and other books loosely based on Psychology of Mind, then collaborated with Joe Bailey on *Slowing Down to the Speed of Life*. A few times over the years Syd Banks has had to remind Psychology of Mind teachers that there are only three principles—Mind, Consciousness, and Thought—that create the human experience, and these must be taught through a feeling of love and understanding. Anything else is off the mark. Anything that inhibits the attainment of people realizing positive results in their lives is off the mark.

perspective on their thinking and realize their innate health, satisfaction and happiness would follow and problems would be reduced.

They had come to understand what makes people who live in well-being be that way. It has to do with the way people hold and use their thinking. Anyone could learn to use their own common sense and natural wisdom as their guides!

Roger Mills was no charismatic leader. Yet within him there developed more of an inner calm, a quiet strength. He now went about his business with a quiet confidence, talking in a near monotone, eyes sometimes penetrating, sometimes darting about, taking it all in.

When Roger learned of Tom Petersen's efforts in inner-city housing projects, he believed that what he'd come to understand could help achieve results there too. So he tried to weasel his way in, in any way he could. After all, his doctoral dissertation had been on community organizing in low-income housing.

IV. Fall, 1987

With the grant money scheduled to arrive in a couple of months, Roger had his foot planted right where he wanted it: firmly in the door. He began to show up at the Modello "office," taking his place alongside other service providers. Pam did not know what to make of him. At least his heart seemed in the right place.

Roger wanted to get residents interested in taking his Leadership Training class. He had convinced Miami-Dade Community College to support it and, to fulfill its requirements, he needed at least fifteen participants. Like Tom before him, it did not take Roger long to realize that the class didn't have a prayer of getting off the ground without Rosie.

Rosie was a force to be reckoned with. One of the strongest, most powerful resident leaders and certainly the most vocal, Rosie would complain about the mayor, the police, the housing authority. She truly cared about the plight of her neighbors and would confront anyone in her path.

Rosie: I've always been semi-involved with something, but just semi-involved, just enough to—if I got mad enough—to go in there and speak my piece. And I wasn't very pleasant, either. But then that was it. Then I would just stop going.

Sam MacKinnon: Rosie had the interests of her community at heart. But constantly faced with all the negatives in Modello, she came to accept much of what she saw happen around her. She limited her protests to what she considered blatantly negative; for example, she would keep silent about drug dealers—unless they carried a gun.

Early on, Tom Petersen had hired Rosie to conduct surveys and represent the residents downtown in meetings with the County, City, and agency directors. In fact, she had helped to secure Dr. Mills's grant by going to support it before the county commissioners with a couple of other ladies. Since her part-time funding was scheduled to end as Roger's began, Tom wanted Roger to hire Rosie. In fact, he insisted.

This puzzled Roger. Tom had a mighty hard time trying to get Rosie to come to work on time. Rosie had a mighty hard time waking before noon. She loved to party late at night.

Tom: I told him he had to hire her, and he didn't want to. It was frustrating, since she came to work late all the time, especially since she only lived two blocks from the work site [laughs]. But she had credibility in the community, and that is essential.

Pam: Rosie was committed. She always had her community and the families' best interests at heart. She was always very sincere. She came to work late every day, but she truly did have people at her door at all hours of the night. She really was the neighborhood's liaison. It was like having two shifts. Gloria would come in the morning because Gloria was a morning person, and then around mid-day it was Rosie's time to come in—so that worked out fine. They staffed an office where residents could come in, and they'd troubleshoot anything. They would call for anyone and get that person a service, or a connection, or help with a bill. They were trained in how to do that, and that's what they did for Tom. Rosie had the afternoon shift, so by noon she would get there and sit in the office, and bundles of people would collect around her. She'd hold court and help people. She really gave people a lot of help. Then when she got the other job, her hours were extended, and mornings aren't her thing [laughs]. And once she digs her heels in, then it would be very difficult.

Tom: I didn't see my main role as changing people's work habits. It was more of a total thing for the community. Rosie's work habits were lousy, but there was a trade-off, and she had a lot of positives.

Roger didn't want to have to deal with potential problems like this. It went against the way he wanted to move into Modello—stay in the background as much as possible and be cheerful. Both Tom and Pam insisted on Rosie. Fortunately he wouldn't have to face it for another month or so.

Roger sat quietly by the Modello basketball court and watched the guys play ball. They ignored him.

"Oh, nice pass!" he began to say. "Good shot."

Still they ignored him.

He began to kid them when they made a bonehead play.

"Hey man, what are you doing here?" A tough guy said.

"Oh I'm just hanging around watching you guys play." Roger smiled. "I've got nothing better to do."

They couldn't figure out this White guy. Was he a narc? After the game he went up and talked to a couple of the guys, and asked if he could shoot a few.

Before long, he even got into a few games.

After becoming reasonably visible from helping out at the meetings, on his own Dr. Mills began going down to Modello to chat with folks as they sat on their stoops or wherever they happened to be.

He learned of the chaos that ruled Modello: women fighting in the parking lots, trying to pull out each other's hair; the men arriving at night and shooting up the place. Two months after Dr. Mills arrived a little child fell into a mop bucket and drowned. Tragedies seemed to occur regularly in Modello.

Rosie: Dr. Mills came into Modello the same time a lot of people did, with the media, wanting to do some things. We were the focus at that time. I don't know why, but we were. Dr. Mills came along, and he was sort of in the background for a while. In the beginning, you couldn't even come into Modello. This man would come in by himself! That's why I thought he had a problem [laughter]. Everybody else would come in a group. One woman, she would come in, and she would have to be with somebody Black—and he'd have to be a man. This man would come in and actually walk around to people's houses, so that's why we thought he had a problem in the beginning [laughter]. But if you want to help people you've got to overcome that fear.

Cicely: He would walk right in that project with all the drug dealers hanging on the corners, all by himself, knocking on doors. They say they thought he was crazy coming in there the way that place was, but God was with him though. He was the first White man that really came into the project like that. He really cared about people. I admire him for that.

Dr. Mills: I just wanted to get to know the people, find out who they were as people, get past the surface appearance, that this is a tough drug dealer, or this is a crack addict, or this woman isn't feeding her kids. I was trying to get past all those stereotypes and labels that we all use and just realize that they're human beings like everyone else. As you get to know people you find out who they really are behind that facade or that front they're putting on.

Ultimately Roger wanted to get the residents talking about their thinking and their states of mind, and help them realize how it interferes with their healthy functioning. At the beginning he knew he couldn't say anything resembling that. He had to build rapport first or no one would listen. For now, he would just be himself and talk common sense when issues naturally arose.

"Oh yeah, you could probably go back and finish school if you really wanted to."

He simply wanted to be encouraging, to show in an informal way that things weren't always the way they seemed.

Dr. Mills had his eye on the healthiest people—those that seemed most intact, most interested or curious, who in some way wanted or hoped something would change—even if they didn't really think it would. He had no intention to try to reach the hard core or drug gangs first. They would be most resistant; it was their community, their culture, their turf he'd be threatening. So he set his sights on twenty or so residents, figuring if they changed visibly, if they started doing better and turning their lives around, others would at least become curious.

Beyond that, Roger was shooting from the hip. He had no set plan. He was practically flying by the seat of his pants. He only knew that he wanted to begin by teaching Leadership Training as a vehicle to get across some basic ideas about how their thinking affects them. He didn't really know how he would go about it.

Roger knew only how he would start. He wanted a core group of fifteen or twenty people out of 120 families to be trained as community leaders. He wanted people that other residents already respected. If he could help this "critical mass" to understand that they could change their thinking, become more hopeful, and see that things could get better if they worked together, it would start a ripple effect throughout the projects. Both he and Pam wanted these leaders to see that they could be the catalysts for change, that change wouldn't happen by somebody from the outside doing something for them. If even ten people caught on and began to see this understanding deeply in their own lives, it would spread. Quality counted, not quantity. Depth of understanding would be far more important than having a lot of people come to meetings.

Dr. Mills pegged the people he wanted. "I'm offering a course on leadership through the Community College. It will help you be more effective leaders in your community. You'll get credits for attending. You can bring along anyone you think might be interested."

When he first approached Rosie with this idea, she half-closed her eyes and shook her head slowly back and forth, her lips slightly pursed. Not interested!

"With all these agencies being around and the media attention focusing on the conditions in public housing," Mills continued, "you really want to define for yourself what you want for your community. Come and take control of this thing instead of letting the agencies control it."

Such logic was tough to fight, but some didn't think anything would ever change and were quite cynical. Others were more hopeful. Still others were angry and wanted to confront. While far from operating out of a common mind-set, Roger believed most residents wanted to have a nicer family life, a quieter, more sane life, not have to deal with shootings every night and to sleep on the floor because a stray bullet might come through the window. Dr. Mills was suggesting this might be possible.

"You could get together with your neighbors and make things better for your community," he went on. "It's your community. It's your program. The Leadership Training will allow you to decide what you want and make the agencies more accountable to you instead of the other way around."

While walking the grounds one day Dr. Mills ran into a woman named Lisa.

"My roof fell in and water's coming down into my kitchen and ruining my appliances," she complained. "It's been this way for two weeks, and I can't get anyone to come out and do anything about it. They don't care about us. Why should we care about doing anything?"

"Hang in there," said Dr. Mills. "Get organized. Come to the leadership training and we'll teach you ways to collectively deal with maintenance in a way that will get those people to respond better. You can't really do it alone."

Lisa never showed up for the Leadership Class.

Wherever he went Roger listened to the residents' complaints and ideas. At the beginning they simply chatted about the weather or their interests such as cooking or food. Sometimes they talked about their kids, sometimes even about how their old man beat on them. They would complain about the shootings, about their children picking up rocks of crack on the grounds because guys would toss them when the police did a sweep and their kids would come home with little rocks. Most residents were too intimidated to take action.

"If I call the police on the drug dealers," they said, "they'll come over and shoot me or my kids or tear my apartment up."

Dr. Mills wanted them to see hope. "Come to the leadership training and we'll help you see how to reach other people and bring them in. Then, once you have twenty or thirty people forming a crime watch and calling the police, they can't single anybody out, and they'll start to see the writing on the wall."

Or, "Maintenance or management will be more responsive if you get fifty people at a meeting saying the same thing."

Or, "If you go meet with the county commissioners and tell them the problem and have a good turnout and get the media there . . ."

These were traditional community organizing techniques, trying to show the complaining individuals that a lot of them wanted the same things, and there is power in numbers. Neither clinicians nor service providers traditionally play this role. Mills found that most of the residents were nice people who wanted the community to improve and their lives to be better. They just didn't know how to do it. They felt trapped. Roger wanted to help them see how things could change, to see hope.

"When would you like to meet? What time of day?"

They reached a common agreement. The Leadership Training class would start on a Wednesday between 1:00 and 3:00. Most people didn't get up and get moving until around 11:00 or noon, and by the time the kids got home from school and certainly in the evening there were other distractions. They would hold the ten week class in Sam's crime prevention office in the middle of Modello.

At the first meeting about twenty people attended.

Rosie: We went to the first class, and here this man was talking about, "Regardless of what's going on in your unit, if your self esteem is high, then it doesn't matter." So, you know, right away I said, "Well, he ain't too bright." [laughter]. I just came to that conclusion. "I'll stick with Tom Petersen or somebody who's going to offer me a job right now, because I don't have time for what he's talking about."

But he came back the next Wednesday, and he called my house, and he was, like, "Are you coming over?"

"Well, not really, because I don't have a baby sitter."

"Why don't I walk over and talk to you."

And I was, like, I don't want this White man coming over to my house! So I said, "No, I'll come over there and meet you." [laughter]

So this became his daily routine. The man would just not go away! [laughter].

I would even tell the other parents, "Look, tell him "No!" I'm going to tell him that you say no, you're not coming to the meeting." And I would tell him, "The other ladies said they're not coming to the meeting," and I would give him their reasons.

He would say, "Well, I'll just take a walk over there."

And I would be, "Will this man ever quit?!" [laughter]

Dr. Mills heard Rosie scream at him that he was overstepping his bounds; he shouldn't go around knocking on people's doors, bothering them like that.

Rosie went to Pam. She and Rosie had a very good relationship. "What am I supposed to do about this Leadership class?"

Pam ran to Tom. "Tom, who is this guy? It's not working!"

In spite of it, Pam saw that Roger seemed really sincere—an odd duck, perhaps, but sincere. At first Pam wondered if he was for real. She did like his attitude, his way with people. He knew community organizing. They both wanted residents to feel ownership of whatever the program, so they wouldn't be mere recipients of services. They both wanted the residents to be the ones to come up with the ideas. After all, it was their community.

In the classes chaos reigned. Everybody wanted to talk about their personal problems and complain about their neighbors or their neighbor's kids or how poor maintenance was. None of it rattled Dr. Mills. He considered it pretty typical. It took him a couple of sessions to get them quieted down enough so he could talk uninterrupted for even five minutes.

Fewer and fewer people began to show up. Roger spent some time with them, then went knocking on doors, asking, "Why didn't you come over? We missed you. What's going on?"

"My old man beat me up."

"I had to go down to the food stamp office."

"My son got shot in the leg and had to go to the doctor."

People struggled just to get through their day. Roger would have to be patient. It would take time. Relationships were the key. Building rapport was far more important than perfect attendance or starting or ending on time.

In the course Dr. Mills attempted to talk about people's thinking and their outlook. He spoke of how people learn to think about themselves—from the way they were brought up, from what they were told, and this became how they think about themselves now. Yet it doesn't mean that is necessarily the way they really are. It was just their habits of thought. His words fell on deaf ears. It didn't take. He encountered mighty resistance.

> **Rosie:** We were real hostile. We did not want to be bothered. We felt things like our roofs leaking, the roaches and the rats were more important than some P.O.M., Psychology of Mind [laughter]. I didn't even want to hear it.

Toward the end of the course the number of attendees dropped to four. Among them was Rosie's friend Patty, who sat in the class, thinking, "What is this White man trying to tell us? Come on, man, be for real!"

> **Patty:** You know, we were almost doing things to make him get away. When he first came in we'd say, "How do you know? You can't tell us!"

Some dropped out who didn't like what he said about thinking: "It's your state of mind and how you see things." Roger could understand their response. They believed they were victims of society, victims of the housing authority. The bad guys were the police or White society.

Still, when people complained about their roofs falling in and how management wouldn't respond, or how the post office wouldn't deliver mail there, and all the things that went wrong, Dr. Mills took those opportunities to inject into the conversation how everyone looks at things differently and has learned to think differently. Everybody operates out of separate realities.

When someone brought up that their neighbor had done them wrong, Dr. Mills would say, "[So and so] has just learned to see things that way. She's not really a bad person."

When someone brought up how bad the police were, he said, "The police are just frustrated coming in here. Look how they see the community. They get rocked or bottled. Their cars get stolen. When they get out of the car, somebody drives their car off. The drug dealers hide, and everybody protects the drug dealers. They feel like the bad guys, so they just get more hostile and aggressive."

One older woman in the class didn't believe the astronauts had ever gone to the moon. She believed that it was just a big trick they did in Hollywood, with sets and mirrors and stuff. "Nobody could ever go off the planet and go up on the moon. What a ridiculous idea!" Everyone laughed.

Dr. Mills responded, "See how everyone sees things differently and believes whatever they want to believe. That's the way the human mind works. That's the power of thought. If we believe something strongly enough, that's the way we see it, and we're convinced that's the way it is."

Whatever their concerns, Roger wanted to help them see that people think whatever they want, that people can change their outlook and how they see possibilities. People change what they do if they change what they think.

They began to hold classes around the community in people's apartments. Sometimes one of the ladies would offer to bake something or serve coffee. The teaching still didn't take hold.

A handful of women involved themselves in the class inconsistently. Toward the end almost nobody came. What Dr. Mills said just didn't seem relevant to their lives as they saw their lives at the time. Despite Roger's continual encouragement, the class fizzled.

Some of the ladies went to Pam and said, "Well, he's a nice man. We don't want to hurt his feelings."

Pam: Not a lot of people made it through that class. But Roger is a real pit bull. He kind of bites on your pants leg and doesn't let go. Then at the end you really appreciate it. He's a very special person. And everyone got certificates at the end, because Miami-Dade gives certificates.

Dr. Mills: Some came back in later; others never did. Some always thought that what I was saying was a bunch of crap. They are still angry, living unhappy lives.

Some of the residents clearly had problems. Gloria, whom Tom had initially hired with Rosie, suddenly disappeared. Her kids couldn't find her. No one knew where she was, only that she had suddenly become infuriated over her job. For financial reasons Tom had had to cut back. He only had money to hire one person to do community work, and he wanted Rosie. So to Gloria he gave the job of managing the store. This immediately proved too much for her, since she had great difficulty figuring out prices and the mathematics of it all. Not only did she become stressed to the max, but she was terribly insulted that she had to be the one to change while Rosie kept doing what she'd been doing. On the day of the grand opening of Modello Mart, Gloria didn't even show up. Now she had disappeared again. Two days passed. Tom kept trying to reach her so they could try to work something out, but she was furious with him. Three days passed. Even her kids didn't know where she was. Later they discovered that she had locked herself in her closet with a gun. She wouldn't come out. People went into her house searching for her and did not even know she was there. She only came out after her kids went to school. She would then shoot her .45 in the air. When it came time for her kids to come home again she would retreat to the closet. Four days later she finally emerged.

Roger had his eye on a very intelligent, attractive woman named Sandy. He had great hopes of reaching her. At times Sandy could be quite seductive and sweet. But she was hooked on crack. Her apartment practically had become the area crack house. Sandy would wake up to people lying all over her floor passed out on crack. She would then be surprised when the Department of Health and Human Services came to try to take her kids away. Then she would scream at anyone in her path.

As the starting time for Roger's grant grew near more problems erupted. Roger wanted all professionals working Modello to be trained in his approach so they'd be more responsive—including the schools and police. He wanted everyone to start seeing the residents as healthy rather than bundles of problems, or as "sick," "scum bags," or "low life." He wanted to "change their eyeballs" so they'd see the residents in a healthier way.

They were not amused.

They asked Pam, "Where did this guy Mills come from?"

As coordinator of all service agencies working Modello Pam had to keep everyone on track and help them know what each other was doing. When Pam saw this problem rearing its head she became nervous.

She had mixed feelings. On one hand, Pam liked the way the agencies related to each other in Modello. They held regular, monthly meetings. They tracked various cases such as child abuse through the office so they knew exactly who was involved with each case. They looked at the family as a whole and coordinated case management to make available a continuum of care. The service providers found the meetings productive, useful, supportive. They wanted to attend. In those years in Dade County such groups did not exist. Pam and Sam and a couple of other providers who were there every day met each time a crisis arose. They would hook up the family with appropriate services. When they needed a bed for drug rehabilitation, Pam would contact Tom and the Task Force. Tom would use his influence to free up a bed. It made their lives so easy. In fact, as Tom was getting ready to leave Modello he joked that he wasn't really needed. All they needed to do was call the agency and say, "I'm Tom Petersen," and they would automatically get a bed or a service.

On the other hand Pam saw many of the individual providers compete over turf. "You shouldn't be working with these kids. They're mine!" Pam had zero tolerance for this attitude. Although she prided herself on her ability to get people to work together, to stop pointing out differences and start finding agreement, she'd been so frustrated by the "professionals" that by day's end she'd be worn out. She could use whatever support Roger could provide.

To the other service providers Mills represented another "piece of turf." They seemed threatened by this new man on the block. Already they were fighting over budgets and didn't need any one else horning in. They resisted Roger's enthusiasm to share what he was doing and train them. Roger wanted his concept to be everyone's. This annoyed them. It resulted in great disagreement.

Pam: In some ways it was understandable. Roger's philosophy has a way of rocking one's world. The other service providers were committed, dedicated people but were threatened by the possibility that they needed to look at life differently—especially those who worked in the drug and alcohol field, for whom Roger's concepts were a complete turnaround.

They would say, "I really object to this!"

"Why?"

"Because you can't give people too much hope that they'll be able to break out of their addiction. You'll only disappoint them."

Pam thought, "That's a professional talking? That's frightening!"

"I don't believe that," Roger responded. "I don't believe that we as professionals can limit someone's potential. If we believe that, how can we possibly pass on anything worthwhile to them?" He refused to buy it.

Clytee Mills: Roger stayed in there and he was patient. He was absolutely embodying these principles. He'd be so exhausted. He'd be red-faced with exhaustion. He gets red-faced. You could see his face and he could barely even talk a lot of times when he came home. He was putting his life's blood into it.

Pam: There were a lot of conflicts. But, my thing was, I wasn't willing to lose any program. Roger would come to me and want other programs out because he thought that their philosophy was too far afield. But I couldn't cut them out either.

For herself, Pam wanted to attend the training that Roger was offering. No one else did—except a woman named Marilyn who'd been brought in by Tom. Roger wanted Marilyn to work as a consultant under the grant to help with parenting issues.

The rest said, "We're not here to be trained. We're here to do our jobs. And we don't agree with what you're saying."

Roger finally realized that he'd better quit fighting to get everyone on board. Basically, it all came down to relationships. If they had a good working relationship then the service providers might become open enough to see that if something worked for a client they shared it made it easier for everyone else.

While marveling at Roger's determination Pam also saw Rosie and a couple of other women kind of hang in there with him, despite calling him a crazy White guy and grumbling about him always coming by to drag them out. The residents were unaccustomed to such tenacity. Usually service providers would become frustrated by their antics and say, "I'm out of here!" Roger's perseverance was a sight to behold. He would find a way to have contact—whether anyone wanted it or not.

Patty and some others began to soften toward him.

Patty: Lots of people come in and try stuff and get frustrated and go right back out. They didn't stick. But Doc did. He stayed. And I'm glad that he did. He's a good person.

Rosie: So finally, I knew he wasn't going to go away [laughter]— and I'm glad he didn't now—so I just started to sit down and get into some of the things he was saying.

Slowly, gradually, by October or November, Dr. Mills began to see some subtle changes in Rosie. Something seemed to be having a bit of an effect on her. Maybe he could feel okay about hiring her.

As November approached and the time for the grant drew near, Dr. Mills asked the women who made it through the leadership course, "What kind of person do you think we should hire as the social worker?"

One of the two grant positions had to go to a resident. Clearly, that had to be Rosie. For the other, the residents wanted a Black male in his late twenties-early thirties to serve as a role model for the kids. Modello did not have an overabundance of positive, African-American male role models.

Dr. Mills posted the job in the paper, screened resumes and interviewed applicants. Over fifty applied. Most had years of experience working with gangs or delinquents or in the inner city. Most were street-tough and street-wise. Roger didn't want any of them.

He saw their mind-sets already contaminated. They held set beliefs about what these kids were like. Many were cynical. "You can't reach these kids after a certain age."

The grant sponsor suggested, "You should hire that guy who worked with gangs."

"No," replied Roger, "He has no hope."

Mills wanted a certain feeling created in the project, and that guy didn't have it.

At one of the early meetings to initiate the grant the supervisor of the new Modello day care center heard that Dr. Mills was looking for a Black man with a degree in sociology or such.

"My niece's husband has a degree in Sociology," she told him. "Right now he's working at Southeast Bank. Why don't you give him a call?"

Lloyd Fields answered the phone. He hailed from Dayton, Ohio, with a degree from Bowling Green. Lloyd had grown up in a middle class family. He had never been in a housing project. The other candidates had a wealth of experience. Lloyd had zero. Roger wanted him immediately.

> **Dr. Mills:** Lloyd was a natural. He was a nice guy, laid back, down-to-earth, a good sense of humor, funny, upbeat, at ease with himself, very low key. He liked people. He treated others with respect. Most of all he had that feeling. He had hope. And he was naive.

Lloyd heard an offer he couldn't refuse: "Why don't you ask your boss if you can take a leave of absence from your job at the bank and go to a training in this approach we're using. It runs for a week. If it makes sense to you, great, tell me you want the job. If it doesn't, we'll just shake hands and go our separate ways, and you can consider it a vacation."

Lloyd's boss said, "No problem. We'll pay you to do it." Little did he know . . .

The training took place at the Institute at Coral Gables. Pam and Marilyn, the parenting consultant, also attended.

Ever since Roger offered it Pam had been looking forward to the training. First, she liked Roger but didn't really understand what he was talking about. Second, she was dying to get away. "Oh fine! A week away from Modello. I don't care what they talk about. I'm going!" she laughed.

She felt a little guilty because Tom Petersen wasn't too happy about it. "There's too much for you to be doing to take the time for this," he said.

But Pam felt burnt out and frustrated. Neither her job nor personal life were going too well. She took things too personally. Pam had the responsibility to coordinate everything going on in Modello, and they didn't seem able to do what they wanted for people. She felt frazzled and brought those feelings to the training.

Among the other training participants seated across the table Pam saw a sophisticated, good-looking, well-dressed Black man. Lloyd had no idea who Pam was, nor what to expect. The course was called, "Psychology of Mind," "P.O.M." for short. It ran eight hours a day for a week. Darlene and Chuck Stewart were the instructors, with help from Rita Shuford.

Lloyd heard them say, "Everybody has self-esteem and common sense. Everyone is born with it. It's something you forget you have, but it's never really lost." The statement struck a chord. Lloyd likened it to losing a set of car keys in your house. They weren't really gone, just misplaced. You could find them again. Anyone could find their health.

Lloyd believed it. It made a world of sense. Everybody has common sense. Most everyone is well-intentioned from the get-go. Nobody is really bad; they just get insecure. They do the best they can, given how they see things. "Their best right could be wrong."

In college Lloyd had learned about Freud, and about "operant conditioning" and all kinds of psychological and sociological theories. None of it washed. Though majoring in sociology he never considered becoming a sociologist or a social worker to teach what he heard. None of that psychological stuff about going back into your past history and trying to face up to all your junk and get angry had made any sense to him. After graduation he considered his degree nothing more than a piece of paper. So he tried banking. It seemed like fun. The day Dr. Mills introduced him to Psychology of Mind his career changed. It was simple and straight-forward, with no scientific hogwash. "It was just plain real. It was right!"

"Your behavior is via thought," Lloyd heard the Stewarts say. "Your emotions are via thought. You get caught up in your thought patterns. But if you can drop those patterns the true health inside you really comes out."

Lloyd: It just nails it for me. And, to me, it was nothing new at all. I grew up in church—still go—and a lot of things that are taught in the Bible are in this approach; I mean, bang, smack dab right, bulls-eye. But I never heard anybody outside the church say it like that—a psychologist teaching it in that way. It was so layman—the true meaning behind the teaching or preaching.

When I teach it, I try to stay away from it being spiritual because people get turned off. But, what you need is already God-given. You've got it right at conception. You have everything you need right there. Instead of looking out, you look in, and what you find inside and grab hold of will manifest outside.

Lloyd didn't need to hear anything else. Over the next four days he heard the trainers say the same things over and over in different ways. Still, it seemed necessary because other people in the room didn't seem to be getting it, among them a woman named Pam. Lloyd couldn't understand their confusion.

Pam could not understand Lloyd's and others' enthusiasm. She fought the trainers all week. What they were saying sounded completely contrary to everything she'd been taught.

"Life just isn't this simple!" she said forcefully. She kept fighting.

Calm, collected, and light-hearted the trainers didn't react to her challenge. In the beginning they had said this type of training would probably be different than any the participants had been involved in. There wouldn't be any information to memorize; there wouldn't be any techniques. If people allowed it would just sink in. It wasn't a matter of knowing a lot; the idea was to feel it, to get into it on a deeper level. So the trainers talked softly and gently and gave a long break every two hours so the trainees could integrate what they learned.

At the end of the day they said, "Just go home and have a good time. Don't think about this stuff. That's what will help it sink in most. Just try to understand it for yourself instead of thinking about how to use it with others. If it makes sense to you, then you'll naturally model it for others and form empowering relationships to teach it to them."

This training was certainly the opposite of encounter groups. No one called people "assholes" or tried to pull skeletons out of their closets. Participants weren't asked to get angry, to "cathart" or beat pillows. Unlike a training such as *est*, trainees weren't made to feel uncomfortable. This training consisted solely of interesting talks and discussions in a pleasant atmosphere. The whole idea was to learn about one's thinking.

It couldn't be that simple! Pam fought hard. It was an insult!

On Thursday afternoon a light bulb clicked on. Pam didn't even know why. It wasn't any one thing she heard. Suddenly she realized that she fought it so much because what they were saying had legitimacy. This meant she would have to readjust her frame of reference.

When they returned from the training Roger noticed that Pam seemed much lighter. The training apparently had a powerful affect. Pam felt it permeate her personal life. She had been so hard on herself when things didn't work out. She believed that something was wrong with her. She questioned whether she knew enough, whether she was doing enough. It threatened her sense of self. Now she felt freed. She didn't know how to describe it; only that whatever she'd learned had a strong personal impact.

Lloyd came back bubbling with excitement. "This stuff is really cutting edge! How come I didn't get this kind of psychology in school?"

"It's just common sense, isn't it?" Dr. Mills responded.

"I could even see how it would help people at the bank deal better with each other and work with less stress."

Roger just smiled.

V. November, 1987 - January, 1988

In November, 1987 Roger hired Lloyd as a half-time project social worker. Rosie provided outreach and community organizing as a social worker aide. Dr. Mills supervised both, at one quarter time.

Lloyd: He actually hired me before he got the money. I didn't get paid for three months. He was saying, "Don't worry about it. It's going to come." Fortunately, I had a pretty good savings. I was living off my savings, man! [laughs]

Pam: We had to lend Lloyd money from the Modello Mart at Christmas time.

Clytee Mills: The grant started just around the time we got married. The reason I know this is we didn't get paid for three months. It put a little strain on Roger, but it put more on me because he handles things beautifully.

Money or not, Dr. Mills gave Lloyd his work instructions: "I want you to go into the schools and talk with the kids and talk with the parents. Just make friends with them and see where they're coming from."

Lloyd wasn't sure he heard him correctly. "Just talk to them? You're going to pay me to just go into schools and just talk with parents and kids? Is that all you want me to do?"

"Right."

"Doc, you mean to tell me that all I have to do is go into the school, pull a couple of kids out of class, and just talk with them?"

"Yes, just get to know the people. That's all I want you to do."

"I'm hired! When do I start," he laughed.

Lloyd: I know why he hired me. He just knew that I didn't know what I was getting into. [laughs]

Lloyd first arrived at the Modello Housing Projects at 10:00 a.m. on a Thursday. He looked around in bewilderment. Dr. Mills had told him a bit about Modello before he appeared, but Lloyd could not have imagined this.

"Oh boy!" he said to himself. "What am I going to do now?"

Kids were running all around.

Lloyd had only been in Florida for a year. He was still trying to get accustomed to November being warm. Now he walked into Modello, and he looked, and it was a school day, and all these kids . . . It stopped him in his tracks. A lump formed in his throat. It seemed like July—all these kids were outside playing, but it was a school day! His eyes moistened. And he saw the drug dealers. And unattended little toddlers running all over the project unsupervised—in their filthy diapers.

"Where are the parents?" Lloyd wondered. "Where's the truant officer?"

He then saw a sight that would be forever etched on his soul. As if in slow motion, in the midst of the craziness, he saw a semi-naked little toddler, running. All she had on was her mother's negligee—just running around with this rag hanging off her. He could tell she hadn't been attended to for a very long time. Tears filled his eyes.

"What is going on here? This is, literally, another world!"

It was the opposite of all he was used to. It reminded him of a Star Trek episode where Mr. Spock and Captain Kirk traveled into another dimension and saw their exact opposites. That's what Modello was.

Lloyd stood in his suit and tie, dressed for work at the bank, eyes opened wide. He hadn't grown up in poverty. In the middle class you were raised to go to school every day. It wasn't a question whether you'd go to college; it was, "Which college are you going to?" Lloyd was raised with morals. Modello blew him away. The rules were entirely different. That meant in Modello he couldn't play by outside rules. If he did he would likely get hurt.

Modello was Dodge City without Wyatt Earp. Police were afraid to come in. The place contained everything one could think of as "bad." At any moment somebody could be shooting. Prostitution abounded. People would steal things from the businesses around Modello and come inside to sell the stuff.

A man approached Lloyd, a bag in hand. "Hey man, you want some of these steaks? Five dollars!"

Lloyd peeked in. A whole bag full of fresh steaks! The man had just stolen them from the Winn-Dixie around the corner and was selling them to get money for drugs.

Lloyd arrived at the office shaken but not letting on. Dr. Mills introduced him to Rosie, and to Pam, the woman from the course! Mills sat Lloyd down to talk but soon left him in Rosie's care.

Many women passing by came through to check him out. One lady named Sandy had been beaten, bruises everywhere, a huge cut on her leg. Tore up! Barefoot. Laughing.

Rosie said, "Good God child, what happened to you? You look like walking death."

Sandy laughed, "Ha ha! I am walking death. My boyfriend just pistol-whipped me with his ouzi."

Then she turned about-face and walked out as quickly as she'd entered. Bewildered, Lloyd glanced at Rosie who kept on talking.

"You know," Lloyd interrupted, "this is an entirely different world!"

"That girl is on crack, and her boyfriend is selling drugs," Rosie offered matter-of-factly. "That's one of the people we're going to have to deal with, sooner or later."

"Oh, okay," gulped Lloyd.

Yet, the people treated him warmly. The minute he opened his mouth, they knew he was green. They looked him up and down.

"You're not from here, are you?"

"No."

"You're not even from Florida, are you?"

"No."

"Where you from?"

"Ohio."

"I knew you weren't from around here. I *know* you not from around here!"

Lloyd: The women saw me as somebody different. And the guys there, a lot of them were drug dealers. They were kind of testing me out. It took about a year before they started warming up to me. The older guys watched me and would keep me at bay. They would let me do what I wanted to do, but I better not do anything threatening like appear to come on to one of the ladies. I didn't know whose lady or girlfriend was whose—and I wasn't about that, but they looked at me as a threat. They weren't sure whether I was so clean cut and wore a tie because I was a police officer or what. They never would approach me directly. I never would approach them unless I knew beyond a shadow of a doubt that they knew where I was coming from. Otherwise if I pushed their "insecure button" they might try to harm me, and I didn't want that at all. So a lot of times, at least for a while when I would go walking around, I would be with Rosie and she would introduce me to people. After the introduction I could then go and talk to them.

"Lloyd," he said to himself, "if you just do things common sense-wise, at best they won't bother you, and if the worst happens at least you got yourself covered some way, or a back-up somewhere."

Common sense told Lloyd, when in Modello lock your car and don't leave anything in it that might draw attention. When knocking on a door step back and to the side in case some hothead shoots through the door. When trying to talk with someone upset, say, "Why don't I come back later," not press the issue and wait until they calmed down. Never approach anyone like you're something special. Just try to be respectful. Don't be seen as threatening in any fashion. When around the ladies don't come on as a man that desired them— even if they make the approach. Always stand back when talking with them, and talk when others are around so it's always safe for everyone.

Dr. Mills instructed him, "Just get to know who you're dealing with, have a good time with them, develop a rapport, and then if they have any problems see how you can help them out."

It was the only criteria. Otherwise, Lloyd was pretty much on his own. At the bank they told him step a, b, c. Not here! Here he heard, "Find out what's going on with this kid, and see what you can do to help rectify the problem." Or, Doc (as Lloyd started calling him) would ask, "What do you think should be done with this person?" Lloyd felt trusted and completely supported.

Pam saw immediately that Lloyd had a wonderful way with people.

* * *

Ever since Pam Gibson had returned from the Psychology of Mind training she had lightened considerably. Before, as a hard-bitten community organizer for HUD for five or six years, she took everything seriously. Roger noticed her now more buoyant, more fun to be around. She engaged people in a nicer way. She laughed at herself more.

Before, the antics of the service providers really bugged her. Now she began to see their behavior as interesting—almost comical. She now could see that while it was okay to bring in a range of services, unless the residents themselves believed that something had potential to change in their lives, none of the services could do much. The Psychology of Mind/Health Realization philosophy brought the missing link. It renewed her hope. She started to believe once again that she and others could affect the way the residents thought about their lives. This, in turn, would allow them to want to take full advantage of the services.

She could now see how many of the Modello women, who believed life didn't offer a whole lot, set up blocks and limited themselves. Pam could relate to that. She had done the same in her own life, in a different, more subtle way. Pam now felt freed from her own limitations, from feeling the world closed off.

From her new perspective the limits and blocks revealed themselves, such as how the residents dealt with the young neighborhood pedophile who had molested some children. The children were brought to Pam who sat down with their mothers.

"We need to stop him from doing this to your children," Pam exclaimed. "I'm not looking for punishment. I'm not looking for this kid to be stuck in a jail cell, but he obviously needs help."

They called the police and arranged for the children to get to the rape treatment center. Then the parents dropped the ball.

The police phoned. "Pam, she didn't bring her kid over."

Pam recontacted the mothers.

"You know, Pam," they said, "this stuff happened to me when I was a kid. You get over it, and you move on. That's life. I was raped too."

A lot of history, a lot of beliefs about how life is, a lot of limitations. If they believed there wasn't much they could do about it, why bother?

* * *

When Dr. Mills had initially arrived in Modello about 80% of its middle school students were truant. Almost no Modello young person attended high school. Most dropped out at their first opportunity. Parents complained regularly about how teachers treated their kids.

Middle school age youngsters were the official target population under Roger's Juvenile Justice and Delinquency Prevention grant. Soon after Roger hired Lloyd he brought him to the Homestead Middle School to meet the principal.

"What do you want to do in the school?" the principal asked.

"I'd like to have Lloyd meet here with the kids from the projects, get to know them and be available, and maybe do some self-esteem classes."

"Hey, if you can do anything with these Modello kids, be my guest. They're my biggest headache in terms of suspensions, discipline problems, and learning problems."

The principal offered Lloyd a room in which to counsel. It became Lloyd's job to work with any student from Modello.

Dr. Mills received another grant for $6000 from the Babcock Foundation of North Carolina to conduct teacher training. He presented his intentions at a faculty meeting.

The teachers groaned, "Oh, the Modello kids!"

Maria Garcia [Homestead Middle School Teacher]: A lot of people teaching—not just here—think that these children are subhuman, because they live in drug-infested neighborhoods, their mothers are crackheads, their fathers are drug dealers, or their mother might be a prostitute. How would I feel if my mother was a whore, and I go to school with these kids and see her out there in the street? Or that my father is in jail for selling dope or whatever, or that my mother or father is a homosexual. These kids are living that kind of a life. It's a very different thing than, say, the way I grew up.

If a kid experienced problems with a teacher Lloyd would talk with that teacher. When needed he served as go-between between teacher and parent. But the more Lloyd worked with the kids, as Doc had instructed, the more he saw a different need.

"Doc, I could do a lot of things with the kids, but if the parents aren't connected, the kids go back to the same situation, and we end up fighting against the same thing. I want all of us to be on the same team working together."

So Lloyd focused on getting to know the parents and being available to help them out. He wanted all residents to know they could talk with him any time. It didn't have to be behind a desk. Mostly he talked under a tree, by his car, in the store, in passing. Walking along, someone would say, "Oh Lloyd, I meant to talk to you about [so and so]."

Lloyd learned quickly that the residents truly respected Rosie, and he gained a lot of respect through her. She knew what went on in their lives. She knew what they needed. The two developed an excellent rapport. She was a huge help to him.

One of them would say, "You know, this is a difficult person," then together they would create a plan for how they might reach her.

In Lloyd's first weeks Rosie brought up the case of a lady who was blasted out on drugs. Hot-mouthed, she would cuss out anyone, anywhere, any time. She would curse her own kids, and say she hated them. She neglected them. One time she said, "Hey Rosie, I'm trying to be a lesbian. I got me a girlfriend and I'm trying to get into this thing." Another time she caught her room on fire and burned the bed. She was "out there!"

"Lloyd, this lady needs some help," said Rosie. "I told her that you could help her out."

"What type of person is she?"

"She'll probably cuss you out. You got to be careful. Just watch her."

Her kids weren't going to school. When they did they came late. Her seventh grader had been truant for thirty to forty days. When she did come to school, she stunk. She wasn't clothed properly. The kids at school made fun of her. She'd fight back and get suspended. She'd get in your face and scream. She always got in trouble because she'd cuss out her teachers and call them foul names.

"You want to go over there?" asked Rosie.

"Yeah, let's go."

"Are you sure?"

"Let's go, but what I want you to do is introduce me. I just don't want to walk up to this lady's door, she not knowing who I am."

Rosie knocked on the door.

"WHO IS IT!!! Who the FUCK is it?!" she screamed from inside.

"Samantha, this is Rosie. I brought the guy in here to talk to you about your daughter Felicia."

"I DON'T FEEL LIKE TALKING TO HIM NOW! Go on back to the office. Get the fuck out of here!"

"Well, he's here now, Samantha, you might as well talk to him. He ain't gonna talk to you for long because it's almost time for him to go home anyway. Why don't you just . . ."

"ALL RIGHT. All right. All right. HOLD ON A MINUTE!

They waited about five minutes, guessing she was straightening up or something. The door opened. Lloyd looked in. He saw only one or two pieces of furniture and a mattress on the floor.

Lloyd said, "Hi, how are you doing?"

The woman started right in. "Well, Felicia, she did . . ."

"Well I don't want to talk about that right now," Lloyd interrupted. "I just wanted to introduce myself, see how you were doing and just try to get to know who you are so you'll know who I am and stuff, so if you feel like talking or anything you can. If you really want me to go I will, but since Rosie took the trouble to come along why don't we just talk for the rest of the time I'm here today."

"All right, all right, all right. I don't want to talk right here around the kids. I want to go to your office. Can we go over to your office and talk? Because a lot of people around here they got itchy ears and they're always talking."

Back at Lloyd's office Samantha opened up almost immediately and started to cry. "Felicia's not going to school, and no matter what I do—I scream at her, I beat her—and she don't do what I tell her to do. And the other kids, they don't ever do what I tell them to do. And when I leave the house and go do something they always tear up the house. They never do what I tell them to do! They never come home when I tell them to come home!"

Lloyd stayed low key and friendly. At first he wanted only to help her calm down and get her bearings. He didn't want to talk right off about the issues. He'd rather talk about anything else.

Gradually she began to settle down. She didn't curse him out.

People knew not to mess with Samantha, but Lloyd was nonthreatening. He really wanted to hear what she had to say. In return, she was respectful. He didn't tell her that she wasn't fit to take care of her kids. He wanted only to help her regain her mental health, her family functioning. To do that he first had to develop rapport, help settle her down enough to trust in what he had to say. Lloyd said as little as possible, just let her talk. No sense saying anything if she wasn't going to hear it and would reject it out of hand.

Once she calmed down and her level of insecurity with it, he said, "Well, here's something you may want to look into. Maybe let's go talk with the teacher about Felicia."

"Those teachers don't like me."

"Well, I'll go with you. We can just talk about how to help Felicia instead of just talking about what Felicia does. We already know what Felicia does. So we can talk with the teacher and just make some kind of a game plan to encourage Felicia to get back into her books. And even more than Felicia, I'm concerned about you, Samantha. See, I'm just a social worker. That's all I am. I'm supposed to be the expert, but I'm not really the expert. You're the expert. You have much more power in helping Felicia out than I have. If I could help you out, then my job is done and I don't need to go to Felicia. We can just sit and talk a little bit, and I can give you some golden nuggets, as I call them. I let you handle it."

Lloyd knew she had the power to make the life changes she needed. So long as he saw that and kept the focus on it and showed her respect and didn't treat her as a bundle of problems, maybe she could rise above them.

Samantha wouldn't take constructive action.

"Just be patient," said Doc during his supervisory sessions. These consisted of coming down to Modello two or three days a week around noon to have lunch with Lloyd and Rosie and asking which clients they were having trouble reaching.

"Keep calling back," Doc said. "Every time you see her or her daughter say hi and be nice to her. Be available and tell them you want to help if she needs it, like to help her talk with the teachers so her daughter won't get suspended. Just back off, have patience, and maybe eventually she'll come around."

Lloyd persevered, but sometimes Samantha would test him to see where he was at. She would attempt to get money out of him. Lloyd held firm.

"Are you sure you don't want a woman?" she asked one day. "You know, I could be your woman."

"No, that's not what I want."

Lloyd was intent on staying the course. When she was with him she would be treated with respect, period. She gradually began to listen.

Slowly, Lloyd began to help both Samantha and Felicia see how she could exist in school in a way that would make it nicer—for herself. Finally, Samantha agreed to meet with Felicia's teachers—provided that Lloyd was present—and, gradually, Felicia began to come to school more often. She still got into trouble but started to pay a little more attention to how she dressed. She didn't smell as bad. Her clothes were less trashy.

Over time Lloyd helped Samantha get into a drug treatment program, albeit not one operating under Psychology of Mind because there weren't any. Samantha didn't make it through. Not long after she left the drug treatment program she moved out of Modello. By this time she had calmed down some but was still pretty wild. Later, Lloyd heard that she went back to drug treatment again and was getting on with a more stable life.

Lloyd considered this an acid test on where he was with Psychology of Mind, and whether he could be successful. In some respects he felt successful. He was able to interact with Samantha in a way no one else had. She wouldn't talk to many people, but she listened to Lloyd a lot. By the time they moved out of Modello Felicia was doing a little better.

* * *

At the school Lloyd's marching orders were, "At first just go out and make friends with the kids at the school. Don't deal with any of their problems. Just create a good feeling."

Creating a good feeling was Lloyd's specialty. Before long many of the Modello students naturally wanted to be around him, to go see him when they had problems. He took referrals when they got into trouble. He asked them to come in and talk individually whenever they felt the need. Lloyd conducted a mini-assessment to learn which students came from Modello. Through the school's locator he learned when they were in which classes. In his first year Lloyd counseled twenty-eight students from Modello families.

This was a far cry from the school's old approach. Previously when a Modello student got into trouble the school sent home a curt note about what the child did. Some parents didn't even know how to read, but since it came from the school they assumed there had to be some problem. They thought the school officials were prejudiced against their kids and didn't care about them. Lloyd wanted to bridge the gap. He knew the parents cared. They only didn't know how to approach the school.

Maria Garcia: The problem was that it was easy for the kids to stay home and nobody would do anything about it. So with all the field workers Roger had out there and all his people getting into that community, that made a lot of those kids come to school because there was always somebody around there. There wasn't going to be a child that went out one morning and say, "Hey, my mom's not here, I'm not going to school," because there'd be another mother there to see them. When they knew there was someone supervising them it made a difference.

Now when the administration received an office discipline referral from a teacher about a Modello student, the office referred the matter directly to Mr. Fields.

Lloyd would ask the student, "What happened?"

"The teacher did _____ to me."

Lloyd tried to appeal to their common sense. "What would you have done if you were in the teachers shoes?" "How could you have avoided this situation?"

Sometimes students would come in so upset they wouldn't respond. Lloyd then said, "Well why don't you just sit here in my office for a while to cool off a little." No sense talking if the kid wasn't responding. Otherwise he'd end up "in preach mode." It wouldn't penetrate. He had to be patient and give it time. When they calmed down he would come back and talk.

* * *

Although the Leadership Class had ended without effect, out of the chaos Rosie, Patty, Carrie Mae and a couple of others could at least begin to serve as a core group to provide direction. Doc asked them what they wanted to do next. Pam hired a few of them to conduct a survey asking residents what they wanted for their community and for themselves.

The survey showed that Modello residents wanted more control over their kids. They wanted their kids in school. Roger took the cue to start a parenting class and organize some form of residents' council.

For some reason HUD balked at the idea of a tenants' council. Dr. Mills didn't want to ruffle feathers. They needed another vehicle.

"How about starting a parenting class?" he asked Lloyd.

"Well, that would be good," Lloyd answered, "but people might be kind of offended and say, 'Who are you to tell me how to raise my kids? I got eight kids already!'

What about a P.T.A. [Parent-Teacher Association]? That might make it easier to get people out. Then, if parenting issues were raised, they could deal with them there.

They agreed. It would be largely Rosie's job to get people out.

VI. Late Winter-Early Spring, 1988

Curiosity brought out the residents. To kick off the first P.T.A. meeting Rosie and Lloyd knocked on doors inviting them to a pot luck dinner. Many came out for the feast.

But as the P.T.A. first began to officially meet, very few attended: Rosie, Patty, Carrie Mae, an older woman named Miss G. who would do anything to have some kind of social event in her life—all remnants of the Leadership class—a new lady named Lisa, and maybe one or two others. Even with all her persuasive powers Rosie was unable to get many to come out. Those who did come didn't arrive on time. When they did arrive they wouldn't get down to business.

Unruffled, Dr. Mills and Lloyd intended to keep it light. They discouraged finger pointing and blaming. At first it didn't work.

"Well, your son did [this]!"

"Oh yeah, well your son did [that]!!"

"Now wait a minute. We've got to have some ground rules here," said Lloyd, "That's not what we're here to talk about. We're not here to talk about problems, per se. We're just here to get to know each other."

Many residents didn't even know their neighbors in the next building. Modello had become such a fearful place that many people wanted nothing to do with their neighbors.

Designed to be informal, people came to the meetings in whatever state of dress and hair they wore in their own homes. No one cared how anyone looked. Nor did anyone care to distinguish between the P.T.A. and the soon-to-be-started parenting class. Because the same folks attended both, they bounced back and forth depending on the issue being discussed. The staff used no set curriculum. They dealt with whatever issues arose in the moment. Dr. Mills wanted this vehicle to teach the principles embodied in Psychology of Mind.

It was anything but easy.

The first official parenting class began in chaos. The ladies came in laughing and joking and could not be settled down.

"Okay, could we start?" Dr. Mills finally said, with patience but edged with lets-get-down-to-business.

They wouldn't.

Dr. Mills began by saying that he just wanted to find out some things about them. "If you want to talk you can, and if you don't you don't have to. You should know that whatever's said stays between us. If there's something that you feel is too personal that you don't want to share with the group you don't have to."

They sat around and talked. It seemed nothing like a class. The ladies thought Dr. Mills silly. It was all a bunch of bull.

Lisa poked the lady sitting next to her in the ribs. "What time does *All My Children* come on?" she whispered. "I've got to find a good excuse to get out of here."

* * *

In February Rosie had knocked on Lisa's door and said, "Come on to this parenting class."

Reluctant but feeling she had nothing to lose, Lisa agreed.

As she sat in that first class she didn't like what she heard. Nor apparently did the other ladies. They gave Dr. Mills a hard time and didn't really listen.

At age five Lisa lost her father to divorce. Her mother remarried, then divorced again. At age twelve Lisa and family were placed by a social worker in the Modello Housing Project. By age eighteen Lisa had her first baby. A year later her mother moved out. Lisa stayed. She had no other place to go.

The neighborhood had changed around her. When she first arrived in Modello in October, 1972 the housing project was fairly new. Residents were a mix of Hispanic, White, Black, Oriental. As the years passed the project began to deteriorate. Everyone moved. Lisa stuck it out. Many African American families moved in and became Modello's dominant population. Only a handful of Latinos remained. HUD records for Modello showed 1% White Anglo. Lisa was the one. She paid it no mind. She was fully accepted and got along well with everyone. Her children were of mixed race.

When Dr. Mills initially came in Lisa refused involvement. Pam watched her walk across the grounds disheveled and depressed. Very, very depressed. Angry. When Pam spoke with her Lisa always talked about what was wrong—with the projects, with the world, with men, how she wasn't going to get anywhere "so just accept it."

Lisa had become suicidal.

She had three children. She felt horrible that they had to live there—that she couldn't do any better.

Growing up Lisa had little self-esteem. At age seven she'd been sexually abused several times. By the eighth grade she'd dropped out of school. She'd never had a father figure. She was bitter. She didn't feel that she belonged. She never felt quite good enough for anybody. Her personal relationships suffered.

> **Lisa:** I was always trying to be who that person wanted me to be. I was trying to satisfy other people. I was always trying to make other people happy so that they would like me, or even love me. But I didn't like myself and I didn't love myself, and I didn't realize that.

Other than raising her children in the mess she was raising them in, her biggest source of depression was her children's father. They'd been involved for six or seven years but weren't married. He promised marriage. Lisa thought, "If I had this man with me all the time, and we could start this life together, this is what's missing. If I had this person, this is all I'd need. I would be happy."

Her man kept promising, "It's not going to be long until we're going to be together the way we want to be. We're going to get married. We're going to get the kids out of this!" Over the years he said it many times.

Lisa put all her faith in him. She was totally faithful to him. She wondered whether he was being faithful to her. So she would make him faithful! She would make something of her life. Maybe she would go back to work.

"Well, you know, you've got the kids," he said, snuffing out the notion.

Maybe she would go back to school.

"You've never completed anything," he grunted. "You're not going to do anything."

Lisa bought into it. She'd been on welfare for two or three years now. It looked like that was all she could do. It stuck in her craw.

In October, the year Dr. Mills arrived, Lisa gave birth to her third child. By January Lisa discovered that her man hadn't been faithful after all. Emotions hung on a thread. She tried to break their bond, but she needed him too much. So confused, so unhappy, suicidal thoughts flooded her head. Serious thoughts.

Thoughts of homicide.

As he went into his bathroom to take a shower, Lisa went for his closet. She reached for his .45.

Head buzzing, baby in one arm, gun in the other, she moved toward the bathroom.

She opened the door.

She pointed the gun straight at the glass shower door.

Something whooshed into her head. "Don't do this! Get out!" it said.

In her other arm she noticed her baby. "Don't do this!" the voice called again. "It's not worth it."

Lisa trembled. Baby in arms, she pushed open his front door and began the two mile walk home to Modello in the darkness.

Devoid of any thought of danger she wandered across the street without noticing the cars, without perceiving any cars. Horns blared! A car careened around her. She jumped, nearly getting hit. Fear overtook her. Shaking in her boots she couldn't imagine handling her devastation.

Finally she made it home. The very next morning the kids began to get on her nerves. The least little irritant drove her up the wall.

"Everybody's trying to run me crazy!" she screamed. "It's always gimme, gimme, gimme. I never get anything back!"

Lisa had to give herself to her kids, but she had nothing left to give. A scary thought gripped her. A terrible, horrifying thought. A thought she could never admit to anyone. She didn't want to be a parent! At least not now. It was too much to handle. Lisa felt horrible.

"How could you think such a terrible thought?!" Lisa berated herself. Then she cried.

And cried. And cried.

Her kids felt the burden. "What's going on with mom?" they asked each other during her crying spells. Maybe they'd done something wrong? They hadn't.

Meanwhile, Pam had her eye on Lisa. Something about Lisa really appealed to her. Pam asked Rosie about her.

Lisa was a hard worker with lots of potential but so obviously down in the dumps. Pam wanted to involve her more, so after Lisa began attending the parenting class Pam called her into the store and offered her a cashier's job.

Lisa's last job had been pulling weeds, working with plants in a nursery. She had never been anything like a cashier. She truly wanted to try it.

"No," she replied wistfully, too afraid she'd fail, too afraid everyone would know she wasn't smart enough or capable enough. "My kids are still a little small," she said.

Pam seemed disappointed.

Lisa walked away grumbling to herself. "A real nice excuse!"

* * *

It took about a month for the P.T.A. to attract a crowd. When they began to talk about the issues they faced in Modello—the police busts, HUD not taking care of the buildings, school problems, truancy, drugs, their kids—people came out .

It took about another month for numbers to dwindle. Rosie practically begged people to come. The residents refused. They thought nothing would change. They'd only be wasting their time.

> **Rosie:** I started to talk with the other parents in the housing project—because a lot of the parents they were, like, "I ain't going over there. No. Uh uh. That man's crazy! There's something wrong with him."

Rosie, Doc, and Lloyd could only assure them that the door was always open.

After a month or two Lloyd began to feel comfortable in his role. His first step: to see the people as basically healthy no matter what they were going through. His second: to build rapport. Third: listen to them with a completely open mind. Fourth, once rapport is established, talk Psychology of Mind principles indirectly as they related to problems the residents experienced, and somehow hope and trust that it would sink in.

Life in Modello never ceased to amaze him. One day in a conversation with one of the ladies who worked in the Modello store, she said playfully, "Well, Lloyd, you know, you're so soft, so sweet."

In his deepest, gruffest voice Lloyd growled, "What do you mean?!"

They had been talking about what it was like living in Modello, and how people there showed love. She told Lloyd that a man would show her love by beating up on her.

"What?"

"Yeah, if I get beat on by a man, I say this man must really love me."

Shocked, Lloyd said, "Well I don't get into that. I don't beat my wife, and I love her. Why do you think it has to be that way?"

She didn't really have an answer. It was simply how she'd learned to see love.

All the women loved Lloyd.

* * *

Clearly, in Modello, the drug dealers were the biggest, most obvious problem. They caused the shootings. They had everyone living in fear.

It was the first thing that struck anyone who drove down U.S. 1 and turned onto the street to Modello. Drug dealers stood at every entrance. Pam had worked in many HUD communities and in every other project unless they thought you were there to buy drugs the dealers would move off. In Modello they would boldly stand.

No one in the community would do anything about it. So long as the residents supported the drug dealing, with its attendant crime, prostitution, and crack houses, the dealers knew they were protected. So long as they kept people in fear they would have no trouble.

The service providers were no more keen on dealing with the drug dealers than the residents. They were the enemy—evil incarnate.

Officer Tom Chaney of the Metro-Dade Police worked the midnight patrol into the wee hours of the morning and weekends in the area encompassing Modello. Modello was the hot spot, the place to go to look for crime. Chaney believed that the Modello residents must be either pro-crime or they lived in fear of the criminal lords operating there. Virtually every Modello apartment became a refuge for the drug dealers. Prospective buyers could travel U.S. 1 or 152nd Avenue, both heavily trafficked, swing onto 284th Street, make their buy, and quickly move back into the flow of traffic.

The police would pull up to any of the Modello corners where young Black men engaged in drug sales and boldly stand and eyeball any marked unit that came along. If they possessed drugs they would carefully set them down and slowly back away from their stash. They'd make no move unless an officer got out of his car and started after them. Then they'd take off like a shot into the maze of the projects and duck into nearly any apartment. The residents would yell, "nine"—a signal that the police were coming. It was "a law enforcement nightmare."

Cheney was shot at two or three times during his stint around Modello. It was a lot safer to concentrate on the buyers than on the dealers.

When Pam had first entered Modello the drug dealers were careful to steer clear of her. People used to come in the store and check her out. They couldn't figure out what "the White chick" was doing there. Everyone thought she was a narcotics agent. The store had to be a screen.

"She's got to be a narc! If they have the money for that store, there must be narcs everywhere at Modello."

Early on Pam had recognized one of the dealers. Lamar was the son of a former client of hers from another project. He'd been in prison for a non-drug offense and was back on the streets selling drugs in Modello.

Lamar became the first of the drug dealers to come into the store and nose around. He would pop his head into the back where Pam worked, ask a question or two, then leave. The visits became more frequent. On Pam's walks around the project to escape her cubby hole she would see him on the corner and go up and talk to him. People thought this terribly bizarre. All the guys would watch. What-are-you-doing-here-lady!?

"How's your mom?" Pam asked casually. "What's happening?" Then she went on her merry way.

One day Lamar meandered into the store and said, "You know, you don't know anything about business."

Pam laughed, "You're totally right. I don't know shit about business. Why? What do you want to tell me?"

"Well, you can't have those things near the door because those kids are ripping you off all the time. Every small thing you put near the door is going into their pocket."

"Well, I never thought about it. That makes sense, we shouldn't put the small things near the door."

"You need to move this over here. You need to move that over there."

Lamar was a talented businessman. He knew things Pam never even considered. He began to give her tips about the way she carried the money out of the store.

"Don't you know that there's about six guys here that are always thinking of ways to conk you upside the head? And it's only because you got some protectors out here that you ain't been hit yet."

"No I didn't. But I'm kind of oblivious," she laughed. "I just kind of get in my car and go."

"Listen, this is what you need to do. . . But I'm going to let everyone know that you're hands off, and nobody can touch you."

"Please do. I really like to feel protected wherever I am."

Slowly, they built a relationship. No, she didn't approve of him dealing drugs. No, she didn't like him fencing stolen goods. But if she told him how she felt she knew it would be the end of their relationship.

One time she had no choice. "Listen, you know I've never gotten into your business, but you can't conduct business in front of the store. I'm not going to have you selling your stolen goods here."

"How did you know that?"

"It doesn't matter how I know, just know that I know it, and I'm asking you as a friend to not do it. I'm not telling you not to do it. I'm not telling you how to live your life, but I don't want that happening in front of the store. You know why we came in here. You know we're trying improve the lives of the residents, and I don't want this happening here."

Lamar responded respectfully. He stopped selling in front of the store.

* * *

Rosie was doing a good job helping the other residents and was invaluable to Lloyd, Pam, and Doc. Unfortunately, because her work schedule had been shifted to the morning she began to not show up for work on time. Roger felt forced to confront her.

Rosie was not amused. "Don't you know that people come to my house anytime twenty-four hours a day and ask me for help!?" She saw it as intrusion into the way she ran her life, and Dr. Mills didn't have any right!

Yet, when Dr. Mills needed her to show up for a 10:00 a.m. meeting with the Private Industry Council or the police department, she would not often make it. If he brought it up she'd become belligerent and storm away. It would be two days before he could talk with her again.

One day when Rosie was particularly late Dr. Mills called her home. One of her kids picked up the phone.

"Where's your mom?" Doc asked.

"She's asleep."

"Go get her."

An hour or two later, Rosie arrived grumpy and bent out of shape that Mills had dragged her out of her house. On other occasions she would get defensive or give an excuse. "Well, my kid was sick." Or, "I didn't feel good." One time she woke up and called in saying that she had to get her food stamps at the food stamp office and wouldn't be in until one o'clock. Then she went back to sleep. Two hours later her kid strolled into the store.

Pam said innocently, "Your mom's down at the food stamp office?"

"No, she's home asleep."

For Roger it was a continual struggle. As her supervisor he felt that he needed to confront her a number of times. He tried to work out a reasonable arrangement with her. Rosie would make an effort for a while, then slip back into old habits, and Doc would have to confront her again. On a few occasions he threatened to write her up, telling her that people downtown to whom he was responsible told him that if she wasn't coming to work on time, he'd have to put her through a disciplinary process, complete with hearings, and they'd maybe have to suspend her. Roger said he didn't want that, but that's what he would have to do if she didn't get her act together.

She'd then come around for a while, then gradually show up later and later.

Dr. Mills found himself in a delicate and tricky situation. He wanted to help everyone gain a new outlook, Rosie included. She had the same kinds of personal problems as others in Modello. He was also her boss. The arrangement wasn't working. Roger proved that he too could get caught up in his own thinking. He sought Pam's counsel. Pam and Rosie had become very close. Rosie trusted Pam and would listen to her.

"Look, is it worth it?" Roger asked Pam, "I'm having such a hard time with this. Should we fire her and hire somebody else?"

Pam did not want Rosie fired. She suggested that Roger just be Rosie's boss and find somebody else to counsel her.

In his heart Roger knew that firing her would be most inadvisable. Rosie knew everyone. She knew their family situations and their histories. She gave the effort clout. If Rosie told the residents to come to an important meeting, they often did. No one else would be able to get residents out like she could, especially to come with an open mind and hear that there was something here that made sense. Mills needed her. He was therefore willing to put up with a lot. He also knew that she needed the job. But it was a continuous struggle.

Struggles seemed to follow Rosie. In the beginning, like many of the other residents, she often found herself in trouble.

Because she was one of the leaders Rosie believed that she should be able to park her car on the grass right next to her apartment. This violated HUD rules. They towed it away.

Rosie stormed into the office. "Who do they think they are, towing my car away!"

Doc looked up from the desk with a smile. "Well, gee, Rosie, you know you're supposed to park it in the lot. Give me a break!" Everyone laughed and teased her about it.

Roger's phone rang late one night. Groggy, he picked up the phone.

"Doc, this is Rosie. I'm in jail!"

She claimed to have been speeding out to get to Sam Mackinnon's father's funeral, driving with a recently suspended license, and she got nabbed.

"Can you bail me out?"

"Gee, I don't know, Rosie. You drive around with a suspended license, and then when the officer stops you, you call him an s.o.b. What do you think he's going to do? No, I don't think I'm going to bail you out."

Roger laughed about it, but he didn't want to be in the position of having to save the residents all the time. He did want to be there to give emotional and psychological support, and show that he and his staff were on their side and would do whatever they could.

"Okay, look," Doc said. "I'll call the State Attorney's office and see if they can do something, but they may not be able to."

They couldn't. So Rosie spent the night in jail. She declared she'd never go back to jail again.

One time Rosie got into an argument with one of her neighbors. Her neighbor came after her with a gun. Someone called the police.

Dr. Mills said to Rosie, "Look, if you're working for us you can't get in to these kinds of things. You're supposed to be a role model!"

* * *

One day Lamar hurried into the store with a man close on his heels, desperately "cracked out," wanting Lamar to sell him something on the spot. Embarrassed, Lamar glanced sheepishly at Pam.

"Get out!" Lamar told the man.

Pam said, "Go ahead, deal with your problem."

Before long Lamar came back in. "How long have you known?"

"Known what?" asked Pam.

"You know what I mean. How long have you known what I do here."

"I've always known what you do."

"Well, why didn't you ever say anything?"

"Because that's not what I'm here for. I'm not here to say anything. Any time you want to talk about it we can talk about it, but I'm not here to stop you."

Lamar was shocked that she had known all along—especially given her purpose for being there—and hadn't rejected him outright. She hadn't said, "You're the kind of person that's wrong with this neighborhood and that's what I'm here to fight." She hadn't said, "You're a bad person. I hate you and I don't want to have anything to do with you!"

An enormous barrier broke.

Lamar began coming in, saying, "You know, I'm clean."

"I don't think you use."

"Because I don't. I never use drugs."

"Oh, that's fine," Pam said matter-of-factly.

"Well, I get high. I smoke every once in a while."

"It's okay. We all have our things that we've done."

After beating around the bush awhile Lamar asked her, "What do you think of what I do?"

"I separate you from what you do. I like you as a person. I consider that we've developed a friendship. Do I like what you do? No. I don't like the impact it has. I don't like what it does to the people that buy it. I don't like what it does to their children. And I know you like these kids. I've seen you with these kids, and you're terrific with them. You buy these kids food. You do all kinds of things. But nobody would have to buy them as much food if your product wasn't on the streets. I don't like what you do. Would I like to see you stop? Of course I would. Would I like to see you do something legitimate? Yes. Can I help you do something legitimate? Yes. But those are all decisions you have to make."

Lamar became quiet. No words came. Then he said, "Okay, I think I'm going to go now. See you later."

* * *

By Spring, parenting class regulars were actually beginning to enjoy coming to the class—not for the content, which they rarely paid attention to, but because it was fun. When a birthday came around they celebrated it. They began to have a good time.

Pam: The parenting class started out very informally as a very comfortable, warm place to come. Roger was wonderful in those things. The women would come in and bring their babies, and he'd be sitting there with babies crawling all over him. It allowed a relationship to form that was not based on teaching. It was just a good, strong relationship, and that's exactly what it should have been. If you had invited these ladies to come in to learn something, they were, like, "I've got to cook lunch." [laughs] But you can have this understanding on your own and you're going to have an impact on people around you. There was no judgment going on. Some people came in filthy, their children could be filthy.

Others came in spotless—there was just a whole range of stuff. But no matter what, everybody was just happy that you came.

Patty: It took maybe a month for us to start listening. We started out giving Doc a hard time—trying to give him a hard time. Not really a hard time—we always did everything with fun. We never got where it was serious all the time. We joked about everything, even when we were giving him a hard time. We didn't really know where Doc was coming from. And a month passed and this guy was still here, and we figured he must be serious about trying to get this project going.

Thelma: We took Dr. Mills through some changes! [laughs]. We told him that he's crazy. Oh, we told him some of everything in the class. And he wouldn't do nothing but sit there and laugh at us. All of us took him through some changes!

It struck them particularly funny when Dr. Mills started talking about their moods.

Thelma: When he come up with high moods and low moods, somebody is going to come off on him, whether it be me or whether it be one of the other ladies. We said, "Are you crazy!? Talking about a high mood and a low mood. We don't think you know your own moods [laughs]. Yeah, we did that to Dr. Mills a couple of times. Rosie told him, "I don't want to hear nothing about no high moods and low moods. Do you know how your high moods and low moods is at?" [laughs]

* * *

Rosie kept knocking on Cicely's door, trying to pull her out to the parenting class. Cicely didn't want to. Rosie persisted as only Rosie could. Finally, she gave in.

"Okay. I'll be over there to the meetings. Sounds okay."

Cicely sat in the back of the parenting class and almost never said a word. If asked a direct question she would look at the floor and mumble softly. Dr. Mills could neither hear nor understand her. While most of the ladies gave Doc a hard time and yelled about their terrible conditions, Cicely never said a word. He assumed she would be one of the hardest to reach.

Rumor had it that Cicely's sons were dealing drugs out of her apartment. Her daughters were prostituting themselves for crack.

A number of people tipped off Dr. Mills that Cicely's two sons were probably the biggest drug dealers in Modello, and if he went over there and saw their stash of automatic weapons and drugs he probably wouldn't be alive ten minutes to talk about it.

Cicely: I tell you, I've been through a lot! It was real rough there for a while. I wasn't taking care of my family like I was supposed to, and I wasn't really doing anything with my life. I was just sitting home, just watching TV every day—soap operas—and having babies [seven children and eleven grandchildren], twenty-four hours around the clock, and laying around. I wasn't doing anything positive in my life at that time. I wasn't going to church then. At the time I wasn't interested in anything. My sons were hanging out with the wrong crew, dealing drugs, and the other guys were stealing. My daughter was on crack, and she was out there on the streets at fourteen or fifteen years old. And I tell you, she got so bad there on drugs that all her hair came out. She was as bald-headed as my hand, and her weight went down to nothing. She was weighing about 125 to 130 pounds, and she went down to 80 or 90 pounds. That's how little she was. That's the way my life was at that time.

Utterly overwhelmed by it all, Cicely felt too embarrassed about what went on in her family to say anything. It seemed as if she couldn't say anything because somebody might jump down her throat and say, "Well, you think you're so good, why can't you keep your kids from dealing drugs and your daughter from prostitution?" So she barely said a word. In the class, no one knew whether Cicely was listening. No one knew whether anything was getting through.

Lisa: Cicely and I had both moved into Modello in 1972, and for eighteen years I didn't know who Cicely was—until the parenting class. We were just like in a little island. No one knew what was going on. We didn't realize that it was our problem. What was their problem, was our problem. We all had similar problems.

Cicely: I was quiet. I didn't have nothing to say. But I was really taking it in at the time. And I enjoyed it, that class. It really helped me a lot. It really did—about how to deal with people with an attitude. It really helped me out a lot. It got me to come out. I care for the people. I felt the love we had for each other.

* * *

From celebrating people's birthdays they all started to go on picnics together. The only purpose was to have a good time—residents and staff alike. They all had a great time!

The atmosphere spilled over into the office. It became a fun, pleasant place to be. The other service providers felt the change. By late Spring Pam began to see dramatic changes in how the agencies related to one another.

> **Pam:** So the agencies began to settle in and become friendly. And they started to see that Roger's stuff brought results that none of them had before.

Meanwhile Marilyn, the parenting consultant, began to help the ladies from the class put together a little cartoon-like booklet on parenting with Miami-Dade Community College. But since going through the same training as Pam and Lloyd she was having a difficult time understanding what they were so excited about. Soon she left the project.

In the parenting class one day Lisa heard Dr. Mills say that no child was "bad." Kids were just afraid sometimes, or insecure, and acting it out the only way they knew how. Lisa thought about her son, now in second grade. She'd been having some trouble with him. He'd become "somewhat overactive" at school. No doubt it had something to do with what was happening at home.

After class as they headed to the store for a soda Lisa pulled Dr. Mills aside and shared her problem. Her son had gotten into a fight at school and ended up in the principal's office. They called Lisa and told her to come in. Lisa had responded defensively.

"Would you like me to go with you?" Dr. Mills asked.

His offer surprised her. She didn't know what to make of it. "Okay," she said suspiciously.

Together they walked to the school for the meeting.

Along the way Dr. Mills said, "You know, Lisa, kids are going to be kids. I know you're upset now, but what you need to do right now is to calm down, because you can see things more clearly without going in there like 'dadadadada!', placing blame, and being so angry at your child for what he did that you're not listening. You want to go in there in a frame of mind where you can explain to them what you want. Something like, 'I'm not condoning my child's behavior, but maybe we could work something out instead of suspension,' or whatever."

With Dr. Mills at the meeting Lisa found herself able to listen, to understand what the principal and teacher were saying without getting upset and placing blame. Doc's presence truly helped. If he hadn't said what he'd said beforehand she'd have gone in tee'd off and blasting, yelling, "I don't care!" and "blahblahblah!" and it wouldn't have done her child any good. She would have showed the school that she wasn't the type of parent they could trust to go to.

After that meeting Lisa began to develop a good relationship with the principal and school. At times her child was "a total character," but when the teachers and principal learned that Lisa really cared about her child and did her best they let a lot of things pass that her son could have been in trouble for.

Lisa offered to the principal, "Dr. Witty, do what you need to do with him?"

Dr. Witty would call Lisa and say, "Lots of times your son thinks he's in more trouble than he is. I don't want to mess up anything on his record. Listen, we need more parents like you."

Lisa began to think, "You know, maybe some of these things Dr. Mills is talking are true."

Although they didn't bring up many problems with their kids within the class, many of the parents began to pull Dr. Mills aside afterwards.

* * *

Doc witnessed Rosie letting the thought creep in that there just might be something to all this. Something seemed to click in her personal life.

Rosie would go into the food stamp office, be given a hard time by the woman behind the desk and essentially be treated like dirt. In response Rosie would tell the woman where she could stick her food stamps and stomp home feeling very self-righteous. Later she realized that she didn't have food on the table nor food stamps to buy it. She'd cut off her nose to spite her face.

Doc said, "Rosie, look, if I yelled at you and put you down would you listen to me after that, or would you just get more defensive and argue back? Look what happens with you and your boyfriend even—or you and your kids. When you yell at them, do they calm down and listen? Do they pay attention to you and do what you want? No, they get defensive or they yell back, or they sulk and they argue with you, and they just get their backs up more. Look at this in a common sense way."

In class Rosie brought up this situation. She could now see how it was self-defeating. She could now see that the food stamp worker probably just had a rough day and faced a lot of belligerent clients who hadn't done their paper work and wanted their food stamps anyway. So when Rosie's turn came the worker started to give her a hard time. Maybe the welfare worker had a fight with her husband the night before, or maybe she was sick of her job and didn't think she could do any better.

"So she's going to take it out on me," concluded Rosie. "And I don't have to take it personally. Instead, I could say, 'You must be having a rough day. What can I do? Just let me get my paperwork done and get out of your hair.'"

Rosie began to discover that when she was nicer to people it calmed them down. When she saw them as human beings, in their separate realities, and treated them that way, they responded. She got what she wanted more, without the upset and turmoil. Even when she had thoughts of wanting to kill Dr. Mills she began to realize that it was just her mood, and she didn't need to act on it. She learned how to settle down, to calm herself and wait until those thoughts dissipated.

Yet, Rosie was still being beaten a lot by her man.

Rosie: I was in an abusive relationship. Very abusive. Before I got involved with this approach I didn't have any self-esteem. I was just at home, having babies. The outside world didn't matter.

Doc wanted to try to help Rosie and others see that what they thought was normal wasn't really so. It was just how they had learned to think, and what they had come to accept.

VII. Spring, 1988

Roger's grant proposed to reduce student discipline referrals to the school principal's office. This could only happen if the teachers knew how to deal constructively with these kids. So Dr. Mills offered a twenty-five hour teacher training course for the Homestead Middle School.

The course would have to be voluntary. To mandate it would spell disaster. Teachers would resent being forced to attend, and during the training they would display every behavior that they would never let their own students get away with. They would grumble, work on their lesson plans or read the newspaper.

> **Maria Garcia:** A lot of us are trying to do the best we can in the classroom, and we kind of feel resentful towards people who think they can come in and do it better. Here's this guy who wears a three-piece suit, in his ivory tower . . .

The teacher training began in February. Over the first year about one quarter of the faculty attended one of three courses. Once a week for two hours they met in the library after school. Roger tried to make the atmosphere relaxed and easy, offering coffee and donuts to help the teachers unwind from the day.

> **Maria Garcia:** The child who has been here every day, who you think has been listening, out of the ten little questions he misses six, and you think, "Why is that happening? Why does he have so many things in his head that he can't sit and enjoy being a kid? Or that little girl in the sixth grade, 12 years old, who comes in all full of hickeys. Doesn't her mother see that? Why should I have to worry about that? Which I do. A lot of us in education, we're

here because we want to be here. I know it's not the greatest paying job in the world, but I want to make a difference. But it is kind of sad for me to think that I've made a difference if I reach one child in thirty years of teaching. I should want to be able to say a whole lot more than that.

Dr. Mills: The basic idea behind the teacher training was to get the teachers to see these kids differently. Their beliefs about these kids were a large part of the problem. Many were saying, "I hope I don't get any Modello kids in my class!" They had the kids stereotyped. As soon as a Modello kid got in their class the kid had three strikes against him. The kid didn't have a chance because the teacher didn't really give him a chance. So the teachers attitudes and expectations kept them seeing the Modello kids in a way that inadvertently kept the kids locked into a negative frame of mind about themselves and school. So much of the teacher training was aimed at helping the teachers see them as basically healthy kids who had just developed an alienated perspective. We tried to get the teachers to see that the child is basically innocent, that the kids basically want to learn, want to do well in school, want to cooperate. We talked to the teachers about their state of mind, how stressed out they were, how they saw these kids, how much they enjoyed teaching, how much of their excitement about the subject matter they passed along to the kids. We had to talk about all these things that they could relate to: about common sense and maturity in their own lives, their self-esteem—because you can't teach something you don't know. If you're not a happy person and you're not satisfied with your work, how can you pass along a good attitude about learning to your students?

Dr. Mills began the training by saying: "Every child is born with a natural propensity to use common sense. It's inborn. Kids don't start out predisposed towards deviance or self-destructive behavior. They actually start out predisposed to function with common sense, to know what's in their best interests. They start out with a kind of a natural enjoyment of learning, with positive motivation that doesn't have 'proving' or 'stress' associated with it.

"It's always amazed me how much little children are natural learners, and how learning becomes aversive when they get into the formal educational system. Somehow that natural desire to learn gets shut off like a faucet. It's shut off because we, as educators, take learning so seriously. We think it's hard. We think grades are important. We create competition. We create stress—keeping the school's standardized test scores up. So our stress and insecurity is passed along to the kids. And guess what? They lose that natural interest in learning. It becomes aversive rather than fun.

"Also, a lot of these kids' parents have not gone to school. They've given up on school, so they're going to pass that on to their children—not consciously, not purposely, but because that's what they see possible for themselves. So what we want to try to do is see how to reengage these students in learning.

"Every child wants to do the best at whatever they take on and if they're enjoying it they will do their best without any pressure or stress or performance anxiety. Kids start out with unconditional self-esteem. Have you ever seen a two year old or three year old whose self esteem is conditional on how expensive their clothes are, or what color their skin is? They just enjoy life. They're not self-conscious. See, that's all stuff we learn from our upbringing, isn't it?

"So what happens is the child learns a set of beliefs. They develop a way of thinking because their parents say, 'You can't feel good about yourself unless _____.' All of a sudden we start to put conditions on their self-esteem or their well-being. 'You can't feel good about yourself unless you go to school looking nice.' We try to impose our standards on our kids because we think it reflects on us, so we try to make their self-esteem conditional in a certain way. Then they develop insecure beliefs, and their self-esteem is conditional. So when they get insecure they act out or get in trouble or react in a dysfunctional way.

"We found, with most of the kids we've been working with, that by the time they get into the first grade they have very insecure beliefs. They think that they don't fit in, that adults don't like them, that other kids won't like them, that they can't learn because they're Black, because they come from the projects, because their parents have dropped out, because of all the negativity in the home, because their parents are yelling at them all the time and telling them they're bad or stupid. So that becomes their way of thinking about themselves.

"Now, you want to keep in mind that they never lose their innate mental health. It's impossible. It just gets covered up or pushed underneath the surface. But it's still there and still has a natural tendency to come back to the surface like a cork being held under water. So as soon as you take whatever insecure thoughts that are keeping it down out of the way, it will pop back up on its own. It naturally reemerges. As soon as you start to show a kid that these negative beliefs are just thoughts, not "reality," this will come back almost immediately. If they find any teacher or a counselor who just starts to treat them as if they're okay, treats them with love and respect and listens to them, treats them as if they're a whole person or a healthier person that health just comes right back to the surface.

"But the child enters school with this insecure way of seeing things, so if another kid gets angry at him or pushes him, or if a teacher looks at him cross-eyed, if he's insecure he'll react. He'll get in trouble, and that will give him further evidence that he doesn't fit in, that others don't like him, that teachers are against him or her. It just reinforces his view. If we have an insecure way of thinking, we interpret what's going on as evidence: 'that teacher really is against me; the other kids really don't like me.' And what's his emotional response going to be? He's going to get angry or feel hurt or feel sorry for himself or withdraw or talk back to the teacher. So the negative emotion will create a negative behavior. And the negative behavior will cause a certain kind of response from the teachers: send him to the principal, or give him an F or detention. So the response will reinforce that thinking that they are against him, that he can't make it in school, that he's not going to do okay. Do you see how it becomes a self-confirming, downward spiral of increasing alienation?

"So most of these kids don't expect to finish high school. They don't think it's the place for them to be. But it's just a cycle of thought that a child picks up. And you can break this at any point—if an adult really believes in you and likes you and connects with you and engages your healthier levels and really inspires you to do better than you thought you could do. You can get through to these kids at any moment. You can turn these kids around. If you build a good rapport with these students, the quality of your relationship will make their thinking relax, and it will bring out the best in them.

"You can't give a child self-esteem. He or she already has it. All you have to do is engage them in a way that it starts to come out of them."

Most of the teachers had never looked at it that way before.

* * *

Many more parents showed up at P.T.A. meetings when the topic of discussion centered around problems with the school. The same phenomenon began to happen any time an issue hit home. Rosie would knock on doors, tell parents about the issue, and ask them to come out and talk about what to do. At first the residents had been quite wary, but with Rosie, Pam, Doc, and Lloyd all asking, "What would you like to see changed in your community?" instead of telling them what to do, the residents became less suspicious and began to come up with ideas.

"Whatever it is you want to say, there will be time for you to say it. It's not just for us five, it's for everybody. Just come in, put your opinion in and let's get the thing going."

The parents would trickle in and see, "Hey, my opinion did count!"

They would sit around in a circle, bring up issues, offer opinions, and make decisions. At least one of the staff would sit in with them. To start the meetings they would ask, "How are you doing?" "What's happening with you?" "How can we help you make your community better?" The staff then stayed in the background while the parents ran the group. They would never tell residents what issues to concentrate on or how to make decisions. Doc kept saying to staff, "We've got to trust the residents' wisdom to know the best thing to do." The parents appreciated it. Any idea was considered okay and, as Lisa said, "There were some doozies."

The staff were there to help if needed. When the meetings bogged down they might ask, "Is there anything we can help you with about getting your kids to go to school on a regular basis?" "How do you feel about school?" "How do you feel about the teachers and administrators?" "How can you bridge the gaps between you and the administrators?" "What would you do to make the school better?" "What do you see happening in the community with your kids?"

They talked about how to resolve the truancy problem, how they could eliminate the drug dealing, how they could get maintenance to be more responsive. The P.T.A. became the focal point to take on all community issues.

When he was around, Dr. Mills wanted to use these meetings as opportunities to teach Psychology of Mind concepts. He wanted the residents to understand that the people who were giving them problems were also doing the best they knew how. They could see HUD workers and welfare workers as human beings who just needed some guidance and help in doing their jobs better. Even the police, school teachers, and principals were innocent and doing their best.

"When you approach these people," Doc would say, "you don't want to go in there with an attitude, or yelling at them and putting them down and making them feel like the scum of the earth— because you don't want people to do it to you."

Certainly the parents had bones to pick with the teachers and school administrators, and the school could not get the parents to come in and meet about their kids. Many parents were dropouts themselves. They were intimidated, afraid to respond when a teacher called them. Nearly everyone wanted to string up one of the elementary school teachers whom they thought racist. She was always on their kids' cases, calling them "little black monkeys." The principal didn't respond. He was an ex-military man who was hard on the kids and gave parents a hard time. The barrier between school and parents had to be broken.

"Look," said Doc, "they're just conditioned to think a certain way. They don't know any better. They're overwhelmed with all these so-called 'high risk' students in the school. The school has a bad reputation. The principal is trying to save his ass and be the tough guy. Keep that in mind. Invite the principal over to a P.T.A. meeting, tell him what you want to do, and ask for his help. Don't go in there and lay the man out."

The P.T.A. decided to ask the principal to come and meet with them. They had a productive discussion. The residents began to see that they had a choice in how they dealt with people. Which way yielded better results—to go storming in there in a rage, or to approach people this way? Once they looked at it, it was common sense.

* * *

As the Middle School teacher training progressed, Dr. Mills talked about 'state of mind' as the most important variable in behavior. A child acting out in the classroom is not being a bad child, he or she is just being insecure in the moment.

From what they learned in the training some teachers began to stop taking the kids' behavior personally. They began to see the kids with more understanding and compassion. They came to understand that these were basically good kids, and that every child is capable of learning, of having positive motivation, of coming up with their own answers. They learned that if a student was having trouble, he or she could be helped to calm down, to see things differently and to use more common sense. The teachers could calm down too.

The teachers raised questions about discipline. Many believed they had to be pretty heavy-handed about punishments and consequences to teach the kids to behave.

Dr. Mills responded, "But you put the same kids in detention or suspend them all the time, and it doesn't appear to help. Another way to look at it is you could establish a relationship with each child, understand more what's going on in their homes, see what's causing them to swear in class or talk back, understand what the child's insecurities are. You could make them feel more comfortable and be more accepting of them, so it would then be easier for them to settle down for you. Try to be more patient, more present with each student, and see each one differently. Just get to know them as people. Every day when every child comes to school, see them as healthy. See each as a child that is able to learn, rather than, 'Oh no, here comes so and so—another day with that kid who's going to give me a hard time.'"

"This is no panacea," Dr. Mills cautioned. "It's no overnight remedy. Sometimes no matter how positive you try to be, no matter how much you try to change the other person's outlook, it's still going to be a very long and gradual process. They may never see things that way, so all you can really do is see it for yourself."

Teacher training evaluations showed that the teachers were helped by seeing that their biggest problem in the classroom was their own state of mind.

* * *

Dr. Mills began to see a subtle change in Cicely. Slowly, she would say something in class. Gradually, she began to contribute. Her eyes would look up a bit from the floor. Her voice became a little more clear. She became a little more involved in the happenings of the P.T.A.

"You know, you can help your children," Dr. Mills said to Cicely one day when he felt the time was right. "You've got it in you. You could see what's going on with them a little differently, and you can guide them."

Cicely was ready to listen but had no idea what to do.

"You could just show them more love and attention," Dr. Mills suggested. "You could do things with them. You could talk to them in a more common sense way, and help them see that they're on a dead end road. You could help them see that they could do more in their lives than just deal drugs on the corner."

It took a while but it began to make sense. Cicely had been taking everything they did personally. She took it all as a reflection on her. Dr. Mills told her it wasn't. Her kids weren't doing these things to her. They themselves were hurting, and they didn't know what else to do.

Slowly Cicely began to see that if she had self-esteem inside her— if it was naturally there like Dr. Mills kept saying—then she could feel good about herself. She could be happy in her life.

"I'm going to start feeling good about myself," Cicely declared one day.

* * *

Rosie brought a new participant to the parenting class. She cared about Thelma very much.

Thelma stayed drunk nearly all the time. Everyone knew it; everyone talked about it. When she went on a drinking binge with the father of her youngest children, a man in worse shape than she, he would beat her unmercifully. Their frequent fights would begin in the apartment and often end up in the middle of the courtyard for everyone to see. Thelma's eyes were continually swollen and painted, and her lips busted up from the beatings. Thelma's boyfriend was also apparently sexually abusing one of her daughters. Again, everyone knew. There were no secrets in Modello.

Thelma: Before Dr. Mills came around, I was like this: I didn't go nowhere. I stayed home. I kept my house clean. Stayed pregnant. I had a lot pressure on me. I was a mother with nine children. My daughter, she was expecting. My oldest daughter, she was sick, and it was like I didn't have anybody to reach out to me. And my boyfriend, my kid's father, he was beating me up. And I was drinking a lot. I wouldn't have nothing to do with my neighbors. I wouldn't even go to their house to use the telephone. And with my kids, as long as they handed me $5 or $10 to get me a bottle—if I just had my bottle, everything would have been cool to me. And when I go to get my lips to that bottle, I wouldn't get no half pint, I had to get me one of those liters. As long as I had my liter of liquor, I was all right.

Thelma was too drunk to care to do anything with her children.

Rosie hated to see Thelma like this. Rosie had been trying to conquer her own battering problems—nothing compared to this—and felt she had to do something. She wanted to get Thelma to the parenting class.

Thelma had met Dr. Mills briefly and had heard him say some things about low moods and high moods and psychology, and her reaction was no different than the rest of the women.

"This man is crazier than I am." she said. "This man, he don't know what he's talking about." She certainly did not want to go to any parenting class.

But Rosie was asking her to come.

"Okay, I'll be there," she gave in.

Thelma attended her first meeting. To her surprise she liked it! She went to her second meeting, and she liked that too.

At her third meeting Thelma walked in 45 minutes late, her face tore up, black eyes, hair in disarray, no shoes, feet caked with mud, clothes dirty, not smelling any too good and looking like she'd just been through hell.

No one raised an eyebrow.

Doc only seemed glad to see her—he always did, no matter how anyone looked—even bruised and barefoot and with torn, dirty dresses. Everyone in the class responded in kind. No judgment. Nobody shifted in their chairs in discomfort. Doc only talked possibilities. He paid no attention to what might be wrong. He wanted only to give everyone a nice feeling about themselves. Thelma would be accepted no matter how she appeared, no matter how she looked or acted, no matter what she had been through.

"Hi Thelma! How are you doing? I'm glad to see you. Come sit down. How are you feeling today?"

To hear Thelma tell it, this incident was a test. Others weren't so sure.

Thelma: I say, I'm going to try him a third time, but I'm going to go in there and I'm going to be myself. And I go in there, and it had been raining, and I was barefoot, and I had mud all over my feet. I say, I'm going to try this man. He claim he's all this and he's all that. And I'll go in there barefooted, mud all over my feet, to see how he's going to accept me then, right? I went up there, barefooted and all that, mud between my toes and stuff, and I stepped in there, and Dr. Mills looked at me and smiled with this great big old smile on his face, like he was not paying my feet any attention, you know. And he started talking to me. He was just asking me how I was doing, and he was glad to see me. He was greeting me, you know? And I'm standing there looking at this man saying, this man ain't paying no attention to my feet, and look how black they are! And he was talking to me like a man should talk to a lady, right? And that made me feel bad. I mean, I made my own self feel bad by me coming in there like this, right? And I'm coming in like this just to see how he's going to accept me. I'm testing him. Let me tell you, I really felt bad. I didn't stay there. I left. I told him I'd be back. I went home, got in the tub, took me a good bath, and I came back. Then I stepped back in there.

Thelma was shocked that the class didn't reject her for the way she looked, for the way she was—not only Dr. Mills but everyone in that parenting group. It proved a breakthrough in the way she saw herself.

Thelma: It looked to me like they saw good in me, you know?

Thelma began to feel better about herself, and her eyes began to open wide.

* * *

Three months into the class and P.T.A. they'd developed such rapport there was almost no distinction between staff and residents. Lloyd was just Lloyd, not Lloyd Fields social worker. Dr. Mills was just Doc. At those times the residents instinctively knew that no one was trying to sell them a bill of goods.

Lisa: They were just like one of us. They ate the same things we ate. If we were having corn bread and beans, they ate corn bread and beans. There wasn't any funny stuff or anything like that.

And when we were going somewhere with these really educated people, it wasn't like, "I don't want them going this place because they're not quite as educated." No, we went. And there were some characters that went with us! But we accepted each other. We went to their house and said, "Hey, how are you doing?" And we'd know what was going on with their lives. They'd introduce us to their families, and we'd introduce them to ours. They weren't like workers. It was like they were just friends—just people.

On their outings Lloyd watched the ladies with great interest. He considered these times an extension of their group sessions. At such times the ladies were living the feeling the staff wanted to create through Psychology of Mind—no talking needed. Still, he waited for moments to interject some pertinent nuggets.

One time in the midst of eating, fooling around, talking freely, Lloyd saw Thelma so happy, talking her head off, something she rarely did. She brought up her son, Tyrone, with whom she had been having problems.

Lloyd asked, "What do you think you could do to help your son Tyrone?"

"You know something?" it dawned on her, "I could go to the school and talk with the teacher and talk with Tyrone when he comes home—just ask him how was school. I could put my arm around Tyrone and tell him I love him."

Before that moment it had never occurred to her to ask, "How's school?" or even to show him much affection.

"Oh, okay," said Lloyd, then they went back to their fun conversation.

One day on a picnic to the beach with the kids where everyone had a good time, Thelma confided to Doc: "There's something different about this program. Nobody's telling us what's wrong with us, or what we need to fix about ourselves or our kids."

Doc smiled. It was fun, yes, feeling like a family, but Roger knew they were learning more than they realized. In casual conversation when feelings were high, they were most open. Those were the times to interject something germane, to casually ask how they might look at various situations in a more common sense way.

If a resident was having trouble with her social worker trying to take away her kids because she wasn't going in for her urine analysis Doc would say, "Look, this social worker has nothing else to go on other than you not showing up for your drug tests or appointments. So because you're pissed at her for threatening to take away your kids, you're making it more likely that she'll do that. It's just common sense, when you stop and think about it."

They talked often about common sense. Doc insisted that everyone has it. It could help them. But when people are upset or angry or down or caught up in things, they don't have access to it. Nobody does. The ladies became fascinated with the concept.

* * *

In May, to celebrate the one year anniversary of the opening of the Modello store, and to have a family celebration day, they decided to hold a momentous community event, complete with barbecue, carnival rides, clowns, and a D.J. on stage set up on the basketball court. About 400 people came out, including parents, kids, friends from other projects, neighbors, relatives. Sergeant Carl Baske from the Metro-Dade Police Department, who had begun to take great interest in Modello and visit fairly often, showed up with a couple of other officers. Everyone had a wonderful time. They laughed and danced and sang and kidded around and played a little basketball at the other end of the court.

Just before the event, one of the prime drug dealers approached Pam.

"You know, Pam," he said, "I really have a lot of respect for what you're trying to do here, so out of respect to you we're not going to sell drugs here today."

Pam: I was thrilled. The next day they went back to selling, of course, but that day, out of respect, they didn't sell. I was very touched by that. I really felt as though I had made some inroads. I considered it one of my biggest successes.

* * *

"No blame" made Lisa first begin to listen.

Initially she had come in thinking, "Parenting class? He's going to tell us how to raise our kids, and everything we're doing is going to be wrong."

Instead Dr. Mills said, "Everyone is doing the best they can at the time, given how they see things, so there's no blame to place on anyone—whatever your situation is. I'm not here trying to tell you how to raise your children. I'm just offering you alternatives."

The parents would bring up some of the "bad" things their kids would do.

"No child is really bad," said Dr. Mills.

"You haven't seen some of our kids!"

Another chimed in, "I don't care what you say. Maybe hers isn't bad, and maybe hers isn't bad, but mine is bad!"

"They just have their own way of seeing things," Doc responded.

This may have been a parenting class, a meeting to talk about their kids or other problems around Modello, but Roger knew that the parents would first have to find the answer for themselves.

Lisa: He was just wanting us to work on ourselves. He just had to help us see how to do it.

Patty: Through having our class I realized I had to pick it up. I had to get myself together so my kids could see that I was trying to get myself together. And I started having a little more patience trying to get settled in that neighborhood. Doc put a lot of light on things that I really didn't understand at first.

Doc and Lloyd never stopped trying to think up creative ways to help them see their situation in a different light. The message was basically the same, but each resident somehow had to be able to see it for herself. That was the trick. They didn't always see the connection.

After someone in class brought up a distressing incident concerning her child, Doc said, "If you feel like killing your child when you're really upset with him, just notice that's how you're feeling. Then, once you notice it, put a lid on it—don't do it—and walk around the block, or go to a neighbor's, or watch TV, or send them to their room, or lie down on the couch with pillows over your head. Do whatever you need to do to try to calm down and get in a nicer frame of mind. Try to get a nice feeling back for your child first before dealing with him. Wait until your mood shifts. When you think about your child, think about his innocence, or think about him in a more loving way or a more accepting way. Then go talk to him, and listen to him, and see that your child has got his own reality, his own way of looking at things. And know that he has common sense too."

Doc would say, "Notice your moods. Notice how you are with your children at the times you're really feeling good and at ease, and how you behave toward them when they're really upset about something—and the results of that."

Doc would ask the ladies, "Do you notice how you see things differently when you're in a really bad mood? Things look awful, and your kids look like monsters, and this place looks like the hell end of the world. But when you're in a good mood, then you have a nice day and enjoy your kids and enjoy your neighbors. Your moods and your thinking are connected."

The parents seemed to resonate with the concept. They could see when they were in a bad mood and having a rotten day, and then their kid annoyed them, it was the straw that broke the camel's back. They'd take it out on their kids. Their kids would take the brunt of it and get screamed at or knocked across the room. If the parent simply noticed the mood she was in—was just aware of it—then she had access to the option to stop taking it out on her children so much. Plus, she wouldn't have to suffer so much herself because she would come out of it faster. The parents noticed that when they were in a good mood, they saw their children in nicer ways. If they noticed it, they had more volition about it. Doc and Lloyd continuously would bring this to their attention.

"When you're in a bad mood, your kid looks like monsters and brats, and you yell at them. Then they get in a bad mood and yell back. Do you see that dynamic? When you're in a good mood, do you notice that you're more loving and interested in your children, and they seem more calm and cooperative?"

All this talk about moods was beginning to make some sense. They began to say to themselves, "I could either knock my kid across the room, or go out and walk around the block, or talk to my neighbor for a while until I calm down. Then I can come back and talk to my child in a calmer way and get better results."

Sometimes Lloyd would ask, "What do you do to discipline your kids?"

"Well, I beat my kids. I wear his ass out!"

"I don't do anything. I just tell him that he shouldn't do it, and I just keep telling him and it doesn't do any good."

"I have to stay on my children's case all the time because my kids are bad. My kids are bad!"

"This one is smart, but this other one acts like a joke."

In response Lloyd would say, "Did you ever notice that if you always tell your kid he's crazy, he acts crazy. If you tell him he's smart, then he's going to try to act smart."

The staff would never tell the parents what to do. They only wanted to help them see things in a different way. They would then see for themselves whether it worked.

Some parents disagreed with their view. Lloyd said, "If what we said bothers you, that's okay. Don't think about it. Just enjoy yourself while you're here."

Doc wanted the class to be an oasis where the parents would gather and feel comfortable. If they felt relaxed and lighthearted they would let down their guard, and maybe some learning would get through. It appeared to be working.

Dr. Mills: We said everyone has an innate capacity to function with common sense. You already know how to be a good parent. It's just a matter of getting yourself in that state of mind where your common sense will help you see what your child needs at any moment. There's really no parenting technique that can help you. You just have to watch your own moods. When you're in a low mood, that's the wrong time to interact with your child. Just wait until your mood changes, and listen to your child and you'll see how they're seeing things and how they're caught up in their own separate reality, their own separate way of seeing things— and then you'll be able to help them. The point of discipline is, really, to help the kids regain their perspective, or regain their own capacity for common sense, as opposed to punishment for punishment's sake.

Lloyd: It was just sitting on the wave and letting the wave carry us, and we'd just flow with the wave. If it goes the way of talking about kids, then we'd probably spend two weeks talking about our kids. It may flow to police involvement and then might flow right back. But whichever way it flowed, our main objective was to get them to understand how thought works, what moods are and how they operate in them, what to look for and what not to look for, what to trust and what not to trust.

* * *

One day, Carrie Mae's son brought a knife to his fifth grade class and cut one of the other kids.

Carrie Mae had a volatile temper. She would "go off" on her neighbors or on her own kids whenever it struck. If a teacher did something to her kids that she didn't like, she would storm down to school. If the school ever called about her child doing something bad, she was known to stomp down the street to the school, take down his pants, and whip him with a belt right in front of the principal.

When she received this phone call from the school, she became livid. Quickly she grabbed her belt. She roared down the street to the school ready to do some damage.

Halfway there something clicked. Into her head popped something she'd heard in the parenting class: "Don't interact with your child when in a low mood. Take a break first, calm down, let off some steam."

"Uh oh," she said to herself, "You're in a bad mood right now. You'd better watch it.".

When Carrie Mae reached the school she picked up her child without saying a word. She brought him home, told him to go to his room, walked over to a neighbor's apartment, and stayed there for three hours—until she found that warm, loving feeling for him return. Then she went to him.

She brought up the situation at the next parenting class.

"It took me three hours to calm down enough to feel like I could talk to him right. I came home and told my son to come out. He was ready to get beaten up, because that's what he was used to. I said, 'No, I'm not going to hit you. I just want to find out what you could have been thinking—why it made sense for you to do that. I want to understand. Are you having problems at school?' And he said the older kids were picking on him, and he didn't know what else to do. He was scared, and this was the only way he could figure to handle it. And I was shocked because I never stopped long enough before to find out what he was going through. And we had the best conversation we ever had in our lives. We both broke down and cried and hugged each other. Then we talked about other ways that he could have handled it, like going to the principal or the teacher, or talking to me."

It proved a major breakthrough in their relationship. Carrie Mae stopped having those problems with her son.

This was the power of understanding moods, of understanding the need to back off in low moods, to calm down, to get back the feeling, to become reconnected with one's own common sense and wisdom—then respond with a loving feeling.

The parents shared such stories, and the rest listened and learned. Many had similar experiences.

* * *

Modello residents were not happy with the police. When they burst into the project on a raid or sting they didn't always know who "the bad guys" were, so anyone who happened to be around would either have a gun pointed at them or be told, "Hey, you better get your butt on the ground!"

Lloyd: When there were gunshots, a lot of kids used to duck into the Modello store. People would call 911, and the dispatchers at 911 would say that they weren't giving them the right type of information, so they couldn't really respond to whatever problem it was. And when the police did come, they would come in like gangbusters, and anybody in the way would get it. They wouldn't care.

Cynthia Stennis [Modello day care director]: The sirens would be blasting, and the kids would be ripping and running, and they could get run over. Because I seen it before, stomping on top of kids and stuff to try to get at one person. Yeah, I was there, and I seen it!

The parents brought up the problem in the P.T.A.. Lloyd asked, "How could the police do a better job? How could they help you?"

They decided to ask State Attorney Janet Reno to come in and sit down with them. She came with representatives from the police force to talk about how they could be more effective.

P.T.A. members said, "What are you all doing about guys on every corner? Whoever comes in here, they run to your car thinking you want drugs or something."

The police replied, "If you want the drugs out of your neighborhood, you're going to have to help us out. If we're coming in, and you know it's a sting, if we say, 'Go into your house,' don't sit there and argue with us. Go in the house, because we've got guns blaring and we're looking for these guys. Don't let them come through your apartment."

"Hey look, if somebody comes running through our apartment, they've got a gun too, and I'm going to let them run through my apartment!"

Slowly, they began to understand each other's concerns. A rapport began to develop, at least among some residents—a big switch. The police began to see that the residents were willing to look at them differently. Therefore, they could begin to change some of their "normal" police behavior.

Whenever Pam and Lloyd knew of a big problem with a family and knew the police would be coming, they would try to be sure at least one of them was present while it was happening to help ease the situation. They would try to calm people down and connect with their common sense, and hear what they had to say so head-to-head anger wouldn't result in violence. If Pam or Lloyd could get even one party to be a little more calm, the other would often respond in kind.

* * *

When Pam first started in Modello many residents would not even speak to each other. They were mortal enemies. "You don't cross my area." "Don't come into my territory." "You don't touch my kids or talk to them." As Roger's philosophy began to slowly pervade the area, gradually Pam began to see those barriers dissolve. Relationships improved. Judgments slowly dissipated. People began to think, "We're all here trying to get by. We may make mistakes, but we're all here for the same reasons."

Roger felt quite heartened to see these subtle changes. He began to see change in people before they even saw changes in themselves. He saw people soften, their faces look younger, their eyes get a twinkle. He'd see it in their step and how they talked. They seemed to enjoy themselves more and look nicer. Doc would go home encouraged and delighted, feeling, "Ah, it's starting to take!"

On other days he left frustrated, thinking, "Oh, I didn't really get that across," or, "I didn't really address what they were really asking." On some days nobody showed up for a class. On others the entire community acted as if it was in a lowered state of consciousness and everything seemed set back two years. People were arguing, fighting, complaining, threatening to kill each other. The whole place was in an uproar, and they couldn't get anyone to calm down. The police had just done a sweep, marching into someone's apartment, pushing them around. Everybody wanted to string up the police and didn't want to hear anything about calming down or handling it in a better way.

On such days Roger would go home discouraged, "Oh, this hasn't taken at all! Fuck it! I'm going to quit. This whole thing's a pain in the ass. It's not worth it. It's not going to work."

But Roger Mills knew enough about moods to know that he too experienced them. If he felt discouraged it was just his mood talking. It was only how he was thinking about it at the moment. Roger needn't take those thoughts seriously. He knew they would pass.

A couple of days later he would go back and find that the residents too had gotten over their mood and were in a more rational state of mind. That was simply how it worked.

Besides, in Modello things changed so fast and so often that most of the time it kept him feeling hopeful and wanting to see what would happen next.

VIII. Summer, 1988

Suddenly ten parents were attending the classes. Then thirteen. Then fifteen or sixteen. Others would drift in and out. A couple of men even showed up from time to time.

Lisa began to truly enjoy the classes. "This is great!" she said.

In response her man said, "You're going to too many classes! And this shit he's talking, you're listening too much!"

Lisa kept attending.

Soon a position at the store again opened. Rosie came by Lisa's apartment.

"You know Lisa," she said, "a lot of people are applying but Pam wants you."

Lisa looked up from her cooking.

"Go on," said Rosie.

Lisa turned off the stove and said, "I'm going!"

Lisa sat in a room interviewed by Pam, Sam MacKinnon and his boss, and others. They made her feel comfortable. They wanted to know if she was honest, what she would do in certain situations. Lisa zipped through the interview.

Thirty minutes later Pam called her at home. They selected her.

Lisa felt fantastic. They'd chosen her! She practically jumped around the room.

After beginning the job, Lisa peeked at the files. Lots of people had applied—lots who had graduated high school—and they'd chosen her!

Carrie Mae trained Lisa, and Lisa caught on immediately. She could do this! It felt great! But the greatest part was that Pam had put faith in her.

Lisa did a beautiful job in that store. She was so proud of herself. She worked there for three years until they closed her baby down.

Doc's help about her kids had opened Lisa enough for her to begin to express concern that her boyfriend put her down all the time.

"Well, he probably just feels insecure at times, shaky about himself," Doc responded, "then he puts you down because he's in a bad space or a low mood or something. But you don't have to take it personally or buy what he says, because it's not really true. It's just his perspective at that moment—how he's looking at things."

Lisa had never thought of it that way.

"Your situation doesn't have to be like that" she heard Doc say, "You can be happy. You can be whatever you want to be. Your children don't have to follow the same path that you did. Whatever happened in your life doesn't have to take control of you now. Whatever happened, put it back in the past. Whatever happened to you can't hurt you now."

"That's not true!" Lisa argued, angry at the notion.

"Lisa, the past can't hurt you now because it's already happened."

But so many things had happened, and they were terrible, and they caused wretched feelings.

"That's not true!" Lisa practically yelled. "They are still with me now. They're on my mind all the time. They happened, and it doesn't matter what happens in the future, because I still have to worry about what happened."

"If you don't worry about it, it will go away."

"Is this man crazy?!" Lisa said to herself, infuriated. "He didn't have these things happen to him. He didn't go through what I did! No way that can be true!"

Lisa could not understand what Mills was saying.

Doc would see Lisa in the store looking terribly depressed, and he'd say, "You don't have to be that down, it's just your thoughts."

"It's got nothing to do with my thoughts," she shouted. "Fuck you! It's my life, not yours. They won't fix my apartment. My bathroom is leaking. My kids won't mind me. They're brats. That's what I'm using all my energy for."

When she was depressed and and in a low mood Roger refused to buy into her victimization, no matter how vehemently and angrily she defended her reality. Lisa fussed and fumed at him, but a few days later in a better frame of mind she always came around and apologized.

"What you were saying made sense," she admitted.

Roger hung in with Lisa. He could see that she was getting something from it—whether she realized it or not. He knew that somewhere, somehow, he could find an opening under the radar—if he could only get in low enough.

* * *

Cicely had begun to open up. Everyone in the class seemed to help. Everyone was supportive—especially Lisa. She became a true friend.

Cicely: With my kids and all, you know it really took me a long time. I didn't know where it was. They had to pull it out of me, but it was in me all the time. Dr. Mills' program has been a lot of help to me. It brought a lot of things in me out of me. I started feeling good about myself.

Thelma: We would go to picnics, and I didn't have that. My parents didn't do that for me when I was coming up. I didn't know nothing about going to picnics or any different things. And the more I would go, the more I would feel good about myself. They made me feel like I was somebody, and they made me feel like I was important, and I still could be somebody, you know? And it changed me.

In class one day Dr. Mills asked Thelma, "Do you think your kids have the same moods that you have?"

"No."

"Why do you think that?"

"Because it's impossible for them to have the same moods that I have, because I'm grown and they're still children."

"That's the difference in what we're saying."

"What?"

"Your kids have the same moods that you have."

"Dr. Mills, that's impossible. How?"

"It's true. We're all born with something in us. We're all born with common sense."

"That's true."

"Now, think about what I just said."

"What?"

"I said that we're all born with the same things inside us, right?"

"Yuh."

"Now, think about it?"

Thelma sat back perplexed. Then came the light.

"You're right! You're right. Our kids do have low moods and high moods like me."

"Why do you say that?"

"Like you said, we ALL was born with that common sense; we all was born with moods. Those kids, they have to have their low moods and high moods too."

"Explain it to me."

"When our kids are acting up, that's when they're in their low moods, so their low moods and their high moods are the same as us because it's the same as us adults do."

"Right. You can watch it for yourself."

Thelma nodded with a smile. "I'm going to watch for myself, and if I see that it's like you say it is, then I'm going to come and let you know it."

During the next few days Thelma watched very carefully. She discovered that her kids acted exactly as she did. If she was in a low mood or upset she would act it out toward her kids. If her kids were low and upset they would act it out toward her. It was identical.

Thelma came back to the next class excited.

"Dr. Mills, You're right! You're right."

Doc smiled. He knew she'd had an important breakthrough.

Thelma: People came there and they said they were going to do this and that, and they didn't do it. They did not do it! They came down and they told lies, that's what they did. When Dr. Mills came in and said what he was going to do, he did it. And he had enemies behind him. And the reason he had enemies behind him was the ones that came in before him said they were going to do this for us, and they didn't do it. Then here this man comes out of nowhere and starts getting these things working in the project, and then they went against him because he did it. Some of the tenants would take Dr. Mills through some changes. They would have meetings, and it was mostly jealousy. Some of them were against him. They would cuss him out. They thought he was the police, that he'd come and tear their house down. They thought bad all sorts of things about him. I really don't know why. But that's life though. When you start out and do something good, there are going to be half for you and half against you. That goes for everything that you do. Dr. Mills, he expected that. He knew that was going to take place.

* * *

They lost some, too.

A month after school let out Dr. Mills came down to teach a parenting class to find that an eighth grader had shot a rival who'd been messing around with his girlfriend. Police swarmed about. Sirens blared. Modello was in chaos. Forget the parenting class; they had to try to help cool down the situation.

The kid was one of the first Lloyd had worked with. He was a quiet boy, at least around Lloyd. He didn't get into much trouble at school, but he was hanging with the wrong crowd, listening to them instead of to Lloyd. It happened over a girl.

The gang had said, "Hey, if you're that upset about it, fight him."

They fought. The other kid beat him up pretty badly. Now he was even more upset.

His gang said, "Why don't you get a gun and shoot him!"

So he did—with a friend. They chased the kid out into the field and shot him. Killed him.

The police whisked them off to jail.

Lloyd had tried. He'd tried to encourage him to stay with his books, to not get so caught up in what the guys that he was hanging with were up to. But his mother was alcoholic and his older brother was involved with drugs and had a powerful influence. Lloyd felt he was getting through sometimes, but the kid wouldn't say much. The more he hung out, the more influential his friends became. Lloyd watched their influence overcome him. He could see it heading for disaster, but nothing he said seemed to make a difference.

Lloyd hurt. A life ended! It shouldn't have happened that way. And over what?

Lloyd: You never want to say you missed that one, or you failed him.

Yet, deep down he knew that he may not have failed. Lloyd tried to talk with the boy's mother. Rosie tried too, but nothing seemed to take hold. It was just one of those things. Lloyd couldn't take it personally. He had learned that much.

The kid's mother was extremely distraught. Lloyd and Rosie tried to calm her. Though the boy was only fourteen and it appeared that the fatal bullet had come from his friend's gun, she was afraid her son would be convicted as an adult and spend the rest of his life in jail. She began drinking and smoking crack even more. She spiraled down hill. As with her son no one could reach her. She did seem to have a special feeling for Dr. Mills, though, so they asked him to see her.

Dr. Mills told her she should first try to calm down, try not to worry too much. He'd have Lloyd see her son at the jail and counsel him. They would speak in his behalf and try their best to get the charges reduced. They knew he was not a bad kid. He was just so upset and distraught he'd acted out of impulse. If she calmed down, started straightening herself out, got her act together more and got some help with her drinking, she would be better able to help her son when he got out. She would be a better, more stable role model to him than his friends in the gang.

She confided that she was at the end of her rope—really scared. Ashamed, she thought her neighbors looked down on her now because of what her son had done. Mostly she grieved.

"You can help him just by the quality of your life," said Dr. Mills, "and the feeling that you're living with."

The mother did begin to settle down. She went into detox. When she came out she went to the skills center to work on her G.E.D. She got a job in the kitchen at the elementary school and was doing pretty well.

Even in a horrible situation at least some good came of it.

As for Lloyd his "failure" became but a blip on a screen. So much of what he did with people began to work. So many people began to change.

* * *

Rosie hadn't expected to see changes in herself. She was there to help her community and her neighbors—and for a job. About six months after working with Dr. Mills, however, looking back she realized she'd changed some. She realized it after it had already happened, after the fact.

It was not unlike what had originally happened with Roger. As had happened with him years ago he could see that the philosophy of "Health Realization"—realizing the innate health that everyone has within—was beginning to penetrate. It was beginning to work on Rosie's mind without her even realizing it, as if she had taken time-capsule medication. Without realizing it Rosie found herself calmer around her kids, listening better, being more loving. They began to respond in kind. Something was beginning to shift in her head, on her eyeballs, and she gradually came to see a different world than she'd seen before. She began to calm down a bit and see things in a more common sense way. In turn she started acting differently. Then after the fact she began to look back and see some change. Dr. Mills and Pam saw the progress.

Rosie: At first it didn't make a lot of sense because, to be happy, you've been programmed to think that's hard work. It's not something that's natural. But he proved me wrong. He proved me wrong! It's not hard work. I don't have to beat myself in the head when I get happy [laughter], thinking that I don't deserve to be happy—because I do. But after we started to really get into it, I mean it really started to make sense. It was a while before I could really grasp it, that it was something that I already had. I already had it!

I was not raised in a housing project. My mother was not a welfare mother. I had a father. My mother and father were married. So it doesn't matter where you come from. If you don't feel good about yourself, then you can forget it. But anybody can feel good about themselves. I don't get upset anymore when I get happy, because there are people who always say that if you get too happy, something is going to happen. So you be so happy and you're wondering, "Why am I feeling so good today? God, something is going to happen! I got to hurry up and go and get myself in a bad mood because something is going to happen." [laughter].

* * *

One late afternoon Dr. Mills came out of a parenting class to find that his car wouldn't start. There had been a thunderstorm that morning on his way to Modello, and he'd left his lights on. Dead battery! Roger kept cranking it. Nothing happened. Without saying a word to the ladies he walked to the store and called A.A.A. to have them come down to start it. They said they'd be there in 45 minutes to an hour.

An hour passed. It began to get late. With Modello Mart about to close, A.A.A. still hadn't shown.

Roger's car was stuck in the middle of the project in front of the community center. At dark, Modello changed into a very different scene. At night, the men came out. They weren't really supposed to be there—they weren't the ones on the leases—so they wouldn't show during the day (except for the drug dealers, who didn't care). At night, the guys pulled in with their big cars and ghetto-blasters to hang out in the parking lot, talk jive and shoot their guns in the air.

Thelma: The project was bad in the evening. It was bad!

By 6:00 p.m. A.A.A. still hadn't arrived. Roger waited another hour. The woman working the store decided to keep it opened so he'd have a place to wait. She didn't want him hurt.

"Where's this A.A.A. guy?" wondered Roger, a bit anxious. Again he called.

The voice on the other end of the phone said, "The guy was on his way an hour and a half ago. I don't know what happened."

The company tried to track him down. Finally, they found him at home. He'd turned the corner to Modello, realized where he was and said, "The Hell with this, I'm not going in there!" He went home and didn't bother to call in. The company finally got the driver to agree to meet Roger on U.S. 1 at a restaurant, then drive in with him in the truck.

Thelma: We were watching him—because by this man walking out to get somebody to come and tow his car, I'm sure he was worried about somebody beating him up. So we were all outside, and we said, "Well, you all, we all got to get together and guard Dr. Mills' car." So we take chairs and put them around his car. I mean, we were talking loud, and we all sat there, and when he came out and turned the corner and he saw us by his car, it was a shock to him. It was me and Carrie Mae, and Rosie, and Cicely— all of them. We sat right there waiting for him to come back. And when he turned that corner and saw everybody who was in that class, all of us sitting there in chairs watching his car until he come back, he just lit up. When he turned that corner, he had a great big old smile on his face. He was really amazed. And we told him,

"We're watching your car so there won't be anything wrong with it when you get back here."

Otherwise it would been stripped clean or stolen for sure. The ladies sent a message: You'd better not mess with this man's car! Dr. Mills felt wonderfully protected and taken care of.

Thelma: And he knew then that we believed in what he was telling us, and we was taking in what he was saying.

IX. Fall, 1988

One day, Sam MacKinnon of the Perrine Optimists, who worked with Modello teenagers, brought a case to Lloyd's attention. Sam had a terrific relationship with the older kids and everyone respected him. He had seen Lloyd's success with some of the women and began to refer an increasing number of cases to him. When Sam spoke with a kid and noticed a difficult situation in the household he would tell Lloyd.

In this case, a crack-addicted mother was prostituting her two teenage daughters to bring money into the house to buy crack. She'd already sold all her furniture. Virtually nothing remained in the house. Pam knew of the case. The woman no longer had any pride or dignity. She'd gone as far to the bottom as Pam had seen anyone go. Her kids' behavior had become erratic. They were missing school a lot. The kids confided to Sam about what was going on, but he couldn't get them to tell the Department of H.R.S. so they could be protected. Sam informed Lloyd.

Sam, Lloyd, Doc, Pam, and Rosie put their heads together. They learned that the woman's utilities had been turned off because she wasn't paying her bills. Perhaps they could use this as an in. Lloyd would go and talk to the mother to help her get her utilities back on. That might lead to talk about trying to get her life turned around. She might even admit she had a drug problem that was affecting her kids. Lloyd would also speak with the kids.

At first Lloyd simply wanted to get to know them and break the ice. "How are you doing?" "What classes are you taking?" "What do you like to do?" "What teachers do you like?"

When it felt right, he got down to business. "How is your mother doing?"

"She's doing okay," was all he got.

Once they warmed up to Lloyd they confided, "Well, she's not giving us food. She's on that crack real bad."

"Well, I'm hoping that you guys can help us out," replied Lloyd.

The mother had nine kids. Lloyd learned that she would sometimes wake them up at 3:00 in the morning and order them to wash the refrigerator or mop the floor. Lloyd tried to imagine the chaos.

They called H.R.S. The investigator said that abuse could not be substantiated. Pam couldn't believe it! In her monthly reports she reported the situation to Janet Reno who became angered that the system was so ineffective. They decided it would be best to make it a criminal matter and arrange a sting.

The staff approached the kids on all fronts. Sam told them, "The only way this situation is going to be straightened out is if you tell on your mom because, if not, you can end up not ever graduating, or your mom could end up dying. It could get worse than it is now. What would you want to happen to your little sister when she gets to your age? Would you want her to go through what you went through?"

Lloyd tried to reassure the kids that something good would come of this.

"For now I just want you to take care of the little things," he said. "Take care of your books. Keep your grades up. Come to school everyday, because if you come to school you get food there. If you go home with food, your mother's going to end up selling it to buy more crack. So come to school. If you need some help with anything you call me up. If you need tutoring or anything like that, just call. If you just need to talk about anything, just call."

Lloyd wanted to keep them out of trouble until the sheriff's department came to take them away from their mother and get her some help.

All the social agencies got together to help. The kids did keep their grades up. They were very intelligent. They truly cared for their mother.

The day arrived to pull the kids and it proved to be one of the most emotional of Lloyd's life. Yanking kids from their family was not a pretty sight—even when everyone knew it was best.

Sheriffs and social workers arrived en masse and charged the mother with neglect.

They grabbed her kids and told the her what she had to do if she ever wanted see them again.

The kids began to kick and scream. They cried and fought and carried on.

Lloyd watched. It was awful! He could barely stand it. Tears came to his eyes. Never would he get used to seeing anything like this.

He watched the sheriffs drive off with the kids down the road.

The dust settled. The mother stared into space. She was so out of it that she just went back inside the house, lit up some more crack, and started smoking. She didn't think much more about it. It was all she knew to do. The house was bare. No food.

One year later an article appeared in the *Christian Science Monitor* about how this mother recovered from a horrible drug addiction, and what she went through after they took her kids away. The court had mandated that if she ever wanted her kids back she had to go into treatment—so in she went. She made it through. When she came out she never returned to Modello.

Not long after coming out of treatment, she spotted Lloyd with a group of Modello kids at a Metrorail station. She swaggered up to him. Lloyd could not believe it was the same person. It blew his socks off. When they had taken her away she looked like walking death, a toothpick, tragic. Now she looked entirely different. She had put on fifteen to twenty pounds. She looked good!

She said to Lloyd, "I just came from looking for a job. I just want to get my life together. I should be getting my kids back in a few weeks, and I may be getting married!"

She did get married and began to work at the hospital as a nurse's aid. She got her kids back and the family became a solid unit again. The kids returned to school and were doing well. Lloyd could not believe the turnaround! No one could. Her success affected a lot of people.

Pam: Before this incident happened, I can only remember hearing judgments cast by the other residents. "She's really bad!" they would say, but they didn't offer to help even the kids. Later, slowly, people would come into the office and say, "I'm really kind of concerned. Is there something we could do for one of her daughters?" Or, "Her kid keeps coming to me every day asking for bread." And the residents started slowly to feed the kids, asking them over to dinner. People began to speak to the lady. It then turned into, "There's got to be something that can be done!" There were a lot of crack kids in Modello, but everybody separated themselves from her. "Well I will never be like that. She's too far gone. She's like dirt. I don't want anything to do with her!" And slowly, "Maybe she's not so different. She used to be a nice person. Isn't there something that could happen?" And there was! That woman was not touched by P.O.M.; she was touched by people who were touched by P.O.M. People had a change of heart toward her, and you felt it. It touched her. And suddenly, you heard, "Maybe I can do something."

That first year Lloyd saw many terrible situations occur all the time. Child abuse abounded. One child died from it. But watching them take away this lady's kids hit him most. He never witnessed anything so horrible!

After the first year, or a little into the second, incidents of that magnitude seemed to die down, then pretty much disappeared altogether.

* * *

The staff decided to throw a dinner for parents and teachers at the Homestead Middle School so they could get to know each other. The intent was not to talk problems or about their kids but simply to have a good time. The principal told jokes; the entire event had the atmosphere of a party.

Parents and teachers both began to realize, "Hey, these are nice people. They're down-to-earth, ordinary people, just like us."

After this very pleasant evening the parents became increasingly involved with the schools. They seemed to care a lot more whether their children attended day-to-day.

Maria Garcia: We had community dinners. Of course not everybody came. That's what happens. But the ones that came, you could see the difference in them because they were not that hostile any more. The way they treated the teachers was different too. It wasn't like us against them; it was us with them. And it made such a big difference for that kid to know, "I had dinner with your mother last night, and I know she doesn't play that game." All of a sudden that little look in his rebellious eyes softened. It made a difference. It really did.

The parents came to the dinner expecting to find typical banquet food; instead they were served collard greens, fried chicken, sweet potato pie, and pigeon peas and rice.

"This is great!" they said.

"Miss Lisa?" asked Lloyd, sitting next to her. "What is pigeon peas and rice?"

"You don't know what pigeon peas and rice is?" laughed Lisa. "You ain't ate until you've had some pigeon peas and rice!"

Someone else chirped in. "You don't know pigeon peas and rice? You gray, boy? Where are you from?"

"Well, you know, I'm from Ohio." said Lloyd, taking the opportunity to act the fool. "We don't have pigeon peas up there, or conch salad, or guava, or a lot of things you have."

If they were laughing at him, Lloyd smiled, at least they weren't mad at him. It began a beautiful friendship with Lisa.

That September the staff rented busses and took the ladies to a play in Coconut Grove. The women had a great time, laughing and yelling out the bus window like kids on a holiday. Everyone was on a natural high. It was the first time the ladies had ever been to the theater to see a play. Lisa said she never experienced anything like it. It was fantastic!

* * *

Immediately after the first teacher training had ended in the Homestead Middle School, Colleen del Terzo was hired as Assistant Principal. Roger and Lloyd immediately pounced, explaining the philosophy and approach they were trying to instill in the school. They found her very receptive and responsive. Within her first three months she went to visit the Modello P.T.A. to see what she faced and to gain insight into the students' lives. She found the volume and magnitude of problems overwhelming.

Colleen del Terzo: I did all the discipline for the middle school. Every day these kids kept circulating through my office like a revolving door. I was new to the job, so there was a high stress level. I'm from the Islands, so I'm comfortable with that kind of poverty, but part of my stress could have been my own culture shock, seeing it so real and in my office. I came to realize that there were a lot of home problems creating the kids problems. I heard about the drugs, whose mom was on drugs, who had just gotten off crack. Then I realized that I needed help. That's when Lloyd Fields and Ben Williams [a school counselor] and Ms. Dawkins [the school secretary who grew up in Homestead and knew all the mothers] and I kind of formed a team. For the kids at Modello we were a very central core. All of us would chip in with what they needed. At that moment in time the chemistry was right. We were friends and gave each other support. We could count on each other.

"Lloyd, work with this kid for a couple of weeks and let me know what happens," Ms. del Terzo would say when she had to discipline a Modello student. She knew Lloyd would follow through.

When a situation became too intense, she would call in Lloyd. Lloyd would help calm her down and give her time to recoup so the next time she had to deal with the kid she could be civil again. He would help her see the student's good side.

When she wanted to send a kid packing Lloyd would say, "Wait, I'll bring the mom in tomorrow, and we can talk it out. "

"Okay, I'll hold off," said Colleen, knowing that if Lloyd hadn't been there the kid would have been out on his ear. She didn't feel she had a choice. She had no time to wait for the mother to come in whenever the mother saw fit, because if nothing constructive happened the kid would "break loose."

Lloyd, and later Cynthia Stennis, checked student attendance. If truancy was a problem they dealt directly with the parents. Lloyd would drive the parents to the school. When needed, he or Cynthia secured glasses or clothes for the kids. They took parents to appointments. Lloyd attended the school's official child study team meetings to help develop alternatives when a kid might be shipped to the alternative school. Sometimes if the mother couldn't understand what school officials were saying, Lloyd would explain it in a different way.

Colleen del Terzo: We had constant communication with parents. By the time the kid got off the bus the mom had already gotten the message. Before this, I would go three or four days without talking to the mom because there were no phones and I couldn't just jump in my car—so the effect of the whole punishment would die. Then there were the fights between the Black group and the Hispanic group. Then were the fights among the Modello kids when somebody three doors down pulled a knife on somebody, and it was all because the mothers' started fighting. We definitely saw a down in all that behavior. Those kids really started to shape up, to come to school and behave, to get good grades. Then the teachers asked if they could refer other kids.

By the fall of 1988 Dr. Mills moved the teacher training into the two elementary schools that served Modello and Homestead Gardens. There he received a warmer reception than at the Middle School. While a number of Middle school teachers had incorporated Psychology of Mind principles into their teaching, over time some relationships seemed to sour.

Maria Garcia: At first everybody was really willing to listen and a lot of people attended the inservice workshops. Then it got to be like the program was about Roger Mills, and that's not what it was supposed to be about. When he presented to the staff it was like he was up here and we were down here. I didn't know where all the energy went after a while. At first he was here all the time, got his program going, got us all hooked. Then we didn't see him any more. Then of course the murmuring starts. "Oh he only cared because he wanted the statistics to write a book or be on the Today Show." "Well he's a consultant. He got what he wanted. He's going to go and write his grants and keep the money coming in." Because that's the way we teachers are. And I felt bad about those comments because I felt they were directed at me. He was very nice to me, but I think a lot of the staff got the feeling that he's very arrogant and pompous, and they'd go the other way when they saw him coming. The teachers would talk sometimes and say, "Oh I see what he's saying!" But there were others who, if a kid acted out, would give snide remarks and say, "I thought this Modello project was supposed to be wonderful." When I was doing the stand back-reflect-don't get excited approach, a lot of the others weren't because they were putting the man in front of the program. But some things in his program, in his book, really did work and really could make us stop and think about it before we act.

Nonetheless, the successes spoke for themselves. The Teacher

Education Center picked up the funding because they liked the first year's evaluations.

> **Dr. Mills:** The teachers that picked this up started saying, "Gee I didn't know that kid was so sensitive, or so bright, or so compassionate, or such a nice kid." Three weeks before they were saying that the same kid was incorrigible, should be thrown out of school and put in a juvenile detention home. Then all of a sudden they're seeing a whole other side of that child that they didn't even know existed. And all they did was change their mind, look through new eyes, give him another chance. As soon as they see these kids as just insecure, their feelings change toward that child. Instead of feeling judgmental, angry, resentful, they feel compassionate, patient, understanding—and it happens just like [snaps fingers] that!

One middle school teacher, who appeared fairly racist and seemed to hate the kids from Modello because they were the biggest troublemakers, sat for about two months in the teacher training without it connecting. She resisted the idea that these kids were basically healthy or well-meaning or had any sensitivity or anything positive going for them. Yet, for Martin Luther King day she said, "Well, I have to do something for Black History Week, so I'll ask all the minority kids in my classroom to write an essay about what it's like to be a Black student in America or come from a Black family."

She came back and said to Dr. Mills, "I went home after one of your teacher training sessions and decided to read these papers. By the end of the evening I was in tears. Some of the papers that these kids wrote were so beautiful and so touching, and so moving. I didn't ever realize that these kids were capable of seeing their lives this way or having those kinds of feelings. I thought they were all mean, nasty, little brats, trying to ruin my life."

This teacher had taken a new look at these students. When she did her students started to change. They became different people, more responsive.

> **Dr. Mills:** As soon as their thoughts change, their feelings change. The common denominator behind all this is thought. That's where the simplicity is—if you can see it. As soon as people see a certain interpretation as valid, they get angry or have some other feeling. The angry feeling is produced at that moment because of their thinking. The problem is that most of us are thinking so fast that

we're literally caught up in the effect of our thoughts after the fact of our thinking—so it seems like emotions come from someplace else. But that's the appearance. That's the illusion. The feelings really come from whatever your thoughts are at the moment.

Other teachers reported that they started to enjoy teaching more. They started to see that their stress came from a lot of their own thinking—about their job, their situation, their kids. They began to pay attention to the mood level in the classroom, to be more flexible, to joke around with kids, to be more down to earth, to be more themselves. When the teachers began to see the kids differently, they began to engage them differently. Like the parents, they began to see that kids respond to love, to caring. The quality of the relationship makes the difference. They then began to experience more success with those kids in the classrooms. Some learned it better than others.

Maria Garcia: I want to tell you that it made a big difference, but I honestly don't know if it did or not. I really do think some people were trying out what they were learning, but Roger was saying that you can change your learned behavior, which I agree. Learned behavior is learned; that means you can unlearn it and learn something else. He was saying that some of these kids have gotten beat to hell, and they come to school for safety, but in turn that's what they live, so they want to beat somebody else to hell. A lot of them have lived that way. A lot of these kids would come to school in the morning when their fathers or their stepfathers beat the hell out of them or their mother. I understand those things, but I can't take it personally. I'm sorry that he had a bad night. I'm sorry that he has to sleep in a room with four other kids. I'm sorry that his little brother wet the bed, the same bed he sleeps in. But I have another goal. I can keep that in my mind, have it underlie which avenue I'm going to take that day, but I can't say, "Oh you poor thing, so you don't have to do this." Because that's not what life is.

* * *

Someone on the P.T.A. came up with an idea to celebrate Black History Month. They brought in guest speakers from Miami, Tampa, and Orlando. They held parades where everyone involved their kids. At these events the parents would pitch in and bring a dish of food.

On one picnic they visited Botanical Gardens. They put on a big Christmas party, complete with Santa Claus.

Dr. Mills and Lloyd approached the head of the area P.T.A. to see if the Modello P.T.A. could be considered a legitimate chapter. Yes! Now they could legitimately approach the Board of Education with concerns and apply for grants. The City and school recognized the Modello P.T.A. as a force, making it all the more important to the residents. Later they became the official tenants council because the same people were involved. This allowed them to officially go before the city council to make demands.

The women who officially "completed" the parenting class changed visibly. They began to look more together, dress nicer, wear makeup, have a spring in their step and a sparkle in their eye. They had more presence and began dealing with both children and boyfriends in a healthier way. They began to get along with their neighbors.

The rest of the community noticed. The parenting class became an oasis of hope and health in an otherwise crazy place. Other residents began to ask what was going on. What were these ladies doing? Out of curiosity other residents began coming into the class. The ripple spread.

Those who attended the class fairly regularly received a certificate from Miami-Dade Community College at a little graduation ceremony. The recognition reinforced their good feelings.

Some, though, never did catch on. Some would rather have shot Dr. Mills than talked with him. Roger shrugged it off. He realized they weren't going to reach everybody. So long as they had a critical mass who, in turn, spread it to their friends and neighbors, soon the majority of people living in Modello would want to approach things in a more clearheaded way, and that was truly gratifying.

> **Patty:** It's just a matter of thought. Some things are not as bad as it may seem, or as serious as it may seem. I learned to take things one day at a time. I'm an understanding person, but I just didn't have enough patience. I began to get more patience with my kids, with Doc, with just about everybody. It helps. We went a lot of places with Doc and saw a lot of different things. But when you see some things in a better state of mind, it really doesn't matter.

Occasionally Lloyd would say something to someone and see a light bulb go on as if he'd pulled a pin on a grenade. The person instantly understood what he was trying to say and experienced immediate change. Most of the changes were so gradual Lloyd didn't know if they had understood anything until he realized later that their lives had become better.

* * *

A short, compact bundle of energy named Cynthia Stennis directed the Modello child care center. The problem was, she was having trouble with her own children. Once again the school had called about Benny, her oldest son of thirteen.

"I'm going to beat his butt!" a frustrated Cynthia exclaimed to Carrie Mae, one of her parent substitute teachers at the center.

Carrie Mae laughed. "My son and Benny are the same age, and I used to have the same problem that you're having—with phone calls and acting out in school and being a clown and stuff where the teacher can't teach the class."

She told Cynthia how she had gone to this parenting class where she came to understand her kids' mood levels, and why they acted the way they did.

Carrie Mae was worth listening to. Although tough with an explosive temper she was also loved by the whole community because she so obviously loved children. She told Cynthia how she used to walk over to school with a belt and beat her child in front of the whole class, demanding, "You're going to do what I tell you! You better apologize!"

"I was worse than you are," said Carrie Mae, "but every time you get a phone call from school about your son, I can see you get upset. I can see that you want to have a good relationship with your son too. I changed after going to this parenting class, and my son changed just by me listening to him. The class helped me realize who I was. Dr. Mills helped me do it. He's been helping all of us. You should probably talk to Dr. Mills. He can probably help you get the situation in hand."

Tired of her child getting in trouble, having attitude problems and not listening to her, Cynthia couldn't help but be curious. Carrie Mae brought her to meet Dr. Mills.

Cynthia took one look at him and whispered in Carrie Mae's ear, "Who is this man? What is he, one of those psychologists? I don't want to talk to nobody like that! I'm not crazy. Don't tell me nothing about this man coming to talk to me!"

Carrie Mae laughed and invited Cynthia to come to one of the afternoon parenting classes, even though she didn't live in Modello.

Cynthia Stennis visited the class. Taken aback, she saw parents sitting there with their hair sticking up on top of their heads, barefoot, with no one paying any mind to their outside appearance. Instead, the atmosphere exuded love. Everyone talked about their good times and bad times, and how they got over what they were going through. They talked about "how their way of thinking was coming before them" every time they got ready to make a decision, and how they would find themselves in the same trap every time they got upset.

> **Cynthia:** The more I sat there and heard them talking about how they changed their lives and how they changed their way of thinking, I started looking at myself. I was saying, My goodness, if this man can help them to get their self-esteem like that, I believe we need that in our project.

After the class Cynthia pulled Dr. Mills aside and told him about her son. Dr. Mills responded that kids have feelings just like she does, and for her son to act like that there's probably something going on with him. He explained how everybody has different mood levels at different times, and it affects how family members are with each other at any given time. He said that her kids have access to common sense just like she does, and maybe if she were more of a friend to her son it might help bring it out in him and give him what he needs.

Cynthia took in his words, then said, "You know, I'm living in the same type of housing project as Modello but in Homestead—Homestead Gardens—which is not too far away, and they could use the same thing there. They need a lot of help."

A few miles from Modello stood Homestead Gardens, a public housing project of 150 units much like Modello, though not quite as rough. Still, it had its moments. Unlike Modello, Homestead Gardens was within the city limits of Homestead and therefore came under the auspices of the Homestead Police Department.

> **Chief Ivy** [Homestead Chief of Police]: There were always disturbance calls, arguments between people. We had our officers go over there. You have to understand Homestead Gardens. You

go in there, and there's a bunch of apartments. You drive in, try to find the apartment. There's driveways and parking lots and courtyards. You're responding to a disturbance call between residents. You get there, and shots are fired. Crowds gather, yelling at the police and throwing rocks. You try to make an arrest. There's a scuffle. Rocks are thrown. Crowds gather. You've got to call for back up. A lot of times there were cars stripped over there. Somebody would steal a car, drive it over there and strip it right there in the parking lot.

* * *

One day Lamar came in and told Pam that he had stopped selling drugs. Others corroborated it. He was no longer out there dealing. Pam felt touched to the bottom of her heart.

Pam: It's not like he turned into Mr. Perfect. He was still fencing gold and stuff like that. But he stopped the drugs. He stopped all that.

* * *

For the first time in her life Thelma felt respected, treated like she was somebody. Lloyd had considered it a victory when Thelma began showing up to the classes. Then she came dressed up more and had her hair together.

"Oh Thelma, you look so fine!" reinforced Lloyd.

They would talk about her family or boyfriend problems. The changes were very subtle.

Thelma kept watching her kids, taking Doc's advice and paying attention to their moods and to her own. Instead of just yelling at them and beating on them she began to get along with them.

* * *

Lisa and Lloyd began to develop a special relationship.

Lisa: Lloyd loved to hug you, and Lloyd had the best hugs! I mean, every time he would see me, he'd just, Oh God, let me get a hug in! It was just great, and that's how we formed this really close friendship. And it was nice too, being able to talk to a man like you would a woman, without anything sexual or anything like that. And I could hug him, and it was just great, because he really liked me just for me. He's my sweetheart, I tell you. He's everybody's sweetheart.

One day when Lisa had become depressed about her boyfriend, Lloyd said, "Look, you don't have to accept what other people think about you. When people are mad or insecure they say things they don't mean. They don't say things to hurt you. You don't have to take it to heart. See, it's just their insecurity, or their way of looking at things. You don't have to take it personal."

Lisa: I wanted step one-two-three and everything's going to be fine, like some of those books I'd been reading. That's what I thought they were eventually going to get to. But it was all in the understanding, and I began to feel it a little. But after we started listening I would hear some of the other ladies and myself say, "Okay, this day I'm not going to yell at the kids," and it would last about five minutes. Then all of us would say, "This didn't work!" But we thought it was this quick fix and we would never have another problem in our life.

All her life Lisa felt someone placing blame on her. Instead, Doc kept saying that people were doing the best they could at the time, given how they were raised—so that's what they bought into. That was the way they did things. Lisa paid close attention.

For many of the ladies the truth of this talk had begun to hit home when they talked about their boyfriends. "Yeah, if I tell him he's a jerk, then he's going to tell me something that's going to hurt me and make me feel bad, and it just goes down hill from there." Now that they began to feel more comfortable, in the class some began to open up about how their old man beat on them.

"To have a man in your life," some of them said, "even if he's beating on you and sleeping with your kids, is better than not having a man at all. At least you had somebody that loves you. And the more they beat on you, the more you know they love you."

Many believed getting beaten was a natural part of a relationship. So Doc would talk about self-esteem and what it is. How everyone is born with it, and they still have it inside them. Their thoughts sometimes just fool them into thinking they no longer have it. But no one can take it away from them.

Lisa listened as the ladies talked about their physically abusive boyfriends. Several ladies came to the meeting with black eyes, busted lips, trying to drink their problems away. Lisa saw her own problem more as mental, but it hurt just as bad. Yet when the others started to open up about their problems Lisa could relate. Though she wasn't physically abused she could feel for them through her mental abuse.

Lisa: We used to sit up in our meetings and we'd actually cry, because we had known each other for years and years, but we were so focused on what was going on with us that we didn't have time to reach out to another person. The usual thing to do was to deny what was going on with you and make everyone think that everything was nice and rosy. For years no one ever thought I had any type of problems like that. Everyone thought, "Oh, great relationship!" But if we saw someone else getting beat up, it was, "I don't see why they stay with that man. They must want this type of abuse." But we didn't realize we were going though similar things. You can't place blame on that person. That's what a lot of us ladies learned. Don't place blame on that person, because even though she's going home and getting the hell beat out of her, that's really all she could do at that time. And some of the ladies got rid of the guys. They just stopped and refused to go for that again. They realized, "Hey, I'm worth a lot better than that. I am somebody! I'm this fantastic person, and I just don't need you."

Lisa began to learn that love wasn't about taking all this abuse and hurt. It was about sharing, not having one person in a relationship give love and the other person putting you down. This stood in sharp contrast to their thinking, "Well, he must really love me because if he didn't beat on me, he wouldn't care."

The ladies slowly began to see how crazy this thinking was—it was not natural to get beaten. That wasn't what they wanted or deserved. Without knowing it they'd been trapped in a cycle. It was what they'd seen their parents do. Lisa could remember seeing her mother go through crazy things, and she had unwittingly concluded, "it's got to be horrible if it's love."

Some began to stand up to their old men and tell them, "No more." Some men had to be thrown out of the house. The men were not on the apartment leases. They were there only because the women allowed it

Lisa: The more we talked about these issues in class the more they connected with me. It opened my eyes to the way things were in my life. I began to see those things in my life differently. But I still fell into my traps. It still takes a while before you can really apply it so you can really realize what's going on with you. Because even when I started really catching on, I thought, "Okay, now I've got to be perfect. I've got to use these methods, and I've got to be perfect, because if I fail and Dr. Mills or any of the other ladies know this, I'm going to be a failure to them." So I still didn't get it. So at times I was trying to be so perfect with this thing but I was going through hell when I was at home. Even after that there were times that if it hadn't been for Dr. Mills, Lloyd, and Pam, and Rosie, Patty and Cicely—if I didn't have that support group, these people that really cared about me—I don't think, I don't know, there were still some rough times there—I might not have been around. Because I was on the verge of suicide about two times after that. I already felt like a failure, and then when I was trying something I was thinking, "You're failing again." So that told me in my mind again, "You're never going to accomplish anything." And this was horrible to me.

X. Winter, 1988 into 1989: Homestead Gardens

By the end of 1988 Roger's initial $5500 federal grant would end. He had been searching for funds to continue and expand the program.

So he approached the Dade County Commissioners through the Department of Youth and Family Development and asked Rosie and a couple of the other Modello parents to accompany him. Lisa wanted to go to save Lloyd's and Rosie's positions.

The residents told the Commissioners how much they were being helped by this program and about the changes they saw in their kids. Janet Reno offered her support, saying that she saw the change too and wanted to see more of this.

By January, 1989 the Commissioners awarded $100,000 from the Dade County General Fund to expand the program. Another $80,000 in County funds came through the Metro Miami Action Plan. Its board, consisting mostly of Black leaders, had been charged with improving life in inner-city housing projects.

Roger could now increase Lloyd's hours from half-time to full-time and his own hours from quarter to half-time (although both put in far more hours than they were paid for). He could also hire two more staff—another social worker equivalent to Lloyd and another social worker aide equivalent to Rosie.

Cynthia didn't know how God worked it out, but Dr. Mills told her they could now move into the Homestead Gardens housing project. Not only that, he asked if she would like to come on board and join his team. She would work for Metro-Dade County and help out families. Cynthia jumped at the chance.

First she had to interview with Lloyd.

Lloyd sat before Cynthia with a stern expression on his face. In his gruffest voice he said, "You know, I'm an ex-con. I was a rapist and I killed somebody. You still want to work with me?"

Cynthia stammered. Lloyd had her scared.

He then he burst out laughing . "No, that never happened. It's not true."

Cynthia breathed a sigh of relief.

Meanwhile, Dr. Mills interviewed prospective social workers. In his first interview a very attractive, vibrant young woman sat before him. Carol Murray talked about how much she truly loved children. Roger found Carol positive, enthusiastic, naturally buoyant. The icing came when he asked about her current work with clients. Carol said she noticed how her mood affected how she saw the kids she worked with and how it played a large role in determining how well she did with her clients.

"Wow!" thought Roger. "She's a natural! She has a leg up on all this because she understands how her own frame of mind affects her clients!"

He wanted to hire her on the spot.

Dr. Mills: But I still had to interview the other forty-nine people [laughs]. I snuck out of the office and followed her out to the parking lot. I said, "I think I want you for this job, so hang around at home until I get through all these other interviews." See, that's what you do. You find a person that has that feeling.

Once again his instincts proved correct. Most of the others he interviewed were social workers or child protection workers with years of experience but who didn't think these families and kids could change very much.

Carol: When I first started in Modello I kind of felt the same way Lloyd felt. "What am I getting myself into!?" Because it was different from what I was used to. Before I got there the people who I'd been working with set me up by saying, "Be sure you don't wear your jewelry in there!" "Don't leave your car there! Take out everything!" "Don't walk by yourself!" So when I got there I was really scared to death. I went to where Modello was, and the office was at the back end of a little store. I was used to a nice office with nice pictures and everything. When I walked back into the store it was, like, there was one desk here and one desk here and that was it! I was really scared, but it all worked out really good. Dr. Mills made me feel very comfortable from day one, and I really enjoyed that.

Dr. Mills: Carol helped a lot. She was like a pied piper with the kids. They just loved her. Every time she'd come into either one of the projects in ten minutes she'd have thirty kids hanging onto her, following her everywhere. So she helped the young girls a lot. She helped them gain more self-respect and feel better about themselves. She and Cynthia really helped the teen pregnancy rate.

In February 1989 Dr. Mills officially hired Cynthia Stennis to work with Carol full time in Homestead Gardens. Doc worked it so his staff were interchangeable. All worked out of both offices in Modello and Homestead Gardens, and in the schools—perfect for on-the-job training.

Because the new grant brought increased staff, no longer could they make do with the tiny offices behind the store, so they secured one of the Modello apartments from the housing authority. When the time came for the office to be fixed up, Roger and Pam asked the P.T.A. to pick out the furniture and furnish it the way they wanted.

"This is your office." they said. "We work here, but we want it to feel like your home."

Before long the office had a couch, end tables, lamps, pictures on the wall, a coffee table, magazines—a homey feeling. In the back, desks and phones allowed them to do office work and provide individual counseling. In Homestead Gardens they were able to secure part of the HUD offices (later, they also moved into one of the Homestead Gardens apartments).

Roger had one more piece of the puzzle to fill. It had been one year and a few months since he had entered Modello; one year since the initial grant. In that time he had seen some positive changes in the women who regularly participated. So he sought another grant from the Dade Community Foundation to train those Modello parents as parent trainers through an internship. The Foundation offered $16,000 to pay a small stipend to Carrie Mae, Patty, Cicely, Thelma, Lisa, and Rosie to receive additional training to work with other parents. Roger figured that they could do wonders to help open doors in Homestead Gardens—a far better idea than the way he initially had to go into Modello.

Again the training was conducted at the Institute in Coral Gables. As their official supervisor Roger wanted them trained without him. Darlene Stewart had departed, so Rita Shuford headed the training, assisted by Ann Thomas and another trainer. Not only would they have classroom training but also three months of supervised on-the-job training working with residents in both projects.

Pam: That training was where the biggest shifts occurred for the women.

Rita Shuford: Roger's work with them kind of prepared them in a way, and opened their minds to possibilities. Taking them out of that setting and putting them into an educational setting where they were getting ready to take on responsibilities themselves—it was just fertile ground. They were ready! I liked them immediately. In a way they seemed like kids who had dressed up and gone to town. But they were going to wait and see. They weren't quite sure what this was really going to be about, and how much it could help them. Initially I think they felt kind of privileged. It was like an outing for them, going to Coral Gables. But they also seemed a little uncomfortable being out of their own setting and coming into a professional setting "up the road." They had pride that they could do that, and I think by that time they were a little more open because of their own parent classes, but there was skepticism. What does a psychologist know about their lives? They weren't real open in the very beginning. Carrie Mae would talk about what was happening with a friend of hers, and she was actually talking about herself.

Rosie: I started to go to the Institute and talk with these other ladies. And I didn't feel they had too much to offer me either—these white women with their nails all did up and stuff. "There ain't nothing they can tell me!" But I found out it doesn't matter where you come from.

Rita: For them to be trainers of other parents we saw that they had to be healthier themselves. So that was our main focus: the health of the helper. We talked a lot about the parents' state of mind being the key, the answer. So the whole focus of the class was how to access a wiser state of mind, how to know when you're not in it, how to recognize when someone else—whoever they're dealing with—is not in a good state of mind, and how to handle that. We said that everything is an inside-out production, so there was an emphasis on "thought."

To begin the training Rita Shuford had them brainstorm: "What would you like to learn about parenting that you think is important for parents to know? What problems do the parents in Modello run into with their kids?"

Rita and her co-trainers then took that information and built a general framework for a twelve week training program, four hours a week. At the next session she asked, "Does this look good, or would you like to make changes?" The ladies liked the outline and offered a few suggestions. Each week the trainers checked in to see how they were doing. "Did any questions come up?" They then began to teach the principles and concepts of Psychology of Mind as they applied to being a parents, and to their children. The class began in January and went until June. Cynthia and Carol joined them once they were hired.

Rita: They were all beginning to understand moods and to realize that self-esteem was something that they could have. They were beginning to see possibilities and have some hope. Given the lives they had been living, I think they wondered how much their lives could really change. Thelma missed a class or two, and we discovered that she was drinking too much, so we incorporated that into what we talked about—how this applies to substance abuse. We talked about whatever showed up. Initially Rosie would sleep through the classes. She would usually have been up most of the night with some problem or other, and she had an abusive boyfriend at that time, and a lot of problems with her children and the boyfriend. She would come and be awake for the first fifteen or twenty minutes, and then she'd fall asleep. Every once in a while something would be said, or we'd be laughing or something, and she would wake up for a little bit, and we always just treated it with humor, that it wasn't a problem. One time she came beaten up—her boyfriend had beaten her with a lead pipe and she had stitches.

Rumor had it that Rosie had locked her boyfriend out of the house. He'd pulled the air conditioner out of the window, came through the hole in the wall, beat her over the head with a lead pipe and sent her to the hospital. She came to a meeting a couple of days later with twenty-four stitches in her head.

> **Rita:** All the women were in kind of a transition stage in their personal lives, in the process of getting more healthy themselves. We talked a lot about what health is, and what it means to live with a sense of well-being, and how their moods play into it, and what their thinking is. Lisa had a lot of questions about self-esteem, thinking she didn't have any. The whole notion that self-esteem is something we're all born with, and it's just a thought that makes us feel one way or the other, was a big one for her. To see that it was just thought that stands in the way, for her that was big "ah ha!"

> **Cynthia:** When I went to the Institute I said, "When I get up there I hope these people don't get boring, because I know they're going to sit around and start talking." So I sat down and they started talking, and everybody started getting involved. They started talking about how kids have moods too, and that's where I found out how my son and I start clashing. He might be in a low mood, and I didn't see he's in a low mood, or I might be in a low mood. So what I had to do was to calm myself down, to watch him. And the things that I learned from the class I passed onto my kids. I've got a thirteen year old son and an eleven year old daughter and a nine year old son, and now they watch me. So when they see that I'm in a low mood, they stay back [laughs]. They go to their room. They go and play with somebody or something and then when they come back they ask me, "Are you ready to talk now?" [laughs].

The trainers went out of their way to make the discussions informal. They served pastries and other goodies to help make the ladies feel comfortable. The trainers encouraged them to relax. They encouraged questions. They invited the women to talk by asking questions such as, "What did you notice this week?" "What did you learn this week?" "What problems are you having this week?"

> **Rita:** There seemed to me to be kind of a gradual awakening. The thing I saw was that they were becoming more confident, their physical appearances were beginning to change. Their faces were more clear, their hair was fixed, they were beginning to take more pride in themselves. They had more questions and were making more connections. There was a deepening feeling of how powerful

the feeling of love and well-being can be. A bonding was forming with them. The feeling of camaraderie started pretty fast, probably within the first three or four weeks. Then one or two people would come one week and you could see it in their faces that they were less strained, less stressed, more open, more together. The group was beginning to notice it. We all said, "Wow, Lisa, you really look great today!" There was just a really nice feeling in that group. They were already applying some of it; they had already begun to understand moods somewhat. We were always looking for their cutting edge: Where were they at? .

When they needed a ride Lloyd would drive them to the Institute. One day he walked into the store to pick up the ladies and ran headlong into Thelma's man.

The guy pointed at him. "That's the captain, right there!"

Puzzled, Lloyd didn't pay much attention. Instead he turned to the ladies. "Hey, are all you ready to go? We're late."

Out of the corner of his eye Lloyd saw the man angrily huffing and puffing. So Lloyd walked up to him with his hand outstretched, "How are you doing? My name is Lloyd Fields."

The man grumbled his name and backed away.

"Okay," Lloyd wondered, not keying into what was going on. He only wanted the parents to get in the car.

Rosie stood in the back, cracking up, waiting to see what would happen.

Once in the car Lloyd learned that the man was intensely jealous of him, thinking Lloyd was trying to take his woman. Thelma felt wonderfully assured that he was going to fight Lloyd and later kick her ass for getting in the car with him.

"Rosie?" sighed Lloyd, "How come you didn't let me know what was going on there?"

Rosie laughed. She loved seeing Lloyd get himself into these predicaments. He was still so naive.

Rita: Probably within the first two or three weeks they were beginning to make changes. The women became more calm, more relaxed. I saw a softening. The women became happier, more hopeful. Carrie Mae moved out of the projects. People began to make more decisions improving their lives. I remember that Cicely's daughter was giving her trouble. Cicely is a very spiritual person, and she brought a lot of spiritual discussion to the group.

* * *

People marveled at the change that came over Cicely. They couldn't believe it was the same person. She began to get involved in everything that was happening. She spoke out. One year from the time she began with Dr. Mills program she became elected as President of the new Modello Tenants Council. [As of the interviews for this book she had been reelected ever since.]

Cicely: A lot of times I used to take things personal. Now when people say things, I don't. That changed me. I saw other people happy who had similar problems as me, and if they could get happy with what happened to them, I saw that I could too. A lot of times people go through problems with their life and they don't need to take it out on anybody, but they just are that way sometimes. I'd see people walking around not being happy and I'd say to them, "How are you doing? What's the matter?" And we would have a conversation. I think they voted me in because I knew how to talk to people. I knew how to deal with people. And I don't take things personal.

Lloyd: She's always got a nice thing to say about everybody. She's always like, "It'll work out. It'll work out."

As soon as Cicely became elected Tenant's Council president she began to go to church. If she was going to be in an important position like that, she felt it was important to be a member of a church.

Cicely: I began to put God first in my life, and things begin to work for me. When you're a member of a church there's a lot of things you can get done that would be helpful to a tenant council, like if you need funds or something like that.

The combination of what she learned about herself through Psychology of Mind and church helped her to be strong.

Cicely: It's the same thing. It's a different angle but it's all the same thing.

She was now ready to deal with her kids.

Cicely: What really changed them a lot was because of me. Before, I was doing nothing. I started being there for them. I started talking with them, having conversations when we were having dinner, taking them out to places, having like a group discussion at night, talking about different things, about life. I let them know I loved them. I let them know I cared. I did try to be a good mother. I tried to bring them up the right way.

She also had to put her foot down. She told Dr. Mills what she told her son: "Look, you're not going to deal drugs out of my apartment any more. I'd love to help you get into school again or change careers, or do whatever I can, but this is not okay. I don't want to lose my lease. I don't want to get evicted. I don't want this going on in my home. You either got to get out of the drug trade or get out of my home."

Dr. Mills knew great progress had been made when Cicely invited him over to her home to visit.

Then there was her daughter who had lost all her color and had become as pale as it was possible to be.

Cicely: My daughter was on that crack, and she was stealing from me and doing some of everything. She was really "out there." It was rough there one time before I was the president. It was bad. A couple of times she had to go to the hospital. But I hung on in there. I kept on holding on to the faith, and I kept on showing her love, and I wasn't putting her down because she was on drugs.

"I love you!" Cicely told her. "That stuff's no good. Look what it's doing to you. You're destroying yourself. Look at you now. Look at your sister. See how she is? Look in the mirror at yourself. How do you feel looking like that?"

Cicely kept talking to her and showing her love.

Her daughter began to break. She heard. She decided to stop. She was able to—for a while—but the crack had too much of a hold. Her friends had too much of a hold. Her daughter was still hanging out with the same crowd who were all "doing that stuff."

Cicely again stepped in. "If you want to get off them drugs, you're going to have to make up in your mind that you're going to have to get off it yourself. And you've got to see, and think about what that crew is doing."

Cicely tried to help her connect to her common sense. That's what Dr. Mills had said to do. That's what had happened to her. But the pathway was through love. Cicely kept at it. Her daughter began to see. Finally, she stopped hanging out with that group which made a huge difference. Her "friends" kept coming to her to get her to do more crack. She talked to them nicely but stood firm.

"Oh, you know I ain't on that stuff no more."

She began to feel strong. Despite her friends, despite other relatives hanging around also being on that stuff, despite her terrible withdrawal, she stood strong—for Cicely stood by her to help her through the pain. Cicely was so grateful and happy!

Cicely: Through my life that's how she changed. You see her now, you wouldn't believe. She's a different person. Oh my God, when she was on drugs, you wouldn't believe to see her now. She was a different person. I just let her know that. She tells people today, "I thank God for my mom, because she stuck with me when I was on drugs." She tells everybody that. She never did go to a drug rehab' place. I guess it happened through my prayers. I kept praying for her every day, every night, to deliver her from that stuff. She's happy too. She tell everybody, "Thank God for my momma."

* * *

Pam: The training at the Institute made a world of difference. The people there train very well. They really know how to present the information. And from that time on, these women just kind of shot off. You saw enormous changes. Lisa just lightened and lightened, and today her face is completely different. She doesn't look like the same person.

Rita: At one point some researchers came in from Barry University and sat in and asked the women questions about what they were learning. That was very enlightening to me because I didn't realize how much they really had been taking in. I saw that they were really understanding how things worked out differently when they let a mood pass in dealing with their children. The other thing I saw during the class was that people were getting out of abusive relationships. As the women were getting stronger the men were getting more insecure. The women were beginning to see these relationships for what they were. I remember Lisa was getting out of one. It took Rosie a while to get out of hers. There was disengagement from the insanity of their lives. Thelma didn't change until later into the group because of the alcohol. But sitting in the class there was almost like osmosis going on. Rosie was beginning to get more and more of a vision of what was possible. She needed a little extra help with getting out of that relationship, and Ann Thomas did a little one-on-one with her.

XI. Late Winter - Early Spring, 1989

Cynthia began soaking it up like a sponge. She learned from Dr. Mills that babies are born with so much self-esteem that they don't worry about "goochi" diapers. They don't worry about what color they are. As he talked Cynthia visualized. After working at a child care center for four years she could see it. It was true. Those babies didn't care who changed them, who said what about whom—all they want is to be happy. Cynthia then began to visualize how babies are brought up, what happens when parents get involved in their lives, what happens when they start going to school. It seemed that kids pick up what they see and hear, and once they reach a certain age they develop a way of seeing life. But underneath it all everybody has this natural thing they're born with, and they never lose it.

Cynthia: It's just trying to get in touch with it and to bring it out and let them bloom and become a flower. Our kids are like a flower—that seed is already there, and all they need is somebody to just pull it out and just let them go and make their decisions. Who am I to tell you that you shouldn't do this and you shouldn't do that? You know what's good for you, and in your own way you know how far you need to go. And that's how we teach.

The trick was seeing it in her own kids.

One evening at home Cynthia received yet another phone call from school about Benny, her oldest. Benny knew exactly what the call was about. He'd been acting out in the class again, being silly and disruptive, being "the clown of class" again. So he scurried away to his room and closed his door.

Cynthia followed him to his room. She opened the door.

She stopped in her tracks.

There she saw a sight she would never forget—a sight that would change her forever. She hadn't gone after him to beat him. But there Benny stood, pants down, a belt in hand, handing it to her, waiting to be wailed upon.

Cynthia's reality crumbled. She became speechless. Her eyes filled. She looked at him, and burst into tears. In his eyes she saw herself, and she saw her child.

She cried to herself, "God, you know what? He must really think I'm a monster—because I never give him a chance to tell me what's going on. All he knows is that when he's in trouble he's going to get his behind whupped and that's it."

It was how she always reacted when he got into trouble. She beat him! What she'd learned in the class flashed into her mind: kids have feelings, and she wasn't listening to her kids. She would just get mad, burst in, and be ready to strike. Now she saw what she was doing. It scared her.

Cynthia: That's when I saw the innocence in myself and the innocence in him.

Cynthia grabbed him and hugged him. "Pull your clothes up and put that belt down," Cynthia kindly said through her tears, "I'm not going to spank you. I just want to know what's going on."

Benny looked at her like, "What's wrong with this woman today? That's not the same mom!" He could feel a difference. This was for real. She actually wanted to hear his side of the story.

"You're not going to beat me?"

"No, I'm not going to beat you. Why would I? Just tell me what's happening. Tell me what happened today."

Then Benny began to cry, and Cynthia cried more. She could now understand what he always went through.

"You know, the way I was raised," she said, "you respect your elders no matter what, you do what you're told no matter what—and I was just trying to do the same thing. I was really trying to be a good mom, and I thought I was, but at the same time I wasn't giving you a chance. I'm sorry, Benny."

In that moment he too saw her innocence. He couldn't possibly hold it against her.

"Yuh," he said, "I understand. And you know I'm trying to be the best son, but sometimes there is a lot of pressure out there, and I never get a chance to talk to nobody."

It was so ironic. Cynthia always wanted him to be able to come and talk to her, but he couldn't because she was always on his case. Cynthia began to feel a shift, something changing within her. She was truly ready to listen.

Suddenly Cynthia realized that her kids didn't know she really loved them. She said "I love you," but those were just words. The words weren't coming from her heart. Her children could tell her how much they loved her, and she absolutely knew they meant it. Yet she found it extremely difficult to tell them what she truly loved about them. Why couldn't she do it? It puzzled her.

Bam! The reason popped into her head. It was so tough for her to tell them because her parents never said it to her. They may have said it just because she was their child, but not because they cared for her so much. At least that's what she felt.

Once the reason struck Cynthia, she could simply let it go. That's what Dr. Mills always said. Dwelling on the past wouldn't help. The past was over. Her parents were just doing the best they knew how to do. No blame! Now that she realized it, she only needed to make sure her kids really knew it.

Cynthia knew that her kids didn't understand how much she loved them because they would never share things with her. They would never ask for her advice. Now she had to make them understand. It was so tough for her to tell them, but she had to!

Finally she blurted it out: "I really, really love you for who you are, no matter what. Do you know what I'm saying? Do you really hear what I'm saying!?"

Whew! She said it. Now all she had to do was see they had all the health and common sense inside them that they needed. That meant that all she had to do was let them learn at their own pace, in their own time, accept them for who they are, and enjoy them for being who they are.

Cynthia: My kids knew that I changed because I was ready to listen to them. Instead of pointing a finger at them all the time and always wanting to beat them, I would sit down and talk to them. And I started to put things back to them. For instance, if there's a problem, I would ask them how they would handle it. That helps them to use their common sense. And when I'm throwing the questions back to them, they feel like I'm giving them a chance to really be in control of their lives and use their better judgment when making a decision. That was a great change. At the end of the week now we talk about if I did something wrong that hurt them, and we'll talk about it. And if I hurt their feelings they let me know, and I have a chance to tell them what they did to me. Or if I wasn't pleased with something I'll tell them, and they'll know the next time not to do it again. So we just respect one another now. Instead of just being the parent all the time I'm like a friend with them. I haven't had any more problems since then.

* * *

As her first job assignment Dr. Mills instructed Cynthia to knock on doors in Homestead Gardens. Her task was simply to build a rapport with the parents to find out what was on their minds, what they liked and disliked about the community and what changes they might like.

It shocked Cynthia when she first began knocking. Since she lived in Homestead Gardens she had pretty much kept to herself. She would go to work, come home and not get in anybody's business. She stayed by herself. All kinds of drugs and fights took place outside her unit, and she didn't want any part of it. She lived all the way in back of the project. Now when she knocked on doors in the front part it was embarrassing. She discovered people who had been living there for three years who she went to school with and didn't even know it.

Dr. Mills put together a little questionnaire with a rating scale. Cynthia used it to ask what the residents wanted in their community. Most said they wanted G.E.D. classes. Cynthia asked how often they spent time doing homework with their kids or interacting with them, or going out to the movies with them, or talking with them. Most scored very low on communication with their children. She also asked what type of activities they wanted if they had a chance to go on a field trip.

About 80% said "Disney World."

Cynthia: They tried to put Dr. Mills on a test to see if he was going to be a man of his word. They had to pick someplace they just knew they weren't going to go [laughs].

Cynthia focused mainly on what the residents said about their kids.

She asked, "Well, how would you like to have a good relationship with your kids?"

"Yeah, I would like to have a good relationship with my kids."

"Well we're having a class. It's like a P.T.A. meeting or like a parenting class."

She then told them what had happened over in Modello. They couldn't believe it. Because the housing projects were only a few miles from each other many of the Homestead Gardens parents knew some of the Modello parents. They wanted to know who had changed.

"You mean Thelma changed? I knew she was doing all kinds of stuff!"

"Well you ought to see her. She looks so good!"

"Is that right? I remember one time when she_____. Yeah, I'd like to see how she changed!"

"Why don't you come on Wednesday night, and I'll have them come too to share with you what happened in Modello and just really tell you what they're learning. And then maybe you can deal with the problems that you're having, and we can just have a good time and sit and talk. There's no lecture or nothing like that. We're going to talk about pot luck dinners and going places and stuff like that. I'm going to have some chicken and stuff. We're not going to give any papers or nothing, just have a good time and 'conversate.' It'll be more like a family thing, getting together but learning how to be a better parent at the same time."

At the first meeting in February 1989 nearly 100 parents showed up—a testament to Cynthia and Carol's work in getting them out. Roger smiled. Hiring them was one of the best moves he'd made.

Rosie, Patty, Carrie Mae, Lisa, Cicely, and Thelma came over from Modello to help kick off the parenting class. After the dinner where people were able to relax, talk over good times, build a nice rapport and meet Dr. Mills, one at a time the Modello parents shared their stories about what had happened in their lives, and how their relationships had improved with their children—all because their thinking had changed. All the ladies had to do was to speak from the heart.

In the audience the parents sat in rapt attention. The Modello ladies had the same problems they had. They could relate 100%. This was completely unlike having some agency come in and tell them what to do about their kids, which commonly would trigger the response, "They never lived in a housing project! How can they come in and tell somebody how to live or what to do when they haven't experienced it?"

> **Cynthia:** When the Modello parents were talking, the Homestead Gardens parents were seeing themselves, because we're all living in a housing project and we're all going through the same things. We're all going through the same problems with our neighbors, with everybody taking things personal. The Modello parents were talking about different situations that they were in, and how it was so much easier for them now. Every parent from Modello had their own problem that they ended up solving, so parents out in the audience were able to identify. Everyone was saying, "Oh wow, you know, that is true!" If it was an abusive relationship like with Rosie, they would relate to her. If it was like Miss Cicely who couldn't get along with her kids, they would be able to relate to her. People who were drinking identified with Thelma. Some identified with parents who had kids on drugs, or boyfriend problems. Some identified with Patty about getting along with her husband. Somebody was ready to relate to somebody else standing up there sharing, and that's how we started it. That was the first class.

After the session the Homestead Gardens residents ran up to the Modello ladies and said, "Oh, I need to talk to you because that's the kind of problem I've got."

"Hey, Thelma," four or five parents said, "you know, I want you to come to my house and talk to me, because I have the same problem. Can you come to my house tomorrow at 9:00?"

"Oh Miss Cicely, I would like for you to come to my house because I'm having the same problem with my kid. Can you come to my house on a Thursday at 10:00 and teach me more about it?"

"I need to really find out how I need to deal with my thoughts and stuff like that."

It seemed each of the parents had their own special person they needed to talk to. So they set up appointments.

Because the Modello parents had the same backgrounds, they were able to break in a lot faster, and Doc could stay more in the background and let Cynthia, Carol, and Lloyd take the lead. The Homestead Gardens ladies decided to meet twice a week to continue the parenting class. From time to time Dr. Mills would come over and help teach the class, but Cynthia was in charge.

At one of the first parenting classes Cynthia got up and told the other parents how her life was changing. The parents respected Cynthia for opening up about her own life. She was just like them and had come through her problems by living this philosophy. It allowed them to be open to having Cynthia come by to counsel them. It helped them be more open to Carol too. She was a stranger, but she was with Cynthia. Besides, Carol was so good with their little kids. As the parents began learning the philosophy themselves and began living it, as in Modello, it began to permeate the rest of Homestead Gardens.

> **Cynthia:** For me to really work with the residents here I had to find it for myself. I had to make sure that I was living it through my life, to see that I can really control my way of thinking and getting along with my family. I had to really see the change for myself and for my family before I can do anything to really work with anybody else. I got into learning more about my moods and my thoughts, and my life was being changed in that I was having a good relationship with all my kids. The way this thing works is no technique, you know, it's just living it. I was seeing how my life was being changed, and I can't even remember how it really changed. It just was a good feeling that I was having.

When a parent was confused about how to handle a situation with her teenager, such as her son coming home too late at night, Cynthia could speak from her own experience. Whenever they had problems that she wanted solved her approach was to throw it back to them, ask what they thought about it. For instance, Cynthia believed Benny should be home during the week at 9:00 but he would come home at 10:00 or 11:00.

"Benny, if you had a child your age what time would you like your child to come home? You want to make sure he's safe, and he's got to go to school the next day. What is a good time that you think, for a kid fourteen years old to be home?"

"If I had a child my age I would want him to be home around 9:00, because I know what's out there."

"Well, if you want your son to be home 9:00, what time do you think you should be home then?—because I'm a parent too."

She saw Benny take pause.

In time, Benny came to adopt this approach for himself. Whenever he wondered how his mother would think about a situation, he considered what he would think and feel if he were a parent. It was common sense.

One day he said, "Mom, you know, I like girls and I'm interested in them. Now just listen to me before I start."

He started to tell her about his feelings if he kissed a girl.

Cynthia thought, "Oh my goodness! This boy?"

"But I'm not going to get into that," Benny said, "and I wouldn't even ask a girl to do anything like that. But I started thinking, if I had a daughter, how old would I want my daughter to really date and be kissing and stuff like that. So I decided I didn't want to kiss a girl right now. I just want to be friends with them and wait until I start growing up."

Cynthia breathed a sigh of relief. There was something to be said about this common sense stuff.

Cynthia told the parents in the class, "So I've seen a lot of change in my kids. They are more aware of their thinking now than they were before. And I'm kind of glad because I wasn't aware of my thinking when I was young. When I became a parent I didn't know how to be a parent because my mom, by me being the only girl for thirteen years, she was kind of afraid to let go. She kept me covered a lot, so it was a long time before I could do anything on my own. Even at sixteen I was still coming in before dark and stuff. She was afraid of me being out there. She was overprotective. I didn't get spanked for things, and my mother always talked to me, but I guess I picked up bad habits from other people. I thought, this is the way I should do it, and that's how I got caught up in it."

As this understanding became clear to her, it occurred to Cynthia how to get it across to the rest of the parents. Instead of going through the principles like Dr. Mills, she communicated it in the parenting class this way:

"I started thinking that my thoughts were like a tape recorder. Because we accumulate things ever since we were babies. When you start looking at people, like your parents, your peers, your neighbors, on TV, everybody, that's when you start thinking, "This is the way life is supposed to be." So ever since we were a baby, we record everything that we see, and there's a memory bank here. So this tape recorder is going on. It's seeing everything we do, and it's just taping and taping. If it's a good experience it's here. If it's a bad experience it's here. So as we go along in life, if our mom told us, 'Don't touch this,' and we get spanked, it's here.

"Okay, growing up, once you get spanked, that tape recorder in that baby's mind is going to remember, 'Every time I touch this, I'm going to get spanked, so something is wrong with touching this.' They don't understand that you might get burned or get shocked. So at that time that baby is going to still touch it, because they still don't understand that it's bad, but they remember the bad experience. Our self esteem is so high at a small age that we forget about a lot of things, but we get to a certain age and we remember, and then we start dwelling on it, and those thoughts throw that self-esteem away.

"If you're in a bad relationship that tape recorder is going. And when you're into a new relationship and everything is going fine, and you're not having any problems, as soon as something happens, or if your boyfriend says something out of line, if you're in a real low mood, the tape recorder is going to remind you of that relationship that's back in the past."

The women were able to relate, saying, "You know, that's true! Because every relationship I get into, everything goes fine until I'm in a low mood, and I start thinking about all that trash what happened before, and I bring it into this relationship. But afterwards I say 'Oh, this isn't true. This is only what happened before!' But what I want to do is control my thoughts before it happens. I don't want to wait until after."

Cynthia held her hand up in the air to suggest a high level. "As long as you're up here," she said, "if you choose to go back and think about something, it doesn't bother you. When you're up here and the tape recorder is moving, there's nothing wrong to think about the past because you can laugh about it and it doesn't mean anything. Even people who have been raped or whatever, if they're up here it doesn't bother them now because it doesn't mean anything any more.

"Maybe the boyfriend comes in and says, 'I don't like what you did!' If you're up here you can push that tape recorder to 'stop' and not worry about what happened in the past, and proceed with your life and know how to get along with him and talk to him—and it won't mean anything. But if you're in kind of a bad mood [Cynthia pointed low] and a situation comes up, the more you get into it the more you want to play that old tape recorder. And depending on your self-esteem you're either going to put it on 'stop' and go on about your life, or you can press 'pause' and think about it and see where your common sense is, or you can just let it keep running. And if you're in a real low mood, you're going to just let it run, run, run. But if you're in a healthy state, you know it's only a thought and you don't have time for that, and it won't be depressing to talk to your boyfriend to see where he's coming from. But if he came to you when you're in a really low mood, you can put it on 'pause' and say, 'Hey wait a minute I don't feel real right now and, baby, I want to talk to you in about ten minutes, because right now I don't feel too good. Later I'll be ready to talk about it.'

"If you stay up here most of the time, you don't have time for the garbage because you're going to keep going forward, your common sense is up, and you know exactly what to say to keep him calmed down. But when you're in a ittle lower state, you're going to play with it just a little bit but you're not going to really let it bother you. But when you're way, way down here, that's when you're going to start making all these negative decisions and find yourself in trouble, because after the fact you'll be saying, 'Oh man, I shouldn't have said that.' We all go up and down, but if we stay up here most of the time you won't find yourself in much trouble as you were before."

> **Dr. Mills:** One of the most exciting things to me was our work with the parent training of trainers internship. They're incredible teachers now, because they're talking from their heart, just about what they've learned in their own lives. When I hear them talk to students or to parents it amazes me, because I think, "Gee, it never would have occurred to me to say it that way. That's fascinating how she said that to those students." Of course I would probably have said it in a more academic way and it probably would have gone right over their heads [laughs].

Before long Cynthia and Carol had nearly one hundred parents out of 150 units involved in the Homestead Gardens P.T.A. and parenting classes.

* * *

Dr. Mills: The only thing that Carol got caught in was that she was young and a little insecure, and she'd really get shaken up if anybody gave her negative feedback.

Sandy's kids had just been taken away by H.R.S.! Sandy stormed into the Modello office. Carol was in the office as Sandy blazed in, blasting Carol with both barrels. She called her a bitch and a liar and shouted that Carol had undermined her. She screamed in Carol's face that it was her fault her kids were taken away, and she knew Carol had been plotting against her. As Sandy continued to scream in her face, Carol started to scream back.

Over the next few days Carol became terribly distraught. She cried, "How could she think I wanted her kids to be taken away from her? It was the last thing in the world I wanted to see done!"

Doc kept trying to tell her, "Look, don't take it personally. This is Sandy's thing. This is what she does to everybody. She'll be back in two days pleading with us to help her get her kids back."

Carol: At that time I was feeling a little insecure, and I would take things very personal when I worked with the parents. I would take it to heart. If somebody said something to me I was ready to get back at them. But they were being insecure, and if I was being insecure I couldn't help them until after I dropped that. One of these parents I was working with, Sandy, would cuss you out from A to Z, Monday through Friday, and then the next week she was happy, like, "Oh Carol, how are you doing? My kids are doing fine, and I love you," and all this. But I had to see that when she did things like that—even in situations where I would be nice— she was just being insecure, and I couldn't take it personal. But it didn't matter that she was being insecure, I had to learn it for myself with Psychology of Mind that it was just me being insecure at times. And once I learned to like me, or to feel good about myself, then I could help these parents. Working with Lloyd and Cynthia and Dr Mills, they were trying to bring that out of me.

* * *

Lisa broke up with her man. Still he would come over to see the kids and try to talk her into being together again.

"Look, I don't need you," Lisa said. "I can be happy without you. I deserve better."

She had been having a ball, happier than she ever remembered being.

"You think you're hot shit, don't you?!" he chided.

But he worked on her. He worked her. He wore her down and convinced her.

She felt her old heart go sailing back to him. And she believed.

XII. Spring, 1989

Lloyd: Then one day when you're not looking for it, that's when all of a sudden it pops up in your face.

During a break at the parent training of trainers session at the Institute Lloyd sat next to Thelma and Rita Shuford. All were talking away about what Psychology of Mind was doing for them.

Out of the blue Thelma turned to Lloyd and said, "You know something, Lloyd? I don't drink like I used to. It occurred to me a while back that I don't need to drink. You know, I drink, but not like I used to. I don't even drink to get drunk any more. I mean, what for?"

It had come out of nowhere. Lloyd's jaw dropped.

"You know?" he said to himself, "She's got something!"

It blew his mind!

Thelma: When I was drinking I couldn't deal with my kids. They were small. A person that's drinking, anything will aggravate them. If the door shuts hard you'll fly off the handle. That's just the way I was. The least little thing they did, it just did something to me because I'm seeing these kids totally different under the alcohol, and they're looking at me totally different because they're not under the alcohol. After Dr. Mills worked with us, and I saw myself, I was drinking but the problems were still there. When I woke up the next morning, that same problem was still there. There was something that I was searching for, and I thought maybe that I could find it in that bottle, but it wasn't in the bottle.

Rosie had offered a great deal of caring support. She truly cared for Thelma and went out of her way to have contact with her.

One day after Thelma's boyfriend beat her up real bad Rosie said to her, "You know what?"

"What?"

"You've got to just stop drinking. You're a nice person. You work hard. You just go to work and you come home and you don't do anything. You don't go anywhere. You've got to just stop drinking. And when you do, everything will just change for you. Everything is going to change for you."

Rosie knew what she was talking about. Thelma heard. She decided to change her life.

> **Thelma:** And after that, I kept weaning, kept weaning, kept weaning from the bottle. I didn't just stop. Like now when I drink, I have a limit. I might drink about two beers and that's it. But liquor? I can't drink liquor, period. But I weaned myself off, bit by bit.

Thelma's relationship with her kids blossomed. Together they would laugh and clown and have fun. They would dance together, sing together, eat together. When they had a problem they would all sit down and discuss it. Her face began to sparkle.

> **Thelma:** Before, I couldn't do it. I couldn't do it because, by me drinking, when I looked at my kids it looked to me like they were the ones that had something against me. That's the way I saw it. But after weaning myself off of the bottle, and I looked out, I see that they're loving me. Before, I couldn't see it, but I see it now, and it made a big difference in them because I can talk to them now. If they have big problems now they can come to me and we can talk about it, and we feel good now, you know? We feel very good.

When Lloyd had first known Thelma in the early days, all that would come out of her mouth was, "Honey, we gonna go have fun! We gonna get some beer or some whisky, and get DRUNK, honey!" She believed she needed to drink to be happy. Now she said, "Hey, I don't need to drink to have a happy life. I don't need to do it." Something had shifted in her thinking, within her very consciousness.

"Woah!" Lloyd said to himself. "We *are* doing something!" Lloyd hadn't completely realized it until that moment.

He was struck to the depths of his soul.

Doc had told him to trust that it would happen. Lloyd saw his role as planting a seed, and maybe—maybe somebody else would come around and water that seed. He never expected results like this.

Lloyd: You know what? That's spiritual! They use that same analogy in the Bible, planting seeds and stuff. It was, like, this particular time it just manifested right before my eyes, where we were just talking about it.

* * *

Assistant Principal Colleen del Terzo had to discipline many students in Junior High School. Of all the students, she remembers Thelma's son Tyrone best.

Ms. del Terzo: He was the one I'll always remember. If I think of that group, I'll think of Tyrone. I was just about ready to kill him. I seriously was.

Tyrone was a leader of a gang. Thelma didn't know. She only knew that he was in continual trouble in school. Again and again she had to go over to the school house to deal with his problems. Ms. Del Terzo phoned Lloyd about him constantly.

Ms. Del Terzo: Tyrone was like the leader, but not the leader. He's smart, very slick. Daily, Tyrone would run his mouth in the classrooms and get into trouble. He would lead gang-style attacks. Tyrone threw a black jacket over a Hispanic kid's head, and his group all mauled him.

With this incident, Ms. Del Terzo brought Tyrone into her office and slammed the door. She read Tyrone the riot act. The police had come in and grilled him. Notified, Thelma walked into the office with her baby in a small cradle.

"Tyrone, this is the last straw with me!" yelled Ms. Del Terzo, nearly turning into a wild woman. "You're going to be dead if you don't do something different!"

Ms. Del Terzo didn't know what she did, but on that day something changed. She only knew that line was never crossed again. She attributed it to "scaring the life out of him." Yet she had also called Lloyd for help.

"Lloyd, you'd better take over. I've had it!" Then she left it up to him.

Lloyd and Tyrone had a talk.

Ms. Del Terzo: After that day Tyrone straightened out. His grades went up, and he shaped up. It was like he'd turned straight overnight. It was months before he was involved in a couple of big events again, but I could give him a break on nearly anything after that because he had given me months of relief.

* * *

The training at the Institute seemed to have a powerful effect on Rosie. Also, she appeared to get a lot out of her few individual sessions with Ann Thomas, one of the Institute trainers. The change that had been sparked by Rosie now skyrocketed. Her life seemed to calm down even more. She began staying at home more, doing less late night partying. She realized she needed to spend more time around her kids. She became a more solid influence on her friends.

Rosie also began to see that she didn't have put up with own man beating on her all the time.

Rosie: I had been in an abusive relationship for about ten years. And after I started to get involved with what was going on with Dr. Mills, I started to change a lot. All of a sudden I'm going against this man. He's telling me, it's either the job or him. He wasn't really doing a whole lot, but he wanted that control. And I just made up my mind: "No way!" And I just started to get involved. He was never abusive to my kids, but I was sort of abusive to my kids, as far as words—and I'm not going to say I don't still smack either, because occasionally I do—but I've learned to be consistent with what I do. And during the time that I got involved with Dr. Mills and the approach I came out of that relationship.

Rosie decided to leave her abusive man. This removed a lot of stress from her life. She became softer and easier to deal with. She no longer needed to be embroiled in fights with her neighbors. She began to settle down to a nicer, more peaceful, ordinary life.

* * *

In the midst of all this, the Modello parent trainers received a stipend to help out other parents in Modello and Homestead Gardens. Rosie shined in this role.

Rosie: A lot of times I don't tell people not to beat their kids because Dr. Mills didn't tell me what to do. What we did was, everyone raised their hands and said, "Dr. Mills, is it okay if we beat our kids?" [laughter] We were missing the point. Because when you get your stuff together, you'll know what to do. You feel like slapping them upside the head sometimes, but then you come to realize you have to calm yourself down. Because a lot of times you're angry with something that happened on the job or that happened in your relationship or whatever. A lot of times your kids may feel that they are being totally ignored, and that's the only way they can get some attention. If they know you're going to beat them or punish them or whatever, they go to school and they act up. Either way it goes it comes back to you.

I learned how to just sit down and deal with it. I talk to my kids a lot, which I never knew how to do. I was brought up to believe a child is to be seen and not heard, and their opinion does not count or does not matter, because I'm your mother. I work. I take care of you. I provide your necessities. So you shouldn't have any complaints. But that's not true, because they do. They have valid concerns, and you just have to sit down and listen sometimes. It's hard. It's not real easy.

It's like smoking. You know you're always reaching for that cigarette. So you always reach back into yourself and you learn. And I learned! Like I said, I was in an abusive relationship for ten years, and I was able to pull myself out of it and I was able to make a clean and complete break.

* * *

Lisa: There was a young girl. She had her first child when she was fourteen and she had a little girl who at the time was about four. The little girl had been fondled by this guy. Well, Pam and I and the other lady in the store, we find out about it, and the police are called in. Her first reaction to the child was, "I told you to keep your little hot tail at home!"—like it was somehow her fault— and the lady dropped the charges. She told Pam, "Well, Pam, it's really nothing, because it happened to me when I was a child, you know." So in her mind it was somehow the child's fault.

I could relate to that because that was exactly what I thought. All the time after it happened to me, even though I could blank this out for years and years and kind of forget that it ever happened, with any relationship I felt like I had to give, give, give in order for me to think that the man liked me. I felt like if I don't do this, the person is not going to like me. Because when I was sexually abused, he would tell me that if I told anyone I was going to put my mother out in the street—because my mother lived with my aunt and she had three kids at the time and didn't have anywhere to go. And I bought into that. So anytime anything like that happened, I wouldn't tell because I was there to protect my mother. I wasn't going to let my mother be put out. And I'm sure she bought into the same thing that I went through, she just didn't have the realization that I had.

And there were other situations. I've talked to the ladies and I've said, "Look, it's not your fault, and if it happens to your child let them know that it's not their fault. I don't care what happens, it is not their fault!"

They should never place blame on themselves. I think it was, like, twenty-three or twenty-four years before I ever told anyone that it ever happened, because I couldn't ever talk about it back then. I would burst into crying. Now I talk about it, and I share it with other people with similar situations, and it doesn't hurt anymore—because that's one of those things that happened and I just got rid of it and left it back there.

I thought I was damaged goods, that nobody was really going to love me because somehow they knew that this thing had happened to me—even though no one really knew. But in my mind I thought they could sense something that I wasn't a good person, and that they just wanted to use me. That's why I was always trying to prove that I was this great person, and I never could live up to what they thought that I should be. And then, inside, there was me, and it took me a long time to learn that this is what I am, and I don't have to prove myself because this is me. I am this great person! And it felt so great when I finally could tell someone.

We used to always say that it sounded so corny when we would tell people, "I really love me." But it's true. Because you get to that point and you realize who you really are, and that's something to love. And when you really feel that about yourself in that way, then you have all this unconditional love to share with others. That's how I am now with my kids.

* * *

One day it occurred to the staff, "Hey, why don't we see if we can get some money from Dade County to take everybody to Disney World!" Initially the residents may have been testing Dr. Mills, but results from the questionnaire showed in black and white that it was the most desired field trip activity.

Cynthia: I don't know how we pulled it off, but we did. We had a bus load from Modello, and a bus load from Homestead Gardens, and they still couldn't believe it! They wasn't sure if they wanted to buy new outfits to go, because they said, "If I go and buy me a new outfit and we don't go to Disney World, we're going to kill Dr. Mills [laughs]."

Lloyd: At the time Dade County didn't understand all of what we were asking, and we did everything before they realized what was going on. They would have never let us do that [laughs].

Cynthia: The bus came about 5:00 that morning. I guess about seven families were sitting outside waiting. The rest of them were in the house peeking out of their door, and when the bus came everybody said, "THE BUS IS HERE!" And you should have seen everybody running out there [laughter].

Lloyd: We took a lot of people, and we were just having fun.

Cynthia: So when they had a chance to experience, not just to go to Disney World but to do something together, that made them feel like a family. Now they don't argue with each other any more. They watch out for each other. Even my next door neighbor! I wouldn't even speak to her because she used to argue all the time. She don't give a care who comes down her hallway, she'll say bad things to them, like "Get off my porch!" and stuff. Now we know how to relate to each other. If the people here are in a bad mood they say, "Right now I'm in a bad mood because_____, come back in about thirty minutes and I'll talk to you then." That makes me feel so good that now we can be like a family. You don't have to worry about your head being knocked off or whatever.

After the Disney trip the Homestead Gardens residents made the P.T.A. official allow them to raise money to continue to go on field trips. As it had in Modello, a considerably lightened atmosphere began to pervade Homestead Gardens.

* * *

Meanwhile, the Modello parent trainers were hard at work helping out anyone who asked for their assistance. Dr. Mills offered plenty of opportunities to learn. In class one day they talked about various situations that might arise.

"There was this friend of mine," said Dr. Mills. "He had called me and said he was going to jump off a building and kill himself."

"What?" Thelma exclaimed. "Well how did you handle that, Dr. Mills?"

"I told him not to go anywhere, that I'd be there, and I went. When I got to him, I didn't mention anything about what he said about killing himself."

"You didn't? What did you say to the man?"

"When I got there I took him out to lunch. I talked about anything but what he called about. I got his mind totally off killing himself. I talked about anything that came into my mind, but I didn't mention anything about him killing himself. And when he got through eating lunch, he didn't even mention anything to me about it. He just seemed happy."

"Really!?"

"Uh huh. That's the way I worked that problem out. And it did work out. In the next two or three days he called me and told me that his life was wonderful."

"Wowwie!" laughed Thelma. "Woooh!"

Dr. Mills explained that his intention was to get the man's mind off his problems. If he had tried to talk to the man directly about his problems it would have kept him focused on how horrible his problems were. It may have even exacerbated it. Instead, he took it in the other direction.

Thelma said, "Dr. Mills, that's nice. You really worked that problem out real nice!"

Thelma couldn't imagine it. If someone had called her with a suicide threat she would have yelled, "Oh God!" and gone running over to the woman with, "Girl, are you crazy?! You can't kill yourself.

You can't be like that. You got kids and all. Hey, come on, let's talk about it!" Dr. Mills had done the opposite and it had worked out so smoothly.

After the class Thelma went up to him and said, "That was really good. I really enjoyed that."

"You did? Did you get anything out of it?"

"Yeah, if I come to that kind of problem I would know how to go about doing it. I would talk about everything but what that person told me was happening with that problem. Yeah, I know how to do it."

Thelma knew that the real message was, don't dwell on the problems. Instead, try to get people into higher spirits where their problems will look different to them.

Thelma soon had the chance to put her new learning to the test. One Homestead Gardens lady told her about a problem with her boyfriend having other girlfriends who lived in the same set of units. She told Thelma that she was going to kill him—literally.

As the woman spoke Thelma listened intently. She kept hearing the woman say, "That's wrong! That's wrong, and if I catch him, I'm going to murder that man!"

Thelma sat and listened.

Before long the woman noticed that Thelma hadn't said a word.

"You got anything to say?" she asked.

"I certainly do," smiled Thelma.

The woman started to laugh.

When Thelma saw the smile on her face, she knew she could get through.

"Oh I'm so sorry!" The lady laughed. "You know I haven't even given you a chance to say a word."

"You sure haven't! I'm so glad now to get in this conversation I don't know what to do," Thelma laughed. "Okay, number one, you got to think about the kids."

"Oh God," she gulped, "I forgot I even had kids."

"You got to think about the kids because if you go out and hurt somebody or take somebody's life you're taking something that you can't give back. It's the truth. You go out there and take your friend's life, you cannot give that man's life back. If you go out there and take your neighbor's life, you can't give that life back".

"It's true," the woman sighed. "So how do you think that I should deal with this problem?"

"If you love this man, you sit him down and you all talk about it. I haven't seen you all. I haven't seen the other people that you're talking about. But by me sitting here looking at you, and looking around, it looks to me like the man takes care of you."

"Yes, he does."

"See, the other women might be nothing to him. You never know. Because men like to be around women, and women like to be around men, but that don't mean they're lovers."

"You keep saying that he ain't doing nothing, but they're the ones that keep coming to me and saying it."

"You know why?"

"Why?"

"It could be jealousy. Stand up and come here. Stand right at your door, and look at your apartment."

She did. "I got a nice apartment. You know, I never paid no attention."

"You know why?"

"Why?"

"Because you always keep in your mind and in your heart what your neighbors and your friends and what your man are saying and doing. That's why you never took time to look at your apartment. There's a lot that you can do, and once you start doing them, then you won't have time for people to bring this stuff on you."

"You're right," she said.

"There's a lot of things that you can do. Go riding. Go on the beach. Anywhere. But make your life happy. It's up to you to make your life happy."

The lady felt so good by the time Thelma left she could not believe it. The woman walked her out to the parking lot. While Thelma was waiting for Cynthia to take her home, she saw the other ladies the woman had been talking about. And she saw the woman go up to them and speak to them nicely.

Cynthia witnessed the scene and said, "I don't know what you did to that lady, Thelma, but she looks like a totally different lady."

Thelma: I saw her in the hairdressers just this Saturday, and she still has that same spirit. Still has the same spirit! She has a brand new car now. She saw me, and she came right over to me and she grabbed my hand and she said, "How are you doing?" And I said, "I'm doing all right." And she said, "You remember me?" I said, "Wait, don't tell me." And I had to think, and I said, "Yeah!" She has a beautiful spirit—a sweet spirit. But I couldn't have done it without Dr. Mills—off that story he told that day. I took that story and I used it on her, but I used it in a different way—because it wasn't the same as his friend. But it worked!

Lisa: It was just great. Some parents, some days they're smiling and all happy, and other times they curse you out and growl at you. But instead of me getting real defensive I say, "Okay, well hi, anyway." And the next day you don't hold that against them, and you just go right back in there because you understand what they're going through. And when they start talking about things that are really bringing them down and stuff, you point out those good things. Or sometimes you just get away from all that, and talk about anything. I learned that you don't just sit there and talk about all their problems. Talk about anything, and it just gets their mind off of it. And they see that their moods start to come up again, and it doesn't seem the same when they look back on the situations that they're going through. I still have that good relationship with everyone no matter where I am. They see right away, I accept you for you.

* * *

One day a lady in Homestead Gardens wanted a guy out of her house. He was always jumping all over her. She called the police. Cynthia went over to try to help settle the couple down. Cynthia brought the man outside.

"It's her damn fault!" he yelled. "I'm giving her all my money and all this kind of stuff, and when I want to play she doesn't have time. I'm the man, and I'm working, and I'm trying to help her, and she shouldn't treat me like that. I'm a hard working man!"

Cynthia let him talk on and on.

After he'd said all he could and had calmed down some, Cynthia said, "Can you put yourself in her shoes?"

"I'm a man! What do I want with—!"

"No, I'm not telling you like that," Cynthia interrupted. "I just want you to tell me, just try to give me some examples—if you were in her shoes, how would you feel about you coming in like that?"

The man stopped and thought. "Well, yeah, I can understand where she's coming from." He thought some more. "Okay, okay, okay, I'll try to be more, you know, nicer to her. I know what I'm saying, and I shouldn't be saying it."

"Can you find a better way? You know what she really likes, right?"

"Yeah."

"Well, what is it?"

"She really enjoys flowers."

Cynthia looked at him as if to say, "Well then?"

"Okay," said Cynthia, "now I'm going on in to talk to her, and when I do I'm not going to be on her side, and I'm not going to be on your side. All I want you guys to do is to be together. And if you really love her, you will see what you can do to be a better boyfriend, and I'm going to tell her the same thing. And in a couple of days I want you to come back and let me know what's going on. I'm not trying to get into your business, but I'm trying to get your relationship back together."

Cynthia went inside and listened to the woman. In this case the woman participated in the parenting class, so she'd heard how thoughts about the past can affect situations in the present.

When the woman calmed down Cynthia said, "Don't you kind of see that you're bringing things that happened to you before into this relationship, and you should kind of leave that alone?" She then reminded her about the tape recorder and how moods affect it.

"You know what?" the woman replied, "that's true, because as soon as I come in, I'm kind of tense. And then once I get home and I want to relax, I can't because the kids are moving around and stuff."

"I know how you feel because I'm the same way. I need fifteen minutes after I come home from work. My kids know now to give me fifteen minutes time out when I come home so I can settle down and get myself together, and so I can be able better to relate to them. Now they come up to me and say, 'Is it time yet? You ready yet?'"

The woman laughed. "You know, that is true. I do need some time out."

Cynthia talked with her about how those same moods affect her feelings for her man, and her man's feelings toward her.

In a couple of days the woman came in and told Cynthia that

things were progressing. Later the guy came in and asked Cynthia what she thought about their progress.

"Well what do you think, How does it feel to you?"

This couple got back together. The majority of problems the residents wanted to deal with pertained to "bad relationships with boyfriends." A lot of relationships came to prosper in Homestead Gardens.

Cynthia: When counseling parents I don't try to change anybody. I just be myself and to try to pull out the good in them, because I know there's good in everybody. Everybody has self-esteem. Everybody's got love. Every human being has it. It just has to be brought out of them. It's just that other things are on top of it and they can't really see clearly. I listen to them first. That's the number one key is to listen to people first before you start talking to them. I listen to them, and nine times out of ten they are able to listen to themselves. A lot of times professionals don't really listen to clients, and when the clients hear themselves they know what they need to do.

* * *

Doc began to take the parent trainers and staff out of the area to make presentations at conferences. The first was in June 1989 in St. Petersburg at the annual Psychology of Mind conference. They had people in tears.

Rosie spoke first. After getting the audience laughing uproariously about how she couldn't make Dr. Mills go away when he had first arrived in Modello she said, "And you just learn so many different things about you. He just provided, like, the tool for me to open up me, because I learned a lot about me. And I'm still learning. I'm not perfect.

"If I don't feel good about myself, then nothing is going to go right. If I'm not in a good mood, then everything is going to go wrong. And I just really started to listen. For me, it's like a light going on. Everything just started to fall in place. I still yell, but I don't yell as much. In the beginning I was always yelling because I was always upset. My kids were always acting out in school, and there were things going on in my household that had me going, and it was also affecting them, but I didn't realize it. They were having a lot of problems at school. I was always at the school.

"You've heard the saying, "Into each life a little rain must fall before you can appreciate the sunshine." I learned all the cliches, so it was hard to know that all I had to do was feel good about myself and my situation will change. It didn't happen overnight because I didn't feel like it could happen overnight. At first I just couldn't relate. I said, "Well, maybe I'll get a job out of it." But in a way it was like overnight because I started to be more patient as far as my kids were concerned. I even got out of the abusive relationship that I had been in for ten years because I had gotten involved—not just with Dr. Mills, but with me doing something that made me feel good about me—just doing things that I knew I could do, like getting up in the morning and not wishing I didn't get up that morning, and, you know, putting on clothes and fixing my hair and things like that. It just gave me a chance to find me.

When it was Cicely's turn to speak, she stood up, grabbed the microphone with confidence, and said, "I went out and knocked on those doors, and I went to let them know that I loved them and that I was there to help them. And by me going out there showing that I care, I'm not putting them down because of their problems and the situations that they're in. And that is the main thing that we really need all over the world is love. And the people need love. I tell them I don't care how bad your situation looks, if you think positive there can be a way out. Because I know, there's nothing too hard that can't be worked out. They say there is no hope. I know there's hope! I don't care what their situation is. It's not there to take your own life. There is hope in every situation. I know this. And that's what the world really needs is for more people like us to reach out and help people—because that's what they need."

The next year in Minneapolis at the annual Psychology of Mind conference Lloyd, Cynthia, and Carol repeated the feeling.

At this conference Carol said, "At that time I was working a lot with kids, and I was sick at the way these kids were being taken care of. I would take them into my office and I would literally feed them and wash them. I had a towel and a washcloth in my office where I would just take them and I would wash them up and send them back home. It was something that I didn't mind doing and because to me it was showing the parents that, this is how your child can look. But I work with the parents as well. One of the residents would come in to me and say, "Get out, put that child down, she'll mess up your clothes!" And to me it didn't matter. I would get them all and hug them and kiss them, and Cynthia said, "You know, you got to be careful, because you kiss kids on the mouth sometimes." But I wouldn't be thinking about that because that's showing them love. But you don't know what's going on in their house, so you do have to be a little careful."

Cynthia interuppted, "That's true about kissing them on the mouth. It's just that she gets so bubbly." [laughter]

Carol continued, "But that was just a part of me, just working with these kids and just being there for them. Because a lot of times just a hug will really go a long way. Or just to say, "I like your dress," or, "Let me see your grades. You make beautiful grades." To me, that is beautiful for that child. They would come in and show us their homework and bring pictures and just really feel good about themselves. And that really helped a lot.

Cynthia went on. "Carol has a unique way with parents. She would get these parents when they got their monthly check and take them shopping. I probably couldn't have done that, but she can do that. Especially if they're on drugs or something like that so they're not going to use the money properly, she will go and take them shopping, and that shows the parents that she cares."

Cynthia: You have to really have love in your heart for people if you really want to work with them. And even though I'm working there from 9:00 to 5:00, my job is not 9:00 to 5:00. It's twenty-four hours. You have to have the love all the time.

It was all from the heart.

* * *

Residents in Homestead Gardens began to feel a new spirit about living there. Everyone began to take pride in their community. They had their own community garden and raised vegetables. Most everyone took part in it. Before, it was, "Don't you get one onion more!" and they'd start counting. Now they shared.

Still, they went out of their way to avoid the drug dealers, and a few residents such as Ruby. No one wanted to risk being in harm's way.

XIII. Late Spring, 1989

The teacher training in the Leisure City and Homestead elementary schools began to produce results. Twenty faculty from each school attended the trainings.

Irene Edminster [elementary school teacher]: Dr. Mills said in the class that nobody is trying to be bad or negative. Whatever they are doing, regardless of how radical it may appear, this is what they feel they need to do to survive. If you can make them see the situation from a different point of view, the behavior will change. Instead of trying to change behavior, what you need to do is try to change their perception of the situation. The more negative that students are about how things look to them, the more they will see discouraging things, then it will send them down even farther into depression. Until you can raise the level of their thinking about the situation, you may quell their behavior for a while, but you're not going to change their need to use that behavior, because of the way they see it.

Janyce Waters [elementary school teacher]: All of us got the book, *Sanity, Insanity and Common Sense.** That one I saved from Hurricane Andrew. That was one of the few books I put in my plastic container. Thank God I still have mine. When you found out what the real problem was—your own thinking—that was affecting what you were doing and how you were doing it, the release you felt in your mind was really something.

---

*Now out of print.

Ms. Waters had a particularly difficult second grade class that year. The students simply did not like each other. They fought, and the fight at home or in the cafeteria or in physical education (P.E.) class came right into the classroom. It drove her up the wall. Both the P.E. and art teachers had a very difficult time controlling her class, so Ms. Waters always had to stay to try to keep order.

Inspired by the teacher training she began to have lunch sessions with about ten children at a time who were normally at each other's throats. Ms. Waters would simply listen to them talk. After five or six weeks she rotated the groupings and reported what each group had talked about to the full class.

"This person feels one way, and that person feels another way. There's got to be room to allow for what he's thinking as well as what you're thinking."

In the middle of a lesson if a pupil started yelling, "He wrote on my paper!" or "He's copying!" Ms. Waters would stop, take five minutes, take the child outside to make it private, and say, "What is wrong? There's got to be some reason that you really need to act this way here."

Eventually the student would admit that something difficult had happened at home.

"If a problem comes up," she said, "you've got to try to get it out and tell me about it so it doesn't ruin everything else in the class, because sometimes that anger and stuff isn't a nice place to visit, so you really don't want to stay there."

Ms. Waters began to see a calmness pervade the class. The children settled down. By the end of the year she'd start to say, "You can't do that because—," and the students would finish the sentence by shouting in unison, "—you have to care!"

She would say, "Your words come back to you, so you have to be careful what words you're putting out there. If you don't care, you can't expect anyone else to."

Janyce Waters: So there was less destruction, and some of those same kids who are now in higher grades still remember that.

Ms. Waters saw that her toughest kid had potential to become an outstanding gang leader. He had many problems at home and refused to talk to anyone. Instead he took control. If somebody didn't follow his rules, he dealt out some kind of punishment or "emotional blackmail."

One day Ms. Waters happened into the bathroom and saw the writing on the wall. The other children had written their private thoughts about the tough guy, using a variety of choice four letter words. Ms. Waters went to get him.

"You see this comment right here?" she said. "That's what they think about you. See, I try to tell you that you have to be a lot more gentle with some of these people, because they don't always want to be bossed. They have thoughts of their own. And I guess you think, 'Well if I don't boss them all the time there's something wrong with me.' But look what happens when you do that!"

The words were written by the kids he thought he controlled. The tough boy saw it! From that point Ms. Waters saw a change in the way he treated his classmates. He spoke with much less bossiness. His tone of voice changed. In return the other children began to respond better to him. They weren't quite as afraid or intimidated. His perceptions had changed, and with it his actions. He experienced better results accordingly.

Irene Edminster: The kid who is constantly banging his pencil on the table, which drives you buggy, or is always making some disruptive outburst, you can approach him in a way that leaves him much more dignity. Years ago it would have infuriated me when it wouldn't stop after I asked for it to stop, and I would be ready to go at the kid. Now, I much more readily express my feelings: "That's making it really difficult for me to concentrate. Would you be thoughtful and stop that?" Give the child a chance to rise above his behavior by lifting him up with a remark instead of putting him down. I now approach many discipline problems from a much more positive point so the child doesn't feel, "This teacher is on my back again." It gives him an opportunity to be agreeable with you and say, "Sure, I'd love to do that." Of course, ten minutes later he might forget again and you may have to say, "Remember what we talked about?" Sometimes it only takes a look the second time because you haven't put the child down, you've given him an opportunity to change his behavior. Instead of just saying, "STOP IT!", you try to approach it by giving the child an opportunity to help you or the class out, or show a better part of himself. As Dr. Mills used to say, "Give him an offer he can't refuse. You're giving him an opportunity to volunteer to be a better person and help the class out by being thoughtful and kind, and more often than not, kids respond very well to that."

Even with children who are having a lot of trouble, when they're threatened they're going to act out what they think they need to do to survive. You give them an opportunity to act out positive behavior.

Janyce Waters: Another thing Dr. Mills taught me was to separate myself and my ego from their personal fights. That was the hardest thing for me. You have to let them work it out, even if it takes teaching time. But you can't teach until they have the right attitude anyway. I had to say, "If I say you have to work it out, if you don't take care of this now, I will have to accept your decision to get sent down the office or get a note sent home, because everything has a condition. It doesn't come free." I had to learn to separate myself from the stress of thinking, "Why can't I control this?"

Ms. Waters would say to her class, "Only you can control what you did, because only you can control you. You can never change what anybody else does, or reacts to, or likes or dislikes, but you can change the way you react to it and deal with it. So when you hear someone say, 'You dummy!' you have to think, 'Hey I don't have to be what that person says I am, because I like me pretty good!' And if you like you pretty good, other people will like you pretty good. It works like that."

Maria Garcia: One thing I got from it was, if that kid came at you major mad at the teacher next door, if you could reach him and talk to him, then it would dissipate. But if I jumped all over him, then I would just make it worse because I would be taking ownership of the problem. I couldn't help him, and it certainly wasn't going to help me because it would just piss me off in a major way.

Irene Edminster: Where before I might have gotten really frustrated and upset, I became a calmer person, because I see what this behavior really represents. I have a much calmer thought process and can come up with much more positive ways to handle the situation than I would have. Before it was, "I can't do anything with these kids. What's wrong with me? Why can't I get them to behave the way I want them to?" Now I don't see it as my problem. I see it as a multiplicity of things that they come from and the way that they see things, and I don't take it personally. I don't think they're out to get me. Now I try to get them to a place where they can relax, to feel that this kind of behavior is not necessary.

Sometimes the best thing you can do is let it rest, back off and get the child involved in something much more positive. That's something I took away from Dr. Mills. If your mind is clear enough things come to you—ways of saying things. And as you practice it, gradually over the years it becomes part of what you do and how you approach children, and every year it gets a little easier. Either I'm getting better classes or things that I'm doing now that I didn't do years ago are making a big difference.

By around the third session the possibility started to sink in that the teachers could also apply this approach to their personal lives.

Irene Edminster: One day while we were still taking the course, it seemed like everything was going wrong that day. I was hitting every red light on the way home. I was in a hurry to get there, and I remember muttering to myself in the car about some silly thing, that this was going to go wrong too. Then I kind of caught myself short. I realized I was in one of those train of thoughts he talked about, and at this level this is exactly how you see everything. I said, "Oh, this sounds like something we talked about today." I was about a mile and a half from home, and I think I laughed the whole rest of the way. When your mood changes, the way you look at things changes and vice versa. So when you come into the class feeling bad, it may not be the children at all. It may be your level of tolerance and how understanding you're willing to be when you have a splitting headache and feel like something is a burden on you and you can't handle all the stress. The kids react accordingly. They're very sensitive—probably more to your body language and tone than what you speak.

Janyce Waters: In my life I started getting a lot less headaches. I could go home and actually turn the children off when they left. Before, it was, "I wonder what I need to do about so and so." Now I see that you do the best you can and don't worry over all the stuff you can't do. With the teachers that took the course, a lot of them changed. Our personal stress levels went a long way down. And every time I get to one of those spots where I say, "Hey, why doesn't so and so do this?" I say, "Hey, wait a minute, I have to separate myself from what his problem is." That came from the class. The influence of that course works for me in here very well, and even outside of here—even when I sit in traffic. You talk about tempers! Now I say, "I'll get out of here when I get out of here. There's nothing I can do, so I may as well be patient and ride it out." You're not where you want to be but you're still [points to head] here. It's contentment. It works. It really works. And it's still working.

Irene Edminster: The other thing that I found extremely important is that you can't look back at the things that you did in the past with regret. You have to say, it's too bad that it happened that way, but at that point in my life I was perceiving a situation as such. I can do nothing about that. That's over. The only thing I have control over is what I do from here. You have to let go of any guilt you have: "My gosh, what I did to that poor kid because I didn't have an understanding of where he was coming from." You have to be able to let that go and say, "Today I see it differently, and from this point on I'm going to deal with it differently." The past is gone. There's nothing you can ever do to change that.

After the teacher trainings Dr. Mills noticed that the school climate became more humane. The atmosphere had a nicer feeling. Teachers seemed to be more relaxed and more patient with the kids. Nearly half the faculty ultimately went through the training. Teacher patience with students increased markedly.

* * *

Cynthia Stennis: At the same time Dr. Mills was training the teachers, Lloyd and Carol and I were working with the students, teaching them what the teachers were learning.

A lot of the kids had been fighting all their lives. At any moment some youngster could deck anyone who looked at them cross-eyed. Some had been fighting since age two to get food from their brothers and sisters, and they were tough.

One youth from the projects often hurt people. He would break kids' noses, or break their jaws at the drop of a hat. He'd been suspended about twenty times and expelled three. In frustration they had placed him in the alternative school, which only made it worse because it contained all the "worst" kids in the district. There he got into fights every day. Most of those kids had weapons so he was considering bringing a gun to school.

Lloyd began to joke around with him to get to know him, to establish rapport so the kid would realize Lloyd was on his side. Lloyd saw the health in him, rather than think anything was wrong with him, or that he was crazy. Once they had a good rapport, whenever he or Doc would see him around the project they'd lightheartedly start to shadow box with him to get him to relax.

Psychology of Mind posited that this youth's mental health was the same as anyone else's. It was based on his moment-to-moment state of mind. He went up and down like everyone else. He may spend more time at the lower levels, and maybe his lows gripped him more powerfully than most, but in those moments when he rose to a higher level he was like anyone else. The staff wanted to get him into a lighter mood, and therefore in a nicer, more rational thinking process. In that state, for that moment, his common sense, his inner wisdom, would be more accessible. In that state they could talk to him about whether his pattern of behavior—every day going to school looking for fights and defending himself—might be self-defeating.

"Look," Lloyd would say to him, "just ignore it. It's silly. You've got better things to do with your time."

The common sense started to sink in. In two months he began to stop the pattern. He began to function better in school. His grades began to rise. He made it through an entire semester without being suspended even once.

> **Dr. Mills:** I remember the day at the end of that semester when he brought his report card in. He was so excited because he had all B's and C's. For the first time in his life he had passing grades. And he couldn't wait to see Lloyd, his best buddy. He ran in with his report card so excited, "Where's Lloyd? Where's Lloyd? I want to show him my grades,"—even before he went home to show his parents. And he's a beautiful guy. He started to come into our office every day, as soon as he came home from school. This is the key: what attracted him was a nice feeling. He felt unconditionally accepted by our staff. He loved hanging around the office because we didn't see him as a delinquent or bad kid. We didn't see anything wrong with him. We just always treated him as if he was a completely healthy and normal. We saw the health in him, and he responded to that. We talked to him as if he had common sense. And it just turned him around.

> **Maria Garcia:** I saw a difference in the Modello kids in the way they took to learning. They began to have a positive attitude. They weren't screaming at you any more. They were learning to become

a little more mellow. Maybe they were getting a lot more attention and didn't have to scream for the attention. I saw a lot of grades go up because of that. I saw a lot of positive things coming out, but I didn't think it was one little thing. I think a lot of things were involved: the trips they were giving them, the homework center, the mother having some self-esteem about herself. I think the other teachers saw it too.

When talking to seventh graders Lloyd wouldn't think they were listening to him at all. Four years later many of them came up to him to tell him how much he helped them, and how much of what he said had come back to them later.

Among the kids from Modello, office discipline referrals, expulsions, and truancy dramatically reduced.

It had all been the result of a combined effort between Dr. Mills and his staff, the P.T.A., a visiting teacher, the police, and the Perrine Optimist program.

Dr. Mills: I remember driving down to Modello one school day and thinking, "Gee, it's quiet here. What's different? Oh, there are no kids around!" And I started talking with people, and every kid was in school! "That's amazing that they've got every kid in school now." Because before, on a typical school day, you would see hundreds of kids that should have been in school that weren't. It was a surprise. "Gee, all the kids are in school! That's neat."

XIV. Summer, 1989

Thelma still had a major problem to deal with. Her boyfriend was still beating her.

Thelma: Then I see my man, and I see that he's just used to doing that because he didn't know any better. After the years went by and I got to looking at it, I saw that he would do that to me because, down in his generation, that's all his mother and father did: fight, cuss, and shout at one another. So his father did this to him as he's coming up, right? So he felt like that he's supposed to do this to his wife or his lady friend the same way. He wasn't taught any different. After I went through the program, I found out that it was wrong. So I went to him and I told him I had to break up with him.

"It's wrong!" she confronted him. "You can't beat me. You can't raise me no more. I'm already raised. You're grown and I'm grown."

Had Thelma confronted him like this before, it would have resulted in a worse beating. This time he sensed something different—a power, a new strength behind her words. It seemed to come from deep inside her. Besides, most of the beatings came when she was drunk, and she wasn't drunk anymore.

"Hey!" she said to him firmly, "You can't be doing this no more— beating on me and dragging me here and there—so if you have to be like this in here, then you go your way, and I'll go my way."

He didn't like what he heard. Still hooked on alcohol and crack himself, he couldn't control himself.

Thelma: He didn't like it at first. He still hasn't got over it. It's something that's rooted in him. What I'm saying is, it's hard to come out, because he was brought up like that. All this shooting and cussing and fighting, it's just rooted in him. You've got to go at it step by step with him and let him know.

Thelma kicked him out of the house. He kept coming back around. To keep him away she got a restraining order. Every time he came she called the police. She had to change the locks on her apartment.

Thelma: After we broke up, he found out then that nobody out there in the streets cared for him. He realized then that he had a family, and we showed him more love than the people he called friends. And his friends were the ones that always kept us fighting. They went in telling him that I'm doing this, I'm doing that, and they're telling me that he's doing this and he's doing that. And it would get us started because that jealousy was in there. So when I sat down and I talk to him, he didn't want to do it, so I took action first. I tell you what I did, I got me a new man. [laughs] And he knew it! And when I got me this man, I thought he was God, he was so good to me, right? And I wasn't used to that. He's an older guy. I enjoyed him, but I was just swapping the devil for the demon. Because this man was drinking a lot, and he stayed drunk a lot, and I realized that it's not what I want. I'm trying to get away from this stuff. So I got out of that.

Meanwhile, her old man saw the huge changes that Thelma had made in her life. It had been quite a while and she'd only drunk less than an inch from the last liter of liquor they'd bought together— not like her at all!

Thelma: When I was drinking I had to drink it straight. I don't put no water in, no juice, no soda water. I'm not going to water it down. I'd put it out until it's all gone! But now, he saw a big change. And you know what? I saw him begin to change too. We have kids, right? I have four kids with him. And he wasn't going to give his kids up. So I would just stand there, and I wouldn't even look at him. I wouldn't speak to him for, like, two years. I would see this man and I wouldn't say nothing to him. Like once I saw him in this store and he was just staring at me, right? And I see him out of the corner of my eye, but I act like I don't see him. I just go about my business and do what I want to do, but I knew he wanted me. I knew he wanted me [laughs], and I said, "That's the key right there." Then I let him come by and get the kids, and I wouldn't give him no hassle. "You all go on with your dad."

Pam: I couldn't believe the changes in Thelma. She's back to maintaining this relationship, and its a very different relationship. I'm not saying it's perfect. They haven't turned into Ozzie and Harriet here, but I'm talking about major, major leaps in a business where we rarely see an inch. You see people taking enormous steps in their attitude toward themselves, and the way that they look at their kids, and the way that they look at their lives. And the nice thing is that there are no miracles. It's a matter of a shift in perspective. It sounds like a miracle, but then again it comes back to limitations because we as professionals don't think it's possible.

* * *

Lisa studied hard. She had finally decided to try for her G.E.D. Even getting to this point had been anything but easy.

Her man had started in on her again, trying to discourage her.

She heard Pam say, "You deserve better. You're a fantastic person. You have a lot of great qualities." She told Lisa what she was capable of.

At first Lisa didn't believe her.

"You can go back to school," Pam had said.

"Naw."

"You'd be great at it!"

Lisa had been saying to herself, "How can you be this great person if you're feeling so cruddy and make all these stupid mistakes." But she could feel that Pam truly believed in her heart what she was saying. It was hard to listen to somebody tell you you're a great person when you're feeling so low.

But all their talk that Lisa could have better and deserved better began to penetrate. She began to hear. She was not stupid! She began to want what Pam and others were telling her. She wanted to believe. She wanted to find a way to get better.

She decided to go to school.

Lisa: When I went in I was, like, "Oh my God, am I going to do this right? I can't remember this! I can't remember my verbs and my nouns." Math was absolutely frightening to me because my highest level in math was short division. Once I got to long division it would give me migraines.

Pam tried to show Lisa how to do long division.

"Why do you have to have this remainder?" asked Lisa.

"Because you have to," said Pam.

"This is really stupid! It does not make any sense for you to have this remainder, because there's nothing that you can do with it. Why don't you just throw it away?"

Pam laughed. It was hilarious. Lisa had an incredible block.

Doc walked by. "You could do it if you weren't convincing yourself that you can't do it."

Lisa: It was one of my worst fears, going back to school. It took me until I was almost thirty-two before I got my diploma because I used to think that I could not do this, that I was going to be embarrassed and be this failure and everyone was going to laugh and everything. But eventually I started back. And I would come home and just about drive everyone nuts.

Lisa came to work with her books. She would ask anyone in the vicinity, even if she didn't know them, "What do you know about algebra? Tell me what you know."

Everyone helpfully offered ideas.

* * *

Cicely saw her job as Tenant's Council President to try to help the residents deal with problems. She also wanted to get more involved with the school system and to get more programs for the kids so they could have something to do instead of staying on the streets.

Lloyd: Some residents took it as a weakness that Cicely was not the type of person that would jump down your case—ever, and people would take advantage of her. She would say, "You shouldn't do this," but it would be so laid-back that people would think, "Miss Cicely's too soft for that type of job. She needs to be harsh and tell somebody off."

Cicely: I had some for me and some against me, trying to do things to make it bad for me, doing things to try to get my kids in trouble—something all the time. But I didn't let it bother me. They did a lot of things to me. As President of Modello I went through a lot. They called HUD on me. They got together and called the manager, saying I did this and I did that. But my spiritual life helped me to be strong. No matter what happened, I'm still going to hang in there. I'm just this way. When I see something and I feel it's bad, they think I don't have any business saying things I should say. But I'm still going to say what's in my heart. I work with a lot of service providers and some of them are prejudiced. If we're working together there should be no division. We're all here for the same thing, and that's to help people. If I'm out there to help, I don't care what color they are. I thank God for the way I am. I love people. We've all got to love one another and care for one another. That's the way it's supposed to be.

Lloyd saw Cicely begin to exude a quiet strength. She didn't have to yell and get on people's cases to be effective.

One day a young mother came to Cicely and told her that all her welfare assistance had been cut off. She wasn't getting any more checks.

"I don't know what happened," Cicely said. "Let's go back to the welfare office and ask them why?"

"They said I had to wait for a while for some reason."

"Don't give up," Cicely said kindly, "Keep holding on. Keep holding on to faith, but don't give up. It'll all work out."

Cicely went to the welfare office to try to sort out the problem. The next week the lady received two checks.

Cicely: I try to be special to everybody. That's what it's all about. That's what I would like it to be all about: people caring for one another, you know? If the whole world was like that, so many things would be happy. I want to tell the world that if things come up in their lives that they don't think they can bear, they could make it through.

Cicely was living proof.

Cicely: I went through so many things. My momma and dad, they raised me up the right way. But I got off on the wrong path and got into the wrong situations. My momma's prayer is what really turned me around. She kept on praying for me that I would change my life. I had got involved with a married guy, and I was just in that bad situation for a while. It was rough out there. He was on drugs, and that man tried getting me onto cocaine, which I didn't. But I was smoking that reefer. That's the only thing I was involved with—until I stopped. And that man beat on me and all that too. Oh yes! But once I got free I was free, and I would never get into no other situation like that. It's going on ten years now, and I haven't been with nobody else but my kids.

I think I was going through all that because the experience was trying to get me prepared. Because a long time ago, before I knew anything about Modello, I knew that I was going to be working in Modello—that I was going to be the head person there. I don't know how I knew it, but I did. And I guess all that stuff I was going through with my kids and myself was to get me prepared for this so I'm able to help other people. If I tell them about my experience and what I went through, I can tell them that there is a better life. If they think positive about their life, things will work out for them, and because I went through that experience too, I am able to let the young girls know about what's no good.

* * *

Cicely thought, "Someone has to help these drug dealers."

She saw so many guys in Modello either become drug dealers or get on drugs themselves. She watched them sit in a negative state. She also saw that they needed somebody. She saw through their exterior. She saw that they were really reaching out for help. A larger problem was that they were talking to the younger children, being seen as role models. More people needed to reach out to them. So Cicely took it upon herself to go to them on the corner.

"I'll tell you," she said, "I see you're selling drugs. You know what? That's wrong. The drugs are either going to get you down in the ground, or you're going to be in jail for the rest of your life. There's a lot of things better than you selling drugs. You see that fast money? Ain't nothing but trouble behind it. And it's not honest. You get you a decent job and you'd be surprised what you can do with your money. You can save your money and buy your own car, and you'll be independent. The way you're going, it hurts me to see people like you be destroyed. It really does."

She said it with love.

Cicely: Some just stand there and listen at me, and some relate back to me. Some would say, "You know what? You're right. I shouldn't be out here selling no drugs. I should be trying to get me a job." Some would say, "Oh, who's she talking to!" But I don't take it personal. If I see them again, I still talk to them. I feel better after I have it off my chest. If I see a person out there doing wrong I'm going to tell them. Maybe they can have a chance. Sometimes I think if I hold back something's going to happen to them. And you know what? A lot of guys call me from the jail house. I've seen a lot of guys change since I been talking to them. Some are still hanging around doing the same thing, but I thank God that I do talk to them and some do change. That makes me feel good when they take what I say. But some of them are not going to take it. A lot of people selling drugs say, "Hey! Get out of here. I don't want you in here!" But see, that's a human being! The same God made me and the same God made him. You understand what I'm saying?

A while back I talked to a guy at Modello about standing on the corner. And he didn't listen. One day about 4:00 he was killed in Homestead. If he only listened I believe he'd be living today. Some will take it, and some won't. But I think, "Maybe if I said stuff to him he'd be alive." And you know what? Some of them come back and thank me for the talk. "Miss Cicely, I'm glad I had that talk with you, because my life is straightened out now. I got me a job. That makes me feel good."

* * *

Meanwhile, the P.T.A. had been continuing its discussions with the police department. Together they stepped up the police effort. Dr. Mills wasn't even involved.

Chief Ivy [Homestead Police Department]: From a law enforcement standpoint the "team police" concept had evolved because it seemed advantageous to have the good citizens of low-income, high crime communities, who were often frightened, to gain trust by having the same officers patrol the area every day, including foot patrol. They would get out of their cars, talk to the people and get to know them. In doing so they became more than "a white guy with a badge." Politicians also liked it because they could say they were providing services to that community. But a community had to be open to the idea.

Modello residents now seemed open. When the Modello P.T.A. sponsored community picnics and holiday celebrations the police provided loose "security" and a presence. The parents and kids got to know them.

Patty: Before, some of the guys that were dealing drugs would come into the meetings because they used to say they thought we were in there snitching on them to the cops. They would come in and see that, "Hey, we have more important things to talk about than just you guys." But they knew that some of the conversation was about them. And they started to see that there wasn't really too much they could do because we were living here, so we had a better chance of getting them out than they had getting us out.

The community police officers assigned to Modello were friendly, nice people who began meeting regularly with the P.T.A., and they walked around getting to know the kids. Gradually the residents began to cooperate when the police did a sweep. They would tell the police which units were crack houses, where drugs were dealt, where the dealers were. The police became more effective in their busts. Later, in Homestead Gardens two newly assigned officers went through some training at the Institute.

Gradually the drug culture began to change. The drug dealers began to see the writing on the wall. They were no longer welcome. The dealers who had viewed the Modello community as a source of support or protection began to feel it erode. The residents started telling them to move on. The housing authority then moved in and boarded up vacated crack apartments. The dealers' "safe haven" began to evaporate.

Patty: So they slowed down. They didn't stop, but it got much, much better. There was less shooting and loud noise and burglaries going on. I had my radio stolen out of my car one time, I had a battery stolen one time, but that was before we started having the community meetings. The drugs kind of went away, and all the loudness and crime slowed down. They had police teams come in like every day, maybe all day and just sit in the area, and I think you had to be in at a certain time. It really changed.

Officer Tom Cheney: There was a definite change at Modello. The real bad years—from about 1984 through 1988—seem to be over.

One day Roger drove down to Modello and noticed something.

"What's different about Modello?" he asked himself. He couldn't figure it out.

Then he realized: No drug gangs stood on the corners! They were gone, disappeared. No prostitutes were hanging out on U.S. 1. It looked like driving into an ordinary apartment complex.

"Gee, that's interesting," Roger said, "I didn't even notice they had gone."

He hadn't been aware that things had changed so much. But after that he no longer saw drug gangs on the corners selling their goods.

Cicely: Now you hardly see any drugs. There is a few in there, but it came a long ways.

* * *

For the past two weeks, almost no one had been showing up at the parenting classes. Doc asked Rosie and Cicely, "What's going on here? Why don't you go around and find out why people aren't coming?"

The next day they came back with the answer.

Rosie: One day we were sitting around complaining about: "Dog! Ain't nobody attending any of these meetings any more." Now when you get ready to have a parent meeting, and you go knock on someone's door, they're not home, because they're either at work or they're at school. It didn't dawn on us that it was something that we should have been glad about [laughter].

People were getting on with their lives, with jobs, going back to school, in classes at the skills center. That was why they couldn't come in during the day.

That too had snuck up on them.

XV. Fall Into Winter, 1989

Cynthia soon faced her toughest situation. She couldn't let these teenagers sell drugs in the back of Homestead Gardens. She didn't know what to do. She had to try something!

"Oh my God," she said to herself, "how can I change these kids' minds?"

From her training she knew how she needed to begin: to see them with different eyes. She wanted to understand these kids, to learn what made them tick, to see what talents they had. Were there any plusses to selling drugs that she could build upon?

These kids could certainly count well. That was a plus. They were good at knowing who they were selling their drugs to. That meant they had to be discriminating and aware. These kids certainly were not lost cases. They were very smart. They had to be smart to do what they did and not be caught!

Cynthia knew she had to build a rapport with them or she would not be able to get to first base. She had to begin by respecting them for who they were. To be in any position to teach them she had to gain their trust just as she had to do with the parents.

"Cynthia," she said to herself, "you're going to have to use common sense. Common sense doesn't say you're going to save everybody, but you maybe can save a couple of people. They know that I'm watching. They know I'm around. If I called the police on them it would put me in jeopardy. They're so close right here in the back that any mistake might be really costly."

The drug dealers in Homestead Gardens were young—ages twelve to eighteen, with maybe a couple at twenty-one. Cynthia decided that she would just go over and talk with them and make friends.

One day she walked by and said, "Man, how much them shoes cost? Where you get them shoes from?"

"Oh I got them at____."

"Well how much they cost?"

A lot!

"Whoooo!" she smiled, "You all must have to sell a lot of drugs to get them type of shoes!"

The kids laughed.

At least two days a week Cynthia went out of her way to have some lighthearted contact with them. She just wanted to let them know she was there.

One day she came by and said, "Hey, I just wanted to let you know that the HUD Task Force got the police involved and called the Metro Dade Task Force, and if I were you I wouldn't stand on that corner too long. I'm here as a friend. I'm letting you know that they may come and do a sweep without my knowledge at any time, and if you run into a house you can cause that person to get put out. I'm just telling you beforehand because I don't want you say that I'm here to hurt you. But if you feel like that this is not for you or whatever, and if you want some other kind of job, this is what I'm here for.

"Thank you, Ms. Cynthia." they said.

"Because I really care for you!" Cynthia continued. "You're just like my own kids, you know. I wouldn't want my kids up here selling drugs, so I'm just trying to let you know."

A couple of days later she went by again. "So you're still standing out here? Okay. You know what I told you now. I'm telling you it's going to be soon. So you need to stay off the corner."

"Okay. All right. All right. All right. We'll just do a couple more sales and then you probably won't see us after that."

Cynthia could see they were just trying to get her to go about her business so they could make their sales.

That weekend the police did do a sweep. They nabbed a couple of guys, but none who lived in Homestead Gardens.

On Monday the youths ran up to Cynthia and said, "Oh Ms. Cynthia, something just told me not to be standing out there today, because I had a feeling. I remembered what you had told me. And they did do the sweep but they got three other guys!"

"Were they from here?" asked Cynthia, feigning ignorance but showing concern. "I hope they weren't from here."

"Naw, they weren't from over here. Thanks for letting us know, because we're going to be more on the watch out now."

"Well really, you know, you guys shouldn't even be out here because what if you get caught? And if you're underage, you're going to cause your mama to get put in jail. You know you should stop."

Cynthia sat down and kept talking to them. She watched a car drive up. Their attitudes changed. They wanted her to leave. They had a sale coming.

Cynthia decided not to move. There she sat. A "Spanish guy" drove up and motioned to the kids, "Come over to the car!"

The kids didn't move. One of them gave him a sign to move on.

The guy in the car didn't understand. He saw Cynthia sitting with them, but she didn't look like she was there to do anything. The kids kept signaling him to go on.

Cynthia said, "Why don't you go ahead and sell to the man? You do it in front of everyone else, so how come you just don't do it in front of me?"

A boy named Lenny said, "No, Ms. Cynth, we've got too much respect for you. I couldn't do that," and he walked over to the car and told the man to leave.

"For what?" the man said, "You all ain't selling?"

"Man, I told you to go! Go ahead!"

The dude left.

Cynthia asked, "You wouldn't sell in front of me?"

"I got respect for you. I wouldn't do nothing like that."

Cynthia knew then that she could say what she needed to.

"Okay," she said, "well, let me leave so you can go on and do what you have to do." Then, as if starting to walk away but changing her mind she said, "Lenny, you know, you really make me feel bad, because your mama is really trying to live a good life for you. You're out here selling drugs, and this woman is working. And you've got two nephews that are sitting up in there, and you're teaching them that they need to be doing the same thing. You want them to be doing this stuff?"

"No. No, I don't really want them to do it, but I want them to have money and nice things and stuff, and my mama's working real hard and—"

"Yeah, working hard to take care of you so you can go to school and so the other two can go to school. She's going out there to bring in the money. Does she accept money from you?"

"No, because she says she don't want to have nothing to do with it."

"So that should tell you right there that she doesn't want you to do it. Has she ever told you not to do it?"

"Well she don't really know."

Cynthia knew Lenny loved his mother and respected her. "Lenny, you are breaking your mama's heart! Why would you break your mom's heart like that? What happens if you're out here selling and you get caught? I bet she thinks you're in school. But you know I'm going to have to tell her that you're not in school. I won't tell her that you're out selling drugs, but the school thing is part of my job. If anyone lives in HUD, all kids need to be in school."

Cynthia saw Lenny thinking.

She continued, "Lenny, how would you feel if somebody sold your mama some drugs?"

Lenny used all kinds of cuss words to describe what he would do to somebody who offered his mama drugs.

"Well Lenny, you're selling somebody else's mom drugs. Who are you to sell somebody else's parents drugs? Don't you know that what goes around comes around? I know you've heard that. You've got two nephews living with you—a niece and a nephew and a sister. What if somebody was trying to sell them something? You're doing the same thing!"

"But I don't offer. They come to me."

"That's got nothing to do with it. It's the same thing. You're selling it! I'm really surprised that you would do something like that. And if they pick you up right now, today, your mama would be put out, and where are you going to go? Did you sell enough drugs, save enough money, so you can get your mama a house? Because you're surely going to be taking care of her. What you going to do then?"

Lenny mumbled almost to himself, "Yeah, if I do get put out, and my mama gets put out, what am I going to do?"

"Do you have enough money? You're talking about buying a car.

You better be thinking about saving your money to get you a place to stay."

"Well, I don't know what I'm going to do," said Lenny. "But you know what? I'm just going to do enough up this week, and then I'm just going to quit."

Lenny: It was hard being short on things to the point where you wonder where the next meal's going to come from. That's a lot of pressure to go through, you know? It was hard, being a person that likes to have things. I like to be amongst the rest of the people, you know what I'm saying? We weren't getting in trouble. We were just hanging around, talking amongst each other about what we should do.

One Friday night, Cynthia woke up to pounding on her door. She peeked out. It was Lenny! He looked scared. What time is it? Two o'clock in the morning!?

Cynthia would never forget the night as long as she lived.

"What are you doing knocking on my door at this hour?" Cynthia squinted out the door.

Out of breath and talking a mile a minute Lenny blurted, "Ms. Cynth, I know what you told me. I know you told me not to be selling no more but the police are after me and I threw it over by the garbage can and I promise that I won't sell it no more. I promise! I just need somewhere to go! Because I know they're just going to go straight over to my mama's house."

"You know that's when your mama's going to find out that you're selling drugs. They'll come knocking on your door and you're not at home. She's going to want to know where you're at, and here you are. You're going to sit right here until the police come. I know they're going to come looking for you here because they know you live in this project."

As predicted, knowing Cynthia worked there two policemen knocked at her door. When they saw Lenny they immediately went after him and grabbed him roughly.

"Don't be rough with him because he's not going to go any place," pleaded Cynthia.

They searched Lenny all over for the drugs. "Where did you put it?" they demanded.

"I threw it away."

"Where?"

"I'm not going to tell you anything, because I know you're going to make me go to jail. But I already talked to Ms. Cynthia and I'm telling you I'm not going to be selling drugs no more. You won't even see my face over there. I'm going to be trying to clear it up. That'll be my part," Lenny cried.

Something about what he said and the way he said it made the police believe he was serious.

"I'm not going to tell you anything," he continued crying. "You can take me to jail if you want to."

"No, we're not going to do that," said one of the police officers. They told him what they would do with him if they caught him again. With Cynthia's encouragement they left.

Cynthia sat Lenny down on her front porch to calm him. It was now 3:00 a.m. She began to explain to him about the tape recorder and how things happen in life.

"You could be in your bed asleep right now, resting, so you could get ready to go to work tomorrow at Burger King or whatever. And I know you don't want to work at Burger King making minimum wage compared to the money you were making, but it's better to make minimum wage than be running from the police where you might get killed. What if it was a bad cop and he shot you in the back? You could have been dead! Or what if they take it out on your mama? Or what if you sell drugs to somebody and the drugs are no good, and they go up to your house and kill your family? Do you want all this?"

"No," said Lenny, "but see, it's just this peer stuff. Just to see the other guys get cars and wear nice clothes, and here you the only one in school that don't. You know what I'm saying?"

"You don't worry about the outside. It's got to come from here," said Cynthia, pointing to her heart, "in what makes you feel good. Just tell me one time selling drugs that made you feel good from what's inside here?"

He couldn't name one time.

"I know it makes you feel good that you can buy these cars and just flash out your money, but inside you know that's wrong. You know you have to be killing other people's families. You're part of a murder—whether you know it or not. Because if anybody sniffs it enough to make them go crazy or kill themselves, you might as well say you're an accessory."

Cynthia could see Lenny deep in thought. He hadn't considered all the ramifications. Guilt began to rise in him. He began to feel sorry for what he was doing to people without really thinking.

Lenny thanked her and hugged her. He told her, "I'm going to go home and get me some rest, and I'm going to talk to my momma because I know they've been over there already. And I'm going back to school!"

He did. One week later two more of Lenny's friends enrolled, but the others stayed out on the corner.

One day Lloyd called Lenny into his office.

"You know, the way you guys are all standing out there, it looks like you're all feeling down, feeling bad about yourselves."

"Yeah, we've got to catch the bus every morning to go to school, and other people are driving cars, and other people go home to fabulous homes, and we've got the kind of homes we're in."

"It's not where you stay," said Lloyd, "it's who you are! That's what people are going to respect you by, not by where you stay or what you've got. It's the person himself. Everybody's somebody!"

Lenny thought about being judged by who he is, not by what he has or should have. Sounded good!

Lenny repeated it to his friends. "Everybody's somebody, no matter what they've got." The concept made them feel hopeful.

"God didn't make no junk."

Lenny: By Lloyd not being kin to me, and taking time for me, that showed me he cared. I feel like if he ain't no kin to me and he cares, then I should care, just to give him a little something back. You know what I'm saying? He took time out, he came to the school, checked up on our grades, and hey, he'd know our grade before we would. He'd know what classes we needed to do a little more work in. He and Cynth picked up our report card for us, and signed us out, and that showed that we had somebody that cared about us, not being kin to us, and not having your own family take the time out or whatever. So I just figured I had to show them a little, and that's why I made it.

Lenny decided to take charge and help out his friends. He began to wake up early, then he woke his friend who lived next door. Since they mostly lived in the same row, on their way to the bus stop they would get up each of their friends so no one would miss the bus.

After that they didn't miss many days of school. Lenny himself had perfect attendance.

Cynthia worked with Lenny and his friends to let them know they could give back to the community and help all the kids get back into school.

"Then you'll still have kids looking up to you, not by selling drugs but by being a positive role model for them. And if you've got to get a job working in Burger King or whatever, at least you know that your mama can sleep at night, that nobody's going to knock on her door, and you won't have to run from any police officer. And then you've got a reference to get a better job. Right now you have no references. I know you want to get a job making six, seven, eight dollars an hour, but when you fill out an application, who can you say you worked for? Nobody's going to hire you if you don't have references or any background of working. You've got to start from the bottom. If you work for Burger King for three months, then you can say that the reason you quit is that you were seeking better pay, even if it's just ten cents more an hour."

Cynthia continued non-stop. "Lenny, I know you're doing the best you can, and I know you're trying to get over this way of life. But you can still get something out of life and without trying to scheme anybody. Just be who you are, work, and feel good about yourself. Even if you only bring in $100. You can do a lot with $100.

> **Lenny:** Dealing with Cynth and them, it showed us that, as life goes on, we're going to get those things we want. So we just worked hard and cared about school. When we were doing bad in our progress, they came and tutored us. So they showed me they were interested in helping me. I just had to get a little feedback back to help my own self. And they took us to various trips and showed us that life had more meaning to it. By our staying in the projects it doesn't mean we can't get bigger things like everybody else. Lloyd said we should just keep believing and keep working hard and it's going to come. So that's what we started doing. Quit worrying about it and take one day at a time. One day if it's meant for you to get it, you're going to get it."

Lenny went to work after school. After a while he came to Cynthia and said, "Ms. Cynth, I never learned how to save until I was working at Long John Silvers, because when I put that work in and

I got that check, my first check was a hundred and something dollars, and I saved that check longer than I would have if I was selling drugs. Because when you sell drugs and make $500 up to $1000 a day, that money goes by so fast. Because the people selling for you, they're going to cheat you out of your money, or lie and say they got robbed or something. And I was spending a lot of money, expecting myself to keep up with the Joneses, you know, paying $200 for a pair of shoes, when I could have paid $45 for them someplace else. So I was sending more money out than I was taking in, even though it was looking good all at once."

Gradually, Lenny began to understand that he no longer had to deal drugs to be cool, that he didn't have to prove to anyone that he was cool. The fact is, he was cool! He could be positive and do positive things and still be cool.

Lenny: It was like our life didn't mean anything, but after a while we just cut that out. Everybody just started doing their own work, doing things around the house, and our parents felt good. Most of all, I felt good. I started doing my homework and passing all my classes. I felt good then. I was somebody that came home with A's and B's, and I didn't have to go to summer school or night school, and I graduated on time. After everyone started doing work and seeing our grades get better, it was fun. Everybody was talking about, "I got an F last semester in science, and now I got a C," and everybody felt good about themselves. Cynth said everybody was back doing the work. Everybody was laughing about doing their work, and everybody came through! One of our partners, he had to go to night school the whole year. This showed a lot of him. He had to go to summer school and day school, and he stuck in there. I told him, "Don't give up! You hang in there with school, you'll feel good. Your mama and everybody will all be proud of you." He just hung in there so he wouldn't let nobody down. And he graduated. Everybody graduated. We were helping each other out as friends. We hung together every day. We were a little family and we stood by each other and told everybody everything was going to be all right.

Cynthia claims that it was Lenny's idea to start a Student Tenant Council, after he had seen the Tenant Council taking their parents on trips and making decisions about what was happening in the project.

Cynthia and Lloyd responded, "Hey, it's possible to do anything. What do you want us to do?"

"Well, what we want to do is get everybody who's twelve and up to do fundraising so we can go on field trips. I was thinking of maybe helping tutor some kids out to the school and, you know, do some of the stuff you do."

Lenny talked it over with his friends. Before long other teenagers from Homestead Gardens saw that Lenny and his gang—tough guys all—weren't going for the drugs anymore and were giving back to the community.

Before Cynthia and Lloyd knew it, by October Lenny and his friends had rounded up about twenty-eight students from Homestead Gardens to be part of a Student Tenant Council. They opened a bank account to hold their fundraising money for field trips. Then Lenny and some of his friends began to talk to some of the younger kids in the projects.

Lenny: Cynth had conversations with us, but by Cynth being a lady, you know, she talked to most of the girls, and by Lloyd being a man, that's man-to-man talk, you know what I'm saying? But Cynth helped us out because Cynth was the one who had the parent council. So one day Cynth asked us, would we like to have a Student Tenant Council. Everyone agreed. We voted in a president and a vice president and stuff like that. So that was our idea of doing that. And after a while it got fun and interesting, everybody coming to the meetings and talking about ideas, and talking about your problems, and you get your expert advice from your peers around you. So that was pretty nice there.

It was the first time a Student Tenant Council existed anywhere in Dade County. With police assistance they started a crime watch prevention program, and the word quickly spread that if anyone planned to do anything wrong in Homestead Gardens "you'd better get on out" because it would be reported. Before long, troublemakers stopped coming in. Before, if someone told on anyone else it was considered "ratting." Now it was a matter of neighborhood pride.

Chief Ivy: Sometime back, at Homestead Gardens we had what's usually "police-community relations" in low-income housing: we would respond to calls and do our reports and get the heck out of there. We'd arrest people out of there, chase people into there, have rocks and bottles thrown at us occasionally, have conflicts with the population there. We didn't do much service there for the people. But as time passed, and I don't know why—I wasn't aware of the work Roger was doing there—we saw that they would make contact with some of our officers, and we said, "Hey, maybe we ought to pay more attention here." We were putting together a community policing program called S.O.S. (Start off Smart), and we were looking for target areas. Homestead Gardens seemed to evolve into an area that was receptive. We started noticing that they had some leadership there. They had the Tenant Council. The appearance of the place improved. I had no idea why at all, but it was happening. So we decided, hey, lets link up with HUD in Homestead Gardens. The idea was to not just go and do things to people, but to actually go and try to help solve their problems, anything from substance abuse to child abuse neglect, incorrigibles, truancy, drivers license, skill development, G.E.D., a nursing program. It was a real partnership. We asked the schools to flag kids from Homestead Gardens if there were any problems. Roger's program allowed us to go in there and apply our program because its very difficult if you don't have some core of key leadership where you can get to somebody that knows somebody. We couldn't have done our program unless Roger had come in there to set the stage for more development.

* * *

The final piece to the drug picture came unexpectedly when HUD brought in Orange Hayes as new Modello housing authority manager.

Hayes was a politically connected, no-nonsense Black man, assigned to clean up the place, having made a name for himself cleaning up a housing project in North Miami. He wanted all trouble out of Modello, pronto. People said that his approach was to talk tough and carry the big stick of eviction. In Modello he wasted no time.

All the constructive action in Modello had convinced HUD to renovate the housing units. When a family moved out, Hayes wouldn't fill the vacancy. He would renovate the apartment. Then, like checkers, he would move another resident family into the new unit, fix up their vacated unit, and so forth. It all made sense, except Orange Hayes also wanted the remaining druggies and troublemakers out. He began to evict people. Because he didn't want any new troublemakers coming in, many units became vacant and remained that way.

> **Pam:** Orange came the last year I was there. HUD wanted to give special attention to Modello. He was a long time public housing manager, so they sent him down. His style was very much kick-'em-in-the-ass. He would have meetings and tell the women things like, "The free ride is over, and if you think you're going to lay up with these men and have their kids. . ."—that kind of tone. Of course I found that very insulting. I was always amazed that people swallowed it. He would say those things and people would kind of nod their heads. The positive side of it is that it really was a turnaround of attention that Modello got from HUD's management staff—a big move from HUD to turn the place around in terms of management and appearance. They did get it cleaned up. He evicted an enormous number of people, a lot of families—that's his style. So you might say there was a drop in some activity [laughs]. I think he got rid of some problems. He would have no tolerance for drug dealing, and a lot of other things.

> **Dr. Mills:** I was really at odds with him. I thought he was much too heavy-handed. He was more of an autocratic kind of guy. He used to walk around with a golf club and say if people would have any more babies he was going to evict them. He would threaten to evict people if they had beer cans on their lawns. He tried to do it by intimidation. He was an ex-military guy.

Roger went to meet with him. "These people are trying to help themselves. If you just work with them they'll do three-fourths of your job for you, and you'll have much better relationships with the residents. You should work with the Resident's Council, listen to them and get their help and they can help make your job easier."

Hayes considered the Resident's Council a pain in the ass.

"Look, we've got to treat people with respect," Mills continued. "Ask them for help and be on their side, and they'll rise to the occasion. If you go around threatening them you're just going to get resistance."

"Hey, you're not Black, and you don't understand what Black people respond to! They respond to intimidation."

Orange Hayes went to Lloyd and said, "What are these White people doing here in a Black community?"

Lloyd thought him a character and liked him. Roger saw him

setting back what they were trying to do there with heavy-handed authoritarianism. Pam found herself at odds with him. Thelma thought he was good for Modello.

> **Thelma:** We had to have a strong manager. Dr. Mills was here first with the programs. Then after he came in with the programs and got us going to the classes, then the manager came down and they started evicting people. People were, like, two and three years behind on rent. They were throwing them out. They were throwing the families out where they knew the drugs were directly in their house. This man would write an eviction notice at his desk, and would give them twenty-four hours to get off the property. But what Dr. Mills was doing would have started to get through to them. We had seen it happen with some of the people who stayed around.

In this case Thelma was in the minority. Many other residents didn't share Thelma's view and were up in arms.

> **Dr. Mills:** Drug trafficking was going down before that. If he evicted the worst offenders, obviously that was going to help because they're the ones that are doing most of the drugs. But a lot of the women who came through our program detoxed and got off drugs and cleaned up their act. Cicely cleaned up her own family with her two oldest sons being two of the main drug dealers. The culture in the community did change because the community wasn't supporting them being in control any more. A significant percentage of people were changing their outlook. Maybe he did evict a number of families. I just wasn't aware of it. Eventually he was transferred out and replaced by a woman with a better attitude.

* * *

In November Pam had an opportunity to go to Belize and jumped at the chance. Everyone would miss her terribly. They had all accomplished so much together.

* * *

He did it to her again.

Lisa fell hard. "How could I be so crazy to fall for this again!" she moaned.

She felt right back where she started.

Lisa: It would be my last fall, but I almost didn't make it out. I tried to fool everyone. I put on a smile. I didn't want anyone to know. But even Sam—who is a wonderful man, one of my friends—noticed.

Lloyd walked into the store and took one look at Lisa. "Hey now, are you okay?"

"Yeah, sure." La-di-dah.

"Naw, come on, tell me."

Bewildered, Lisa thought, "How can they see this?" Despite her trying to put on a happy face they knew exactly when something was bothering her. They could see right through it.

Dr. Mills would bug her too.

"You're getting on my nerves," yapped Lisa "Leave me alone!"

He wouldn't.

"Why don't you just leave me alone!"

"You know I'm not going to so you might as well just tell me."

God, he was aggravating! Why wouldn't this man leave her be!

"Do you understand?!" she yelled at him. "I just do not want to talk right now."

"Lisa, you might as well tell me."

Then Doc would send Lloyd or Rosie to bug her. Lisa couldn't hide. They knew all her little hiding places. She couldn't get away from these people! As soon as they thought something was going on, they would start in.

Another broken promise! Lisa had fallen for it again. Old habits are hard to break. She couldn't have been more depressed.

She had gone into work and stood there shaking. She whispered through gritted teeth, "I don't think I can work today." The feeling had come on suddenly.

"Why don't you go home."

Lisa had been functioning well for quite a while, but as Christmas, 1989 neared, her mind began playing weird tricks again. Worse, she was listening to it and believing it, taking to heart the thoughts that her mind threw at her.

Feeling it coming on Lisa had the foresight to have Rosie take her kids to a relative's house. The feeling was all too familiar. Afraid she might do something drastic, Lisa didn't want the kids around.

The broken promise ripped away her exterior and tore her apart. Damn, she'd been feeling so strong too—or she believed she was. And that made her feel all the worse. She'd been doing really well, taking time for herself—and she fell for this?!

"There you go again!" she pummeled herself.

Lisa locked herself in her apartment.

She wouldn't come out.

She couldn't take it any more.

She heard knocking on her door. It was Lloyd, pounding and calling to her. But she was in another realm. A scary realm. SHE COULDN'T TAKE IT ANY MORE!

Lisa's gun lay on the table.

Lloyd kept knocking.

Nothing!

He kept knocking and calling to her.

"Lloyd I don't want to talk!" She cried, yelling out to him. Her hair wasn't brushed. She had on a big shirt, barefoot. Trembling.

"Well, Miss Lisa," he called, " we don't have to talk. I could just sit with you for a while and we could watch TV or something."

Begrudgingly, she finally let him in.

Lisa: Lloyd can be so annoying, but I love him so much.

Lloyd spotted the gun on the table and became quite concerned. He chose to ignore it.

After sitting with her a while and seeing her calm down a bit he offered a nugget,

"You want to give up today, but suppose someone came to you tomorrow to give you a million dollars, and you had taken an overdose or whatever. You see, you wouldn't ever know that this would have happened because you had already taken your life. You have to look for tomorrow because you never know what's around the corner."

In that moment something got through. Lisa began to feel a shift. The fog lifted.

Lisa: And I will always remember that: even though today might be so cruddy, tomorrow's going to be better. Because if I turn out the lights, then I wouldn't be there in case something came my way. It took a long time before I had that understanding. And little by little I'd get kicked and just get back up. And I would look at my children, and I knew how much I loved them. They are my world. They are just so beautiful to me. And I wanted better for them. I wanted them just to see, if I can make it, you can make it, and anybody else can make it. And they see that! They have been so encouraged by it. They prefer me now to then. It wasn't as if I was so horribly mean; it was that I was flaky a lot of times in my little ways. And once I got a taste of it, it was like, "Hey, this is great!" Even though I was going through this stuff there was still something in the back of my mind that said, "It's going to pass." Even though sometimes I would get caught up so quickly I didn't realize it, but somewhere back there it was like, "It's going to get better, and I do have these people that really care about me." I mean, these were just strangers that came into my life, and these people were just great, and I knew that they really cared about me and I really care about them. So that's some of the things that kept me going.

I don't know how, but we did end up moving in together after that. But there's been a lot of work that's gone on in the relationship. It's not perfect, but I can stand my ground. And I know who I am, and he knows that I know who I am now. So in a way it's a totally different relationship. Like I said, no one's is perfect, and you still have these little things that come up. But it's not like it was before. Like I said, I know who I am and you can't change that.

From that point Lisa's life blossomed.

*　*　*

Lloyd: The first two years it really did not seem like I was working. I'm just coming to talk, to help people with whatever, because I'm learning too. I know people can teach me a lot of things, and they did. But all the while I'm having a good time. We were just having fun. That was the essence of what we did.

XVI. Late Winter to Early Spring, 1990

Then something terrible happened.

Cicely: One time, with my son, I was in the bed around one o'clock in the night, and I heard that he shot somebody. And something came over me. I got out of the bed, and I went looking for him. A guy had been shot. He'd got shot about three or four times. And I know what would happen if he died. So I went to see. I said, "Oh God, don't let him die! Please God heal him!" And I believed in it. I believed that he was going to be healed, that he was going to be all right. I kept holding to faith that that boy is going to be all right. And that did happen! He's walking around today.

They locked up Cicely's son. As it turned out, he was probably not the one that actually shot the kid, but he was at least the instigator.

Lloyd had worked with Cicely's kid off and on. He'd been in and out of jail. Lloyd always thought him to be a really nice guy, but the crowd he hung with was too much of a pull.

Lloyd: He was built. Bodybuilder built! He used to get in fights with his girlfriend, and she used to beat him up so bad. If you looked at him and at the girl, you wouldn't believe it. She cut him up in his chest. He just didn't know how to stay out of trouble and get away from people who would influence him. In turn, he would influence them. And the next thing you know he's in trouble again.

Cicely: Like I said, he was hanging around with the wrong crew, around drugs. Now, I warned them, you understand? I warned them before anything happened. And then when it happened I said, "You have to accept the consequences. You do wrong, you have to pay for it." But now they call back and they tell me, "Momma, I wished I had listened to you." I say, "I wouldn't tell you nothing wrong. I tell you the truth, so you won't get into these problems." It took a while, but now they see what I was talking about. When they come out this time I'm pretty sure they'll be getting their life together.

One thing, in this generation, you try to bring a child up the right way, but there's a lot of peer pressure out there. It's really rough. And all you can do is tell them the right way. Once you tell them the right thing and something happens, you know you're going to feel bad, but you know you warned them. If he went out there and got in trouble and you didn't say nothing, that's a different story. I know I told them the right thing—about hanging out with the wrong crowd, about getting yourself involved, finish school, get a diploma so he could have a good job and make good money. But that's the way it is sometimes. You don't want those things to happen, but sometimes they bring it on their own self by being disobedient.

Now I'm going through something with my youngest son hanging around with the wrong group. I've been talking to him every day. "Stay in school. Get an education." I hope that's what he does. All I can do is tell him the right thing. That's all I can do. I often remind him about what happened to his brother. Like I tell him, "If I see you selling drugs out there, boy, you know you got trouble out of me. I'll have you arrested myself. You're not going to stay in my house if you're on drugs. You got to know that. You not staying in my home selling no drugs. It's just wrong!"

As a leader, I have to be doing the right thing. If I do the right thing other people will follow me. If they see my son out there selling drugs, they'll say to me, "How can you tell me about how my life is when your son is out there selling drugs?" You know what I'm saying? I have to be right myself.

Lloyd: Cicely had me work with her third oldest son, and it seemed to have a lot of effect. I just stayed with him. He was a good kid—a real nice guy, fun, good attitude. He just talked too much and was very impressionable, and he liked to hang with his buddies—just your average kid. The difference was, he would listen to me more than his older brothers did.

* * *

Meanwhile, Lenny and his friends decided to stop the drug dealers from coming in to Homestead Gardens to sell. This was their turf, and they would enforce it!

"You can't sell drugs here any more!" they proclaimed. "You got to go along with the program or else you're going to have to move on out."

Word started to spread. Anyone who came over to Homestead Gardens to sell would have trouble.

The Student Tenant Council began to work with the Homestead Police Department to set up a crime watch, complete with lookouts and a system of communications.

Lenny: I stayed in the environment around drugs, and I saw a lot of shooting incidents and stings and different stuff—because that's what we did in the projects. So we formed a crime watch to keep our neighborhood clean. And it helped us all out, neighbors watching out for each other. So if you ain't home, they look out for you and see that your home won't get broken into and stuff. The Student Tenant Council got together and we said, "This is our project! We stay here. This is where we live every night. So there ain't no use in letting somebody else come through and tear it up." So after we got together, everybody just pitched in and told the parents that we were going to look out for each other, and we're just going to be a big family. We said, "By far, this is one of the nicest projects around here, and everybody is going to care about our project." We clean up every day around here. We look out for each other. Now that we've gotten together, we're putting our foot down on crack, sort of like a crack-down.

Lenny and his gang of friends put it all together, starting the ball rolling that cleared out the drug dealers and dramatically reduced crime in Homestead Gardens. Lenny did most of the talking. He was well-respected among the kids, and they listened to him.

He said, "Don't be against one another, because we're in the same gang, you know what I'm saying?

Lenny: As we worked together, you could see things get better. You accomplish more not being mad at people, just being as one. Like I say, everybody has their day. You get up, and it's what you apply yourself to.

Dr. Mills: I didn't even know the teen tenant council was happening until it had already happened. It was the second year of the grant, and I wasn't going down there as much. They're unbelievable kids. The first time I realized what was going on with those kids was when the Today Show came down, and I heard them start talking. They were doing fundraisers so they could go on field trips, and they were doing more on their own than a lot of these after school programs that are funded at fifty to a hundred thousand dollars a year.

Lenny: Getting together helped us with our problems because the problems that you have, you can ask some of your peers and they might have an explanation to give to you, saying what they've been through. Or what you've been through, you give back. So everybody was as one. We didn't look at anybody as different because he got this or he ain't got this. We didn't look at the material things—we looked at the characteristics of the person himself. So it worked out nice. We helped each other cope with different things around us, about what we didn't have that other people have, about how to stay away from trouble, about staying in school, even though it wasn't easy to graduate staying in the projects—things like that. That was, what, three years ago? All my boys, we graduated.

* * *

One day in the spring Cynthia was busily working in the Homestead Gardens office completing paper work when six big menacing looking guys in their early twenties walked in.

"We want to talk to you!"

Cynthia looked up, scared. What did they want?

"Okay, Cynthia, look," they said gruffly. "We here now. What's it going to take for us to get a job. We want a job—NOW!"

Cynthia gulped. For once in her life she was speechless.

They continued, "We're trying to get out of trouble and stay out of trouble now, okay? And we've been listening to you guys, okay? So put up or shut up. We want to know about a job—NOW!"

Cynthia said, "Hold on, hold on, hold on, Lloyd's back here. LLOYD!"

Cynthia practically ran into the back office to get him.

"Lloyd!" she said nervously, "They're here! They want a job."

"Who wants a job?" said Lloyd, feigning irritation at being interrupted from his paperwork.

"They do!" she pointed.

The six huge guys walked into his office.

In his deepest, gruffest voice Lloyd wanted to growl, "WHAT DO YOU WANT!?"

Instead, he squeaked, "Oh, okay! Let me call around now."

Lloyd: These were guys from nineteen to twenty-two who had been seeing what the teenagers had been doing, and they were getting jealous. They were guys that had been in trouble on and off. I think the heat was on them. I think a few were dealing, but they were in a lot of other trouble besides dealing. It sounds sensational when you say "drug dealers," but they were just into a lot of stuff. If it wasn't drugs, it was maybe stealing cars or stealing or whatever, doing something they didn't have any business doing.

Cynthia: So what do we do? We put all that paperwork down and we got in our cars, and we said, "Get in!" [laughs]

Lloyd: We'll take you anywhere! [laughs]

XVII. Spring through Fall, 1990

The word on the streets was, in Homestead Gardens, you had to watch out for Ruby.

Ruby: I was a crack cocaine mother, and in using that drug I was a violent person. So just about anything would set me off—if I'm not high, or when I'm high, anything! If you hurt my feelings, you got to fight. If you said the wrong thing you would have to fight. I mean, fight! Sticks, knives, whatever. Whatever was around, that's what I used because I know, today in the project, nobody fights fair. You had to go for what you know. So we fought! Mainly it was one particular neighbor, and I used to have it out with her.

I had a hard time with my oldest child. He is fourteen, and he is a very good child. He's real good. I was going through a lot of problems with him. At that time I was like Madam X. I didn't have no kind of understanding for nobody. I didn't want to hear nothing from nobody. Nobody could say, "Hi Miss," or I wanted to cut them or fight them or not say nothing to them.

Jamel, Ruby's oldest child, had been suspended from school once again. The school informed Cynthia.

"How come you're not in school?" asked Cynthia when she saw him.

"I got suspended."

"Why?"

"Well, you know, the teachers don't like me and I always get in trouble fighting and doing this and doing that."

"What kind of activities do you like?" Cynthia asked, taking him off guard.

"Well, I love basketball."

Jamel was a huge boy with a football player's body.

"Is that the time you feel good and you can think real clear, when you're playing basketball?"

"Yeah, I don't think about nothing. I'm just in there spacing, and I can do it good."

"Well why don't you join a basketball team? You know Officer Edwards runs this after school program. It includes basketball."

"Oh they probably won't want me because I'm not in school. I know Officer Edwards."

"You never know unless you go talk to him."

Cynthia prepped Officer Edwards. He had taken some of the training and understood what they were doing with Psychology of Mind. So when Jamel came in, Officer Edwards put him right on a basketball team. Jamel couldn't believe it. The officer didn't ask him anything about school.

Cynthia and Officer Edwards had agreed that involving Jamel in basketball would be the best thing for him. The plan was that after Jamel finished playing ball, when he was tired and relaxed, Cynthia would sit down with him and start asking him about school and what he wanted out of life.

The plan worked. Jamel began to open up about his mom and how much he loved her—but she had problems.

"She don't love me," he said sadly.

"How do you know your mom doesn't love you?"

"Well, she don't come out to the school. She don't have time for me. Half the time she's gone, and I'm around babysitting."

Jamel went on and on. Everything was wrong because of his mom.

"Do you think you're unhappy because of what your mom's doing? Is that what's causing you to be unhappy?" Cynthia asked. "You know, you don't have to like what somebody's doing, but it still shouldn't change the way you feel about yourself and what you want to do in life."

Jamel didn't understand.

"Okay, even if you don't like what your mom is doing, are you going to turn and do the same thing because she's doing it?"

"No. No. I'm a better person than that."

"Oh yeah? So how can you prove it to yourself? You can't prove it to me, you can't prove it to your mom, you can't prove it to anybody else—you've got to prove it to yourself. You've got to get yourself together first. Once you get yourself together, then you'll be able to deal with your mom. You know you can do better than what you're doing now because you're not in school. You're showing your sister and your brother that they don't have to go to school. And I've heard through the grapevine that you're selling drugs. I'm not looking at whether you're selling drugs, but I hope that's not what you're doing because if you're in jail I can't help your mom and your sister and brother too. You've got to really think."

As the conversation felt a bit too heavy Cynthia backed off.

"You know, you should feel good about yourself," she declared. "It takes a very big person to tell me what you did."

Jamel became quiet. Through his eye contact Cynthia knew he was listening.

"I would like to see you in school because it would show not only your mother that you can do it, but you can prove it to yourself. Also it might boost your mother up. No matter what she's doing, you've got to feel it in your own heart and in your own thoughts."

"Do you think they're going to let me get back to regular school? I'm going to this alternative school now you know."

"Yeah, if you don't want to be in that alternative school, I'm quite sure I can work out a deal if you can do real good in the next nine weeks."

"Okay," said Jamel, "Can you take me out to the school?"

"I'd like to take both you and your mother."

"Awwww, she ain't going to go!"

"Let me work with your mom. You've got to let me work with her. I don't care how long it takes. But you promise—you do your part and do what you're supposed to do, and I'll work with your mom. Okay?"

Ruby: At the time I really couldn't tell you what was going on with my kids because I don't know myself. My oldest son was a very angry child. He was very disruptive in school. He did everything to try to get attention, or to try to make somebody listen to what he was saying. He was in that kind of stage.

Cynthia appeared at Ruby's door.

Ruby cursed her and threatened her. Ruby's threats carried weight. She was a large, tough woman with a very loud voice.

"Ruby, I'm concerned about your son."

"That's your business!"

"Well I am concerned, Ruby!"

Ruby hollered, "LOOK, YOU GET OUT OF HERE OR I'LL SLAM THE DOOR RIGHT IN YOUR FACE!"

Cynthia thought it best to leave. "Well you have a nice day," she said sweetly.

The next day she went back and got yelled at again.

She went back again. She got yelled at again.

Cynthia went back again. Ruby did not want to listen. Cynthia knew she had to build rapport in some way. She didn't know why, but she felt on solid ground, in a state where she knew what she could get away with. Instinctively she knew that she could say things to Ruby that she would never attempt with anyone else.

"You know what? Your eyes can kill somebody," she said in a lighthearted tone.

"What do you mean by that?" Ruby growled, a slight smile underneath.

"Look, you know your son is really trying to improve himself, and you're not helping any by doing the things you're doing. I don't really give a damn about what you do, but your kids should come first. And I know you don't want the Department of H.R.S. to come in here, because I will do it. I'm not playing with you! Look Ruby, I care about you. I really care about you. And I'll call H.R.S. on your Black ass, and I don't care what you do or what you say to me because I care about your kids. If you don't care for nobody else, care for your kids."

Ruby looked shocked. "Why would you call H.R.S. on me?"

"Because your son loves you. Your son loves you. You send your kids to school dressed up all nice and everything, but if you're not giving him any attention he's going to—Look Ruby, if he's in jail or killed or whatever, what are you going to do?"

"Well, he don't listen to me."

"But what if he changed? If he showed you that he can change I know you can change too."

Cynthia looked her right in the eye. Ruby was used to scaring people off.

"I know your family," Cynthia continued. "You've got a brother that is the Vice-Mayor of Homestead. You've got a sister that's a detective on the Homestead Police Department. You've got other sisters and brothers. I'm not trying to compare you with them, but you've got a good family. And I know they care about you because I see them come here. But what are you doing? You give them a slap in the face. You don't even care for yourself. And even though you're on drugs or crack or whatever, I still see the beauty in you. I know you're good at taking care of the kids. I know you are. I see them. I see when you dress them nice. Jamel is dressed nice. And your house is not filthy like other people I know on crack. So I know you care about something. And when I come here, even though you're cursing me out or whatever, at least you let me know that you're going to slam the door in my face—you didn't just slam it on me. So I know there's some love somewhere. And I'm not going to stop until you let up and let me help you get on your feet. What do you want out of life anyway?"

"Well I want a job but don't nobody want to give me a job."

"I guarantee you that if you can show more compassion and be a hundred percent behind your son—he needs to be back in school tomorrow—I can get you a job, but you're going to have to want to help yourself."

Ruby could see that Cynthia really cared. She could spot a phony a mile away. It was also becoming quite clear that Cynthia Stennis was not going to leave her alone.

"I know you're looking to me as a social worker," said Cynthia, "and that I got it made, and I got this and that, but that's not true, because I was going through the same thing with my oldest son not listening to me and not really giving him a chance to talk. I know what you're going through."

Ruby: By Cynth being a tenant in this project, I knew her, so I knew she wasn't a threat to me. So she was very welcome in my home. I wasn't afraid of having her write me up or something like that, because I knew if she was going to do it she would tell me. I just about knew what she would come over to my house for.

Cynthia finally got Ruby to go with her to the school. Together they got Jamel back into the alternative school—a school for troubled kids.

Jamel couldn't believe his mom actually went and did it.

Cynthia laughed, "I told you!"

They had a long, lighthearted talk. Later they went to speak with the principal to find out who his teachers were. Cynthia then went to his teachers to tell them what she was trying to do with Jamel. Because Jamel had caused so much trouble they didn't even want him back in their classes.

"I'm working with the family," she told them, offering a few pointers on how to work with Jamel. "Don't take things personally if he says anything. I am working with both of them, and it will change. It's not going to be a dramatic change, but you'll see it if you work with him."

* * *

Thelma's man wanted back in. He felt he'd paid his dues.

Thelma: Sometimes he would come and just look at me. I act like I don't see him. I did him like that for about two years. See, he would jump on me, and I had to let him know that that's not the way it was going to be. So after two years I started talking to him, and, oooh, he just had to hold my hand. He didn't know the feeling that he had for me until he and I broke up. Then he realized how much he loved me. And it worked. But I looked at him and I saw good in my man, and I saw that he needed help also. So I hung in there. I hung in there with him. And I kept talking to him and talking to him, like it's just rooted in him.

"You know what?" Thelma said to him during a peaceful conversation.

"What?"

"You know, you can drink all the beer and all the liquor in the bar, but when you wake up the next day your problems will still be there, and then you have to take another drink and another drink, and that problem is still going to be there. But if you do it wisely and right, and just take you a little sip, that problem is still going to be there—but then you'll have time enough to think about that problem. Then you can work that problem out. But if you're drunk all the time you will never work it out. When you come to your self and get to work that problem out, that problem is not going to be hard as you think it is. But if you keep that alcohol in you, it's always going to seem hard."

Her man began to listen to her in a new way.

Thelma: And sure enough, now he is [snaps fingers] straighter than ever. Now he doesn't even get drunk. He might drink about three beers and that's it.

* * *

Pam returned from her trip to Belize to find, sadly, that her friend, Lamar, the former drug dealer, had been busted, allegedly for possession of drugs. But something seemed fishy.

Lamar had gotten married, had his first baby, and was living in an apartment in Homestead. But his friends hung out in Modello. His problems arose when he went to hang with them. Lamar had a bad "rep." The police couldn't stand him. Lamar hated the police. Pam had initially tried to soften it by purposely having him there when the police, who were always in and out of their offices, came by. But the minute they'd walk in Lamar would walk out—conversation over! Pam finally got him to the point where he could actually be in their presence, but he wouldn't say anything.

On this occasion the police had stopped Lamar and some of his friends who were hanging on the corner and pulled them over to the park across the street. They searched him, then left for Modello. One officer stayed behind. When the police came back they suddenly found a rock of crack on him.

Lamar told Pam, "I didn't do it! I've been set up!"

Pam believed him. Lamar had told her many worse things he'd done, horrible things, like hitting women over the head to take their purse, assaulting people simply because he felt so angry. Lamar hurt people. He put them in hospitals for no reason. Why would he not tell Pam the truth about this?

Whether or not he had a rock on him, Lamar had long ago accepted his fate. He ended up doing quite a bit of time for that incident. Once before, in a South Dade sting operation, he'd been busted for fencing stolen goods.

* * *

One day Cynthia said to Ruby, "We're having a parenting class. Why don't you come with me."

"I don't want to hear about that, Miss! What am I supposed to do about a parenting class? That's you all's business. You go on and do that. I don't want to hear that."

Cynthia kept after her.

"Well what you want me to do, lady? I'm not interested in this!"

She said, "Yes you will, you'll enjoy it."

Cynthia came over to her house every day. Ruby would not budge.

"I thought you told me you wanted to change," Cynthia said one day.

"Yeah, I want to change but—"

"Oh okay, I know," Cynthia interrupted.

Ruby: Cynth would know when I'm getting high off drugs. And she wouldn't intervene or interfere in my life when I'm doing that. She would say, "Well, when you really get ready, you'll come." But every day she would come by. "How are you doing? You doing okay? You want to talk?" or something like that. I don't know why, one day I got up, and I just was tired. I was tired of being tired. And I said, "Something's got to change. This is not the way I was supposed to live my life. This is not the way a woman with kids is supposed to live." I didn't want to go to jail and leave my babies. So I asked Cynth and Lloyd what could they do to help me with this violent temper.

Are you ready for a change?" they asked.

"Well I've got to do something more than I'm doing. I just don't know what it is."

"I keep telling you what to do." said Cynthia. "Come on over. We still have our parenting class."

Ruby: And one day I just got ready, took me a bath, threw on some clothes and just came over. And it started from that day.

Without telling Cynthia, Ruby popped into the room of the parenting class. She stood in the back with her arms folded across her chest.

Cynthia was truly surprised and happy to see her. "Why don't you come and have a seat, Ruby?"

"No, I'll stand back here," grunted Ruby.

In spite of herself she began to listen. It wasn't a lecture. Nobody was telling her what to do. That felt nice. As she stood there she tried to grasp what they were talking about. They were saying something about a thinking process, about how your thoughts would make you feel stuff. She didn't understand.

She thought to herself, "I want to know what in hell you're talking about thinking for. I think every day!"

Then something struck her. It seemed they were saying there was a right way and a wrong way to think. Ruby wondered whether she was in that wrong way of thinking. She heard them say that everyone had their own way of thinking, so if someone is talking to you and saying, "You no good, nasty bitch," it's just because that person has her own way of thinking, and her thinking is making her do that. Ruby began to wonder why she would want to go and fight someone for what they said if it was out of their own wrong thinking.

She thought, "Hmmmm, this is all right, here."

Ruby: Before I went to the parenting class I never heard of self-esteem, a mood, a low way of thinking, or other people's feelings. I didn't have the sense to know that other people had feelings too. I just figured, what *I* feel, what *I* think, what *I* do, that was that!

Ruby began to relax a bit, to feel more comfortable. After class she told Cynth that she enjoyed it and would come back to the next one. She did. Then she began to come regularly, taking a seat and participating like everyone else.

The next time Ruby went to the class she met Dr. Mills and told him she was having problems with her son.

"Well, I have this son, Dr. Mills, and he just wants me to give him all my attention and not pay any attention to my other little babies."

Dr. Mills said, "Well, sometimes your oldest son may not feel like you're giving him any attention, so he has to do things to make you look at him sometimes."

The statement took her aback. She had never thought about it that way.

"Now Dr. Mills," she said, "what can I do to have a really loving son and a friendly relationship with my kids?"

"Really listen to your kids. When they talk, really listen to them. When they speak, let them have their say. Show them love."

Ruby knew she often did the opposite. For example, when someone told her that her son did something bad, she would automatically take the other person's side and smack him, without giving him a chance to tell his side.

Ruby took Doc's advice. She went home and watched her son. He came in from school yelling and demanding attention. Screaming!

In her kindest tone she said, "Wait a minute baby. What's the matter?"

"You don't love me!"

"Yes I do, honey, I love you."

Jamel didn't know what to make of her new tone, but as soon as she picked up one of the babies, he stomped into the other room and slammed the door.

Ruby thought, "What is going on with this child?"

Then Ruby got mad. It tee'd her off, and she stormed off behind him, yelling, "Get out of there! Get out! Let's go. You want to fight? Let's fight!"

Jamel lashed out at her. "You don't need to use that stuff! That stuff don't do nothing for you!"

"You have no right to say that to me! You got no right to tell me what to do!

"Yes he does," said Dr. Mills when Ruby told him the story after the next class. "He does have a right to tell you what's hurting him—and what's hurting you. He can see what it's doing to you, and you can't."

The statement again brought Ruby up short.

"You know people say things like that when they're in different moods," Dr. Mills continued. "Your moods and your child's moods may be different at different times. You've got to be aware of that. Your level of self-esteem and his level of self-esteem are different. You might feel one way, and his level might be low and, out of that, each of you is going to react."

"Okay," said Ruby, "Me and him, we'll talk."

Ruby: Whatever Dr. Mills tell me to do, I'll do it. And it works! It really works. Parenting—that parenting class really helped me a lot. Every session that I went to was a change. It taught me something. There's just no other way of getting around it. I changed with the class. My self-esteem was real, real low. As a matter of fact I didn't have any self-esteem. Dr. Mills really worked with me. A lot of times the class would be over and everybody would just leave, but I would just stay there with Dr. Mills and ask him more and more questions. And the love and concern and patience he had with me was a lot. It played a big part with me. Cynthia also took a lot of time with me. They saw I had a lot of willingness to change.

Ruby began to go home from the parenting class and talk with Jamel. "I love you, but I have my other babies and I have to show them love too. You're big enough and you're old enough to understand. Your time will come when they're asleep, and we'll have all the time in the world to watch TV together, talk about things, and stuff like that."

Ruby: It wasn't all of a sudden. It wasn't any spontaneous change. Like I say, each session of the parenting class gave me something. When we were talking about moods, that really did something to me, because the majority of the time my mood level would be up [agitated], and I didn't know how to calm that down into a good mood. And Dr. Mills taught me how to do that.

Ruby heard Dr. Mills say, "When you're angry and you're upset, don't act on that at that moment. Give yourself a little time. Just go and be by yourself, even if it's only ten or fifteen minutes. You'll see the difference."

Ruby: And that worked for me. I was really happy for that, that he really gave me something like that in my life. That parenting class really did help me.

By practicing what she learned in the class and from Dr. Mills and Cynthia, Jamel began to respond to her. He no longer cursed at her. Without being asked he began to take out the garbage. It even began to affect Ruby's life outside the home.

Ruby: One day my neighbor came to my house about one of my kids, and she called me m.f.'s, s.o.b.'s, and that's truly fighting words for me! I sat there, and I listened—and she was so surprised! You know, she had her knife waiting because she knew that was fighting time, words, and everything. She just talked and talked— until I said, "Well, lady, I'm very sorry about what my child did. Now you go on home and you sit down, because I see you're upset." And that surprised her! And I didn't see Cynth. I did not see her. She was there sitting in the background looking at me. And after I did this, she went [clap, clap, clap], and I said, "Now look at this! That showed me that that parenting class did wonders for my brains [laughter], because I had no understanding when people wanted to do things like that. I'd have wanted to fight.

* * *

"Hi Sandy, how are you doing?" Lloyd called across the courtyard.

"Fuck you, Lloyd!"

She always said that—almost every single time! He was used to it. He expected it. But this time it got to him. He decided then and there that he wouldn't let her get away with it any more.

He marched over to her with purpose.

"How come you have to keep saying that to me? Do you think I deserve it? What's wrong that you have to act that way?"

Sandy tried to open her mouth to retort, but Lloyd wouldn't let her. Sandy was not used to this. She was used to screaming people down.

Lloyd continued, "Look Sandy, you may not think that your life is worth any more than that. But I do! I can see so much more for you. I can see so much good in you. All this stuff that you put out—the way you live your life—that's not what's really real. That's only what you think is real right now. That's only what you see. But I see that you could have better. I see what could be for you. I care about you. I see the beauty of you—inside."

He saw Sandy's eyes begin to moisten.

"Lloyd, shut up, you're going to make me cry."

And she turned and walked away.

XVIII. Into 1991 and Beyond

On December 30, 1990 Dr. Roger Mills departed from Modello and Homestead Gardens, having gradually phased out over the past year. In his wake he left behind two housing projects and many people that would never be the same.

The time felt right to leave. For one thing, the years of budget cuts had begun, making it more difficult to secure funding for prevention programs. For another, Dr. Mills was receiving increased requests to go around the country to teach how Modello and Homestead Gardens achieved their results. Besides, he already played a lesser role in Homestead Gardens than in Modello and had no doubt that Lloyd, Cynthia, Carol, and Rosie would be able to handle it now. He knew the effort would continue without him.

Before Mills left, Janet Reno came down to hear Tenant Council concerns. After the meeting she told Dr. Mills that she was amazed at how together the women were at the meeting.

"I've never been to a meeting of public housing residents where it hasn't been total chaos," she said, "where people haven't been yelling all at once, complaining about personal problems, not being able to stay on their agenda. This group was organized. They had an agenda. They knew what they wanted and they told me. They answered my questions. One person spoke at a time. They were all respectful of each other and with me. It was like going to a board meeting of a corporation. Any other time it would have been total chaos."

Irene Edminster: The first time the P.T.A. met down here, Janet Reno came down and it was a yelling match. "What are you going to do for us?" "Hey, somebody's forgotten us!" And two years later after he had gone in and worked with these people she came down and couldn't believe it was the same set of people. Not only were they calmer and able to discuss problems, but it also showed in the way they dressed, in the way they stood. You could see that they perceived themselves from a very different point than they had two years earlier.

The Tenant's Council wrote a grant to the Ford Foundation to purchase a VCR and TV to run an after-school program. Out of thirty neighborhood associations that applied, Modello received the highest rating—and they wrote the grant on their own. Before, a lot of them didn't even know what a grant was.

The County commissioners had been impressed by the results of the project, especially its effect on the parents. Since Mills's first grant, the budget had nearly tripled. The County was impressed at the significant decrease in child abuse and neglect. Homestead Gardens in particular had seen a significant drop in teenage pregnancy— thanks largely to Cynthia and Carol (although this had not been a stated goal of the grant).

Roger felt comfortable arranging for the County to take over the program.

Fairly quickly, they transferred Carol downtown to another housing project. Rosie found herself in trouble with the HUD site manager who thought her a rabble rouser and wanted her out. The best laid plans . . .

* * *

When Thelma's son, Tyrone, reached high school he returned to his old tricks. One day he and his gang left school and proceeded to another school to beat up a kid. The police picked him up. At 9:00 that morning the police phoned Thelma. Tyrone was in jail.

Thelma took charge. She had always told her kids, "If you go to jail for stealing, I'm not your momma. Don't even claim me. Don't even tell the police that you live with me. Because I work too hard for you." They knew she was serious.

The police said, "He's too young to be here. You've got to come and get him."

"I'm not coming," responded Thelma.

"If you don't come and pick him up, we're going to have you arrested."

"How can you do that?"

"Because he's under age. We have to release him in your custody."

"Okay, what time do I have to come get him?"

"We'd appreciate it if you'd come right away."

"What time do you close?"

"Nine o'clock this evening.

"I'll be there ten minutes before nine", said Thelma.

"You mean to tell me that you're going to let him sit here all this time?"

"I certainly am. I got until 9:00 tonight to get him out, right?"

"True."

"Look officer, I feel like this: if I come in there right now, and I get this child, it's like he'll only have been in there about an hour, and the next thing we know he'll be right back there. I want him to know what it's like being locked up. My understanding is that he's the head leader of this gang."

"Okay," said the officer, "I'm glad you spoke with me. If that's the way you want to handle this, I'm going to work along with you."

"I certainly do appreciate this," said Thelma.

"I'm going to do my part in handling him, and when you come get him you do yours."

"Okay."

Thelma went to get him at 8:50 that evening. She found that the officer had a little talk with Tyrone.

Thelma: Oooh, he took him through some changes! He went on back up in the cell and told him, "If I come in here and see a hole in my wall, you're going to get it! If I come in here and these floors are messed up, you're going to get it!'

Thelma signed him out.

"Momma?" he said.

"What?"

"I never want to go to jail again. That man came in there and told me if I put any hole in that wall, he said he was going to beat me to death in there."

"He did?"

"Uh huh. I thought that man was going to kill me."

Back home, Thelma waited until Tyrone was in the right mood. If she'd talked with him then she knew it would have been "a big booboo." Thelma watched carefully. She would not let him go right back to school, although he wanted to. Thelma called the school and told the principal that she was going to keep him out for two or three days and would bring him back herself. They agreed. Thelma waited for the rest of the day before talking with him.

"You feel like talking?" she asked.

"Yeah, because I want to talk with you."

Thelma had no intention of sugarcoating the discussion as her mother had with her. When Thelma was sixteen her mother hadn't told her how life was. Thelma wanted no secrets. She wanted her kids to be as open with her as she was with them.

"Tyrone, you can't do things like that. You've got your smaller brothers, and they watch you, and they want to follow in your footsteps. You can't be going around here going to jail and bullying and taking people's stuff. How would you feel when they got to the same school as you, and the old teachers tell them how their brother had done all this. You were wrong!"

"I know I was, momma."

"You can't be in a gang, thinking that you can go around here hurting people and hitting on people, thinking that you can control everything and get what you want. You can't do it like that! You got to get a job and work and get what you want. Be independent. You will never be independent in a gang. And thinking that you can walk around here and bully and take everything you want, you can't do that! You could have your life be cut off just like that! [Thelma snapped her fingers sharply] Because if you try to take somebody's stuff and you walk up to the wrong person, they'll blow your brains out right there. People work hard for their stuff. You can't do that, Tyrone."

Tyrone looked at her. "Yeah, momma, you're right. You're right."

"You can't go to school houses thinking that you can teach your teachers. Those teachers are getting paid to teach you. I'm telling you the truth. They're taking their time to teach you. They don't have to do that. They can kick you clean out of their school because they see you do not want to learn. Why would they want to waste their time on you? But it's good that they take their time out with you, because they know that you can do it. They know you're just in that gang, and you picked this up. That's why they're wasting their time with you. Honey, you can't do that!"

"Momma, you sure are right."

"Tyrone, I think you owe your teacher and your principal a big apology."

The school could not believe the change that came over Tyrone. He told them that he now wanted to help guys steer away from gangs. He was serious!

The principal decided to hold a special assembly. Tyrone went on stage

Thelma: He went out there and said to them, "I advise any young guy my age to not be in no gang." And they had him on TV, telling about how he came out of his gang, and the principal was so proud. Tyrone's speech changed their whole school around. He told them how much problem he gave to his teachers and the principal, and how bad his gang was, and whatever they had wanted to do in the school they would do it. And he told them about when he came out of the gang how he went through changes, because they didn't want to accept him coming out. And he explained to them that he just feels like he's doing the right thing, not being in a gang in a school and stuff. I mean, they had a big show, starting from about 7:00 in the morning until about 5:00 that evening. And the guys who were in the gang with him, a lot of them came forth and said how they were glad to be out of the gang, and stuff like that. They cried, and I did too. I was wiping my eyes too. Ooooh, he had been in a hole, and he just came up out of that hole and turned his whole life back around, and he hasn't changed back yet. I was really amazed. I was so—ooooh!

Tyrone sings now. He does a lot of things. He sings in a band, he ballet dances, and he works with charcoal. He keeps himself active. And everybody that knows him says he's different than any of the guys out here, because the guys 16 and 17 years old will be out selling drugs. He doesn't hang out, period.

If it hadn't been for Dr. Mills and the Psychology of Mind and the class I'd have been the one encouraging him to do wrong. I know I would have. I'll tell you the reason why I say that. I would have been encouraging him to do wrong because I would have been totally an alcoholic, and the only thing I'd have been looking for was some money to get me another bottle, and whatever he did would have been all right with me. That's how I would have looked at it if I hadn't gone through the courses and went through the program with Dr. Mills. If I didn't go through it, my life would have been totally destroyed, and my kids' lives totally destroyed too. Because I wasn't setting any kind of example, and everything they did would have been all right with me. But now I can look at them with respect, and they give me respect, and I feel proud about myself, and I feel proud for them.

* * *

Ruby knew something huge still stood in her way. On her own she began to realize what she needed to do. She needed to rid herself of her crack-ravaged boyfriend—only she didn't act quickly enough. Within the next few weeks tragedy struck.

Ruby and her boyfriend had an argument. Ruby's brother was visiting. He got into the middle of it. Ruby's boyfriend stabbed her brother—and killed him.

In near hysteria Ruby told Cynthia what had happened. "What am I going to do now?" she cried.

Cynthia listened for a long time, then said, "You know, I'm not telling you that's what you get, but you're going to have to give yourself a little pat on the back sometime Ruby. If you know that things are not going to work, why are you in this situation? Something has got to be green on the other side. Let me just counsel with you and see what we can do to try to change your life around where you can make better decisions. I'm not going to tell you what you need to do, because nobody knows what Ruby needs to do but Ruby."

Ruby: I had two brothers. One is dead now from an accident that happened to me in this project. That happens when you're doing drugs. Accidents happen. And I went into treatment with that. Because the accident happened in October, and I went to treatment in November. I never did face that. I never faced my brother's death. Because I thought at that time when it happened that I did it. But in treatment I found out that I was not the one who hurt him like that. Like I said, I've really been through a lot. But I came to the conclusion to go into treatment after being in the parenting class. The parenting class was doing little things to me, making me see better at the glass. See, before I didn't have a glass to look out of. I was just doing what I wanted to do, and fuck the world!

Like I said, every time I went to the parenting class, something happened. What happened, I can't tell you. It was just that something would lock in, and I would take it home with me and I would say, "This is good!"

Ruby realized that so long as she was addicted to crack she could only do so much for her kids. She had to get herself right to be able to really help them.

Ruby: One night I was right in the midst of getting high. I was going to get high because I had everything to get high with. And my baby woke up. And for some reason I lay down in my bed with my baby and went to sleep. And I got up the next morning, and I say, "Now look at that, I went to sleep and didn't even use that stuff." And I knew I didn't need it. I always thought I needed that early in the morning to get me through enough to clean up, or I needed that shit to function a little bit that day. So I say, "If I can go one day without it from this morning to the night, I really don't need this."

Ruby went to Cynthia. "Cynth, I'm going to go to rehab'."

"Are you sure that's what you want to do? Are you positive? Ruby, if you do it for me it's not going to work."

Ruby kept repeating, "It's for me! I'm not doing nothing for you. What am I to gain if I'm going to do something for you?"

"I understand what you're saying, but I want to make sure you know what you're doing. Don't go there trying to prove anything to anybody, because it's not going to work. You have to really want to stop, to stop. If you know that's what you need to do, then it will work."

"I do!"

Ruby talked with her family.

Her sister, a school teacher, said, "Ruby, it won't be any problem for me to keep your kids, because two of your kids go to the school I teach in, and your baby goes right down the street to the day care. So that won't be a problem."

Ruby then called H.R.S. and asked for someone to come down to talk with her. They interviewed her and told her they would put her in a treatment program.

"Okay, "said Ruby.

She then called Cynth. "I'm ready. I already worked out everything with my family. My sister's going to take care of my kids, and Jamel is going to go to my mother's house while I'm taking care of things. But one thing I want you to do for me is see if HUD can keep my apartment, because when I come back I don't want to lose my apartment."

Cynthia said she would. She arranged with HUD to board up her apartment and keep it for her until she returned.

H.R.S. sent somebody to pick her up. Ruby left for the New Directions treatment center, where she stayed for four months.

In it were many people with similar problems. It made her feel comfortable to know she was not the only one in the room with that problem. The treatment program was not based on Psychology of Mind, but it provided what she needed. While Ruby had been willing to go into treatment, she was far from ready to admit or accept that she was a drug addict. They told her that admitting it was the first step for recovery. It took her a while. Finally she did.

> **Ruby:** And from that day on everything was fine. I was perfect. I was okay. I did what I was told. I studied what I had to study. I listened. I listened a lot. I don't care where I'm at or where I go today. I like to listen, and that's pretty much what helped.

Ruby emerged refreshed and ready to go to work. She appeared at Cynthia's house one weekend.

"Cynth," she said, "when you get back to work, the first thing I want to you to do is talk to the manager and tell her to move me out of that building, because I know the temptation there. I know what I need to do. I need to get out of that building and I need a job. I want to do something with my life so I won't be home."

Cynthia arranged for Ruby to work at the West Homestead Elementary school as a cafeteria aide. Later, Ruby realized it was not the kind of work she wanted to do.

"I know it's a job and everything," she told Cynth, "and I'm going to try to keep it as long as possible, but I want to counsel people. I want to help others so they can know that what it's all about is your own thinking, and knowing what you need to do to take care of your own life. But I'm taking it one step at a time, to fulfill my life."

Jamel was reinstated in the regular high school and joined the football team. Ruby saw "great, great change" in his behavior. Instead of coming in the house "looking all mad" like he used to, Jamel now communicated with her on a completely different level.

"Hey, old girl, what's happening? How's your day been?"

"You're not going to give me no kiss? Come and give me a kiss. How you feel today? How was school today?"

Ruby: I let every day go take its own course. I let my God do the work for me with my child at the beginning. I said, "God, whatever it is that I need to do today to work with my child and let him know that I love him and that I don't mean to harm him or hurt him in any way, let that be done." And then I would leave it alone, and let whatever happens, happen. In the course of me leaving him for the drug treatment center, he felt so alone because he always had me to mess with. If he got mad at school he brought it home and he took it out on me. If he was mad at me, he automatically took it out on me, and it was always a hollering match, a fighting match. He would say, "Don't take your problems out on me!" And I would tell him the same thing, "If you're mad at your friends, don't bring this shit to me!" When he got mad he would say, "Mama, just don't mess with me. I don't feel like being messed with!" And that used to make me mad because I would always want him to tell me what was wrong with him. But I was the problem! So, like I say, when I was in treatment he got lonely, and we started to talk over the telephone. I didn't have phone privileges for the first thirty-five days in treatment, so when I did call he was all happy to hear from me, and he said, "Mama, something is going on with you, because your voice don't sound the same. Why are you talking to me this way instead of cursing me?" Instead of saying, "Fuck you!" I said, "I love you!" And every day he would call me, and we would talk fifteen to twenty minutes on the phone every day.

So when I got home I sort of knew what he was thinking towards me, and it even got better since I came home. If he comes home and tells me, "Mama I just had a bad attitude to my teacher today. I'm sorry," and I say, "Well I'm not the one to tell it to, because you didn't say anything wrong to me. You go on and tell your teacher you're sorry for what you did." And when he does that, both of us can feel it, and me and him get along just great.

I have a little problem with the food he puts in him because he's a big eater. I mean, he's a big dude: 6'2" and he weighs 320 pounds. I say, "Boy, if you don't stop you're going to hurt yourself."

But he's just like a big baby now. He's just like one of my babies. When he comes in at night he's got to hug me. He's got to kiss me. He tells me he loves me, and that makes my day—all of my kids. At first my kids wouldn't hug me, or kiss me, or tell me they loved me. But today they do, and I'm the same way to them.

Everybody has problems, of course, and maybe in the course of a day maybe one of my kids does something that makes me mad. But I don't shout at them like I used to. I sit down and let my steam off, and my kids never know what I'm doing. Or they bug me so much that I'll yell, "You all have got to be quiet!" Once I do that I know I need me some space. So I'll go in my room and I'll turn on my TV and just lock my door, and they're there knocking on the door. "Mom let me in here!" But I ignore them. Because if I don't, I'm going to lash out. I'm going to say the wrong things and hurt their feelings. And I'm tired of hurting their feelings. It's all about them, and at the same time it's all about me. I have to have a line between my kids and me. I know what's good for my kids today, but I also know what's good for me. Before we just couldn't communicate, and I was always lashing out at him or throwing something at him. I just couldn't be the way I am today with him because of the drugs and not knowing where I'm at.

Cynthia: Ruby is amazing! Ruby has changed tremendously. She's now drug free.

Ruby: And I'm married now, so all the good that's happened to me in a year in a half? Not bad. Not bad!

* * *

Lisa finally felt ready to take her G.E.D. test. It had been a long row to hoe.

First she had enrolled in a nursing program, but when it came time to take the exam she had no money to pay for it. She had lost her job at the store.

In 1991 financial problems forced the Modello Mart to close. When HUD started renovating Modello, many families were transferred to other projects and others moved out, so they no longer had enough residents to support the store. It was a blow. All the residents watched out for the store—even the drug dealers. It belonged to all of them. Nobody would mess with it. Once in a while a kid would steal a bag of chips, but they would just talk to him and tell his parents, and it never happened again. When that kid came back in they treated him as if it had never happened, so long as he assured them it wouldn't happen again. So there were no problems. That it closed hurt Lisa. She is still sad about it.

Besides, her income vanished. She had no way to pay for her nursing test.

Lisa applied to be a cashier at Winn-Dixie. She needed the job badly. With her three years experience in the Modello store, and a great letter of recommendation from Pam, she figured she'd get it with ease.

The store manager said, "You don't have your diploma. I really don't even want to interview you."

"But you hire fifteen year olds and they don't have a high school diploma!"

Lisa left in tears. She had a family to support, goddamnit! She hurt.

If I don't have that diploma I can't do anything," she kicked herself. "A simple little job like this that I know that I'm qualified for, I can't do if I don't further my education? I'm going to get it. I'm going to show them that I can do it!"

Lisa [laughing, two years later]: Now I wouldn't even want a cashier's job. That's, like, below me now.

She simply had to get her G.E.D.!

Lisa: I talked about it with everyone for about a month. It was just so wonderful because this actually was the first thing that I ever started that I completed. I remember that when I got the results of that nursing test—that was in 1991—I said, 'In 1992 I'm going to get my G.E.D.!' And people were like, 'Yeah, she's talked about that for years.'" But I worked extremely hard. I was more determined than I'd ever been in my life. Every time in my life that I ever tried to do something, something or someone would try to discourage me. Again it was my kids' father. He was okay as long as I was a little happy, but if I was too happy and too determined it was kind of scary for him or something, and he would have these little wise remarks, "Sure, this is another thing you've started. You've never completed anything!" Well, that gave me even more determination. "I don't care what this person thinks!" He honestly didn't believe that I had the courage to go after this.

Her man too had been laid off, so they were as poor as they'd ever been. Lisa walked miles to and from the skills center in Naranja without a red penny in her pocket. At times she came home and the cupboard was bare. There was nothing in the house to cook, even though they tried to save every penny for meals. She had to scrape everywhere. It was rough. But she went to school. It would have been so easy to say, "Forget school." She needed to do it.

Besides, she was thrilled with the concept of education. "Hey, this is great!" she would say. "Fill your mind with all these things. It's a fantastic feeling. I mean, you don't need drugs. You don't need tranquilizers. You don't need anything!"

Lisa: Once I got into doing it, it was, like, my mind opened up. You just get a little bit of this, and that's how it is with P.O.M.. Once I got that little taste, even though I was falling back here and there, it was like, "This is pretty good. I think I'll go for some more."

The big day came. Lisa felt prepared and brave enough to say, "I'm going to take my G.E.D. test!"

She had been working up to it. She befriended a fellow student who had been in the class for a long time. The young lady had kicked cocaine and was thrilled to make it. In class she thrived, but when the time came to take the test she was too scared.

"I think I'll put it off for a couple more months," she said.

"Look, what do you have to lose?" Lisa convinced her.

For the G.E.D. test to be held at the skills center twenty-five students had to take it. When the time came to turn in their money, although she didn't have any to spare, Lisa wanted it so badly she was ready to lend money to everyone to get them to take the test so they could make the limit.

"Look, we're going to do it!" Lisa said excitedly to her friend, every day giving her a big hug. "You know, we just have to keep thinking positive. You're a great person. Whatever happened in your past, leave it back there. So what if you got strung out on cocaine. Look what you're doing with your life now! This shows that you want to change. You're doing great!"

The day prior to the test Lisa came down with a virus, sneezing and coughing, her nose running and spread halfway across her face.

"I'm going to take this test no matter what! I don't care if they have to wheel me out!"

For an entire month they had to wait for the test results.

Lisa's friend trembled. "Oh my God, I think I failed."

"Look, we did not fail. We absolutely tore that test up! We did great!" said Lisa.

One day Lisa walked in to find her friend sitting glum.

"Hi! How are you doing?" said Lisa.

"The tests are in."

"Oh my God, I don't want to see this," Lisa feigned.

"I didn't pass," said her depressed friend.

Apparently her friend had forgotten to enter a code on one of her tests and received a zero on one section, so it wiped her out.

"I know I can't do it," she kicked herself. "I shouldn't have even tried."

"Look, don't think that way," Lisa fussed. "Look, you're going to do it again! So what if you didn't pass. Maybe when I go in there, I may not have passed. But I'm taking it over. This shows that you tried."

Lisa went in and learned that she passed. She broke down and cried.

"Get this girl a chair!" someone yelled. "She's going to have a heart attack in here."

"Yeah, but I'll bet none of you know C.P.R.," Lisa laughed through her tears. "You just don't understand!"

Lisa turned to a large group of new students entering the center and shouted, "Look, you see this piece of paper? Do you realize how important this is?! Get on those computers. Get on those books. Get this piece of paper, because without this piece of paper you can't do anything you want to do. You've got to have it!"

Lisa flew home on a cloud. A couple of weeks later she went back to the school and saw her friend still hitting those books. Lisa felt proud. She sat down with her and helped her with science. Her friend's spirits were up once again.

Lisa's graduation could not have been more beautiful. Everyone wore their caps and gowns, graduating the way she always dreamed. No words could ever describe how wonderful she felt. Cicely came over from Modello. Her school friend happily surprised Lisa, although she'd been hesitant to come, and leaped into Lisa's arms and gave her a huge hug. Her friend Lisa had stuck by her and encouraged her to stick it through. She would make it too!

Lisa: Knowing that there are people out there that really care about you, and when they point out these little special things, you find them, and it just starts to blossom with the person. Then they learn, "I can do this too!" In order for me to go for my diploma Pam talked to me for maybe two years. She pushed, along with Lloyd and Sam. They were, like, "Look, get in there and do it! I'll help you." It took that. Any time I would feel down and say, "Well, I'm just going to drop out of school," they were like, "Uh uh. No. Get back in there!" And I couldn't wait to get to school. That's just how it is with work now.

The elementary school hired Lisa as a teachers aide. She loved it, and they loved her.

* * *

Thelma had finally let her man back into the house but with a completely new understanding.

Thelma: Now he's all right. He's getting there. Sometimes we have our ups and downs. You can't stay honey every day. And its good to have ups and downs because that's what makes things better and makes you stronger [laughs]. Now when we have problems I say to him, "I don't want to see you for another two weeks. You go to your place and I'll stay here because we're seeing one another too much." So he'll go to his place, and after about two days I start to miss him, and he'll come over again. And then we'll be so glad to see each other that we'll have a good time! [laughs]. Now things are all right. He worries about the kids a lot—about their schooling. It's good to have a man around when you've got a kids sixteen and fifteen because they hear that voice from that man, and it's a heavy voice.

Rosie: Thelma did something for me the other day that just brought tears to my eyes. Because I had been sick, and I had been in the hospital, and she came up to me, and she was trying to give me twenty dollars. She said, "Because you were sick." I said, "I know, but why?" And she said, "Well, you weren't able to work." And I was, like, "Well, I was getting paid." I said, "You got nine kids, ten with your grandbaby, and yourself, I could never take your money, but thank you for the gesture." Because from the old Thelma it was always "self." She would have never thought about offering me or anybody else anything. But that's just what happened to our community. People are just closer. I could go over to somebody's house and say, "Can I help do something?" Whereas it used to not matter what was going on. The only thing I could think of to do when everybody was sitting around gossiping was to just put that person down. But we've all grown a lot. We all have.

* * *

One day Cynthia bumped into the president of the Student Tenant Council, one of Lenny's best friends.

She said to him, "I don't see you guys in the morning any more getting ready for your jobs. Since the city created a lot of jobs I thought you all were working."

"No, I go to work after I come home from school."

"School? What do you mean? You graduated already."

"Yeah, I'm at Miami Dade College."

"What?!"

"You didn't know I was in Miami Dade College? Yeah, we're in college now."

"Who is we?"

"Me, Lenny," and he rattled off a number of their friends.

"No! You're kidding! All these kids in college?"

Hence the reason she hadn't been seeing them getting ready for work. Lloyd had been working with them for a while, trying to instill the virtues of a college education, reminding them about it every time he saw them. Apparently, it had paid off.

Lenny: When I was younger before I moved here I would get into a lot of trouble in school and stuff. Me? I never thought I'd graduate. I always thought I was going to get kicked out of school and everything. And the principal used to tell me that I was going to fail because I stayed in trouble. And this June 18 when I got my diploma, I didn't even believe it myself. Me, graduating? And I made it on time. I didn't have to go to night school or summer school, so I feel good about myself. I'm in college now. I don't want the people growing up to go through what I went through.

I want them to learn as they were small, because I didn't have anyone teach me that when I was smaller. I had to learn as I grew up. So I'm just trying to set an understanding for them so they don't have to go through the same thing that I went through. Be somebody! That's what I'm doing now. I'm still in the project, but it doesn't matter. You know what I'm saying? I feel I'm somebody, and one day I'll have what I want.

Cynthia: That's how it works. That's how they just proceed. They just keep going and going and going on with their lives, and we don't see them any more, and we're wondering where they're at, and they're taking care of their own business [laughs]. They didn't even come and tell me. I would think they would come and tell me, but I guess it's so normal. They're just going about living their lives and forget about whatever—but I'm happy for them.

Lenny: When we first started this I did little speeches, and Lloyd said there was something good about me in the way I expressed myself, and people liked the way I talked. He said, "Just keep up the good work and it might lead to something." He's the one that got me into communications because he told me I was good, and the people liked what I did. And I say what the heck, I'll just take it and it might lead to stuff.

Cynthia: Lenny and one of the girls in the Student Tenant Council were able to go to Denver, Colorado to talk about what they were doing here. And when he got there you could just see the light in his eyes, that he was able to travel and be asked to teach. He could not believe it! It felt so good that he was able to go out and talk with other teenagers about this. In fact, last Monday he had the privilege to go to New York and talk to other kids about being positive, and that you don't have to sell drugs to be cool, and stuff like that. He enjoys that.

Lenny: The main thing we did was make it a better environment, feeling good about what we got. We thought about people who ain't got nowhere to stay, who ain't got nothing, and I say, "At least we do! We've got something." So we take pride in keeping it up, cleaning it up, and not marking on the walls and stuff, and just feeling good. Because I figure like this, life the greatest gift of all. With life, that's the gift—you know what I'm saying?—we should be happy about it. So that's what we felt good about—having pride in what we've got, being happy with what you got.

Because I feel like this, if it comes to you, it's meant for you. If it didn't, must be it wasn't meant for you. Life wasn't made to make everyone happy—only the ones who choose to be. Life is here, it's up to you to like it. So I choose to be happy with whatever I've got. I just want to send a message out there to everybody. I hope everybody takes the right steps. Don't be a fool, stay in school. Leave the drugs alone. Have fun. Live life to the fullest. That's it. That's all you can do.

* * *

Dr. Mills: When I took Ruby out to speak to others she had people in tears. I was nervous about her, because it was the first time we had brought her anywhere. She sure found a lot of love in her life where she didn't have any before. She's just a loving person now.

Ruby: I came from a dysfunctional family and I didn't want to admit that, and those chemicals, that beer, that liquor, that cocaine, that weed—it all did something for me to hide the truth. It hid the truth from me, so I used it. And it does help your feelings [laughs]. Drugs do wonders for your feelings. You can feel real bad, but you get high and you feel real good. But then when it goes away, there's that same bad feeling, so you got to get some more drugs to bring that good feeling back. So really what I had to learn was that I don't need anything to make me feel good. I don't need anything to make me feel bad. I don't need anything to make me cheery. Whatever mood I want to be in, I can put myself there. Those drugs don't do nothing but hurt me. You have to accept and admit that you, only you—not Tom, not Dick, not Sandy—is doing this to you. You're doing this to yourself. I could tell you I got high because you hit me. No! I got high because I wanted to get high. By you punching me gave me a reason to get high because I wanted to do it any way. But today, I'm happy all the time [laughs]. I'm happy all the time!

Psychology of Mind is a self thing to me. It's a self thing. Psychology of Mind is just helping you with your thinking process. Some people think it's hard to do, but it's very easy. You just have to listen in order to really grasp it.

If it wasn't for the parenting class I wouldn't have made it. I would have been dead or in prison somewhere, and I know this. I know this. Mmm hmm. Yes.

XIX. The End and a New Beginning

In approximately three and a half years at Modello and Homestead Gardens Roger Mills had seen incredible changes. He'd arrived armed only with hope and a new approach to changing lives. Somehow, intuitively, he had faith it would work—although he had no real plan except how to start. Sparked by Janet Reno and Tom Petersen, many people and agencies had helped to provide the structure and process in which to operate. Everyone contributed their part—including Orange Hayes. But the approach that Dr. Mills and his staff brought in—Psychology of Mind / Health Realization—proved to be what caused people's lives to be so touched from within that their very lives changed. Even those who had no idea what the approach meant saw the change and knew something important had happened.

> **Chief Ivy:** Homestead Gardens was initially like the other places, although larger. If you take Coral Gardens—or as they call it, "Drive You Nuts"—which is "Section 8" Housing right next door—you have basically the same types of people and situations. So you've essentially got a control group and an experimental group. One you apply this program to, and the other you don't. Homestead Gardens began doing much better. I don't know what the other variables would have been in there, but there have been significant changes in people's lives. I think Roger's onto something—if you can implement the concepts, which Roger seems to have had some success at. What Roger teaches really brings people to do more than they have before.

Pam: And slowly, bit by bit, all those problems disappeared. I'm not going to say it was all P.O.M. because a lot of factors went into it. There was a much heavier police presence. But even that was the result of P.O.M. affecting people enough to want to work with the police.

Dr. Mills: The results were kind of like what I saw in Saltspring Island in the beginning. I couldn't believe the levels of mental health among those people—how far people had come in their lives. We started to see the same thing in Modello.

And its effects spread further.

Carol: I'm in Perrine in another housing project, and there I'm using the same principles that I learned. When I first started, two or three kids would come in, and I would get to know them and just kind of show them a little love. Now I have fifteen older girls coming in day-to-day. When they get home from school they come straight to my office, and I'm beginning to build a relationship with them. I talk with them. I get into the schools and find out what they're doing. I take them to my house they spend the night with me. I take them out to dinner. Some of them had never been to a restaurant. They said they didn't have anybody to take them, to just do things with them. I think if it hadn't been for what I learned in Psychology of Mind, and what I learned about myself, I wouldn't have been able to help them.

I have a little girl, and she was raped, and she is a 13 year old girl [beginning to break down crying] and I got her to a special school, and she stopped going. But I know that when people see her they don't give her love. They don't see that this is a beautiful child. This is God's child! And I go out of my way for this girl, and she is just a doll. I don't see the side of her that was raped— whatever the circumstances were. And this is a child that they have given up on. The mother was a crack addict, and she's getting better. She's working with me, but everybody there is, like, "She's a hopeless case," and they've been making cracks and stuff. But to me she's special. I've been taking her to go shopping, and they're trying to say that there's something psychologically wrong with her. There's nothing psychologically wrong with her! People in school tell her there's something wrong with her, and she stopped going to school. I was trying to get her to go back but I'm thinking, 'Why should I try to get her to go back into that school? She just needs love. She needs a lot of attention.' And that's what I'm going to recommend. This is how I see the children at this time, like I saw them at Modello. To me I guess, that's just the gift that was given me. I think it's just the relationship that I build with the children and with the parents. I don't get as stressful as I used to, and I don't take the things personal. I thank Dr. Mills again for what he has done.

One day Dr. Mills received a phone call from Jolene Parrish from the group, "Informed Families." She had learned about Dr. Mills's results and asked about his approach. Roger invited these mostly well-to-do White parents from the Miami suburbs to come to Modello to see for themselves. When they arrived, they were completely taken with the Modello women. This resulted in an invitation in early 1991 for Roger to teach a parenting class for Informed Families. To assist him, Roger brought in Cynthia, Cicely, Rosie, Thelma, and Ruby.

Before long, Roger received a request to help apply his approach in a suburb of Denver, then in the Mt. Hope housing project in the South Bronx, then in Coliseum Gardens housing project in Oakland, California. The wisdom had begun to spread.

Dr. Mills: When we were talking to the residents in the Bronx, I let Cynthia take the lead to connect with them and break the ice. Then I would come in later and talk a little about the theory and tell them why those changes happened. Cynthia was really on a roll. She told her story about her son, and she broke down. I think she got hit by it more than she ever had before, just because of the feeling in the room or something, and she started to cry and had to stop for a while. Then she started talking again about how she saw her son change, how she wanted the program to come into Homestead Gardens, how they got other residents involved. And she told some stories like Ruby's—and it really blew people away. After she talked about an hour and a half, I then said, "Here's what people are learning about their thinking," and it actually brought the thing down. Cynthia said to me, "I was going to say that, but you just said it in a different way." I should have let her go on her own, and the same point probably would have gotten across to the group more powerfully than me.

Roger had started the train rolling; now he couldn't stop it if he wanted to. These women had changed their minds, which in turn changed their lives, and they would never be the same. Even after he left, they continued to get stronger. Whenever he heard them speak to others they continually amazed him. Roger himself began to break down in some of his own presentations at the sheer power of what had happened to their lives.

Rosie, once beaten, abusing her kids, continually getting herself into trouble, now looked stately and elegant, no longer the abuser or abused, the power emanating from her channeled now in constructive ways.

Lisa, once depressed and suicidal, now a powerful, self-assured, beautiful woman, working in a school helping teachers to be better able to deal with their students.

Cicely, once so afraid, so timid she could barely speak, her family completely out of control, her face looking ravaged by life, now looked so serene, so kind, so angelic, spreading love like Johnny Appleseed as President of the Modello Tenants Council.

Thelma, once a severe alcoholic, severely beaten constantly, now alcohol free (without treatment), radiant, a wonderful, loving mother.

Lenny, once a teenage drug dealer, hardly ever in school, now keeping his housing project safe and drug-dealer-free, in college, making it and doing well.

Ruby, once a crack addict, always in fights, her son out of control, now had kicked it and developed a beautiful family relationship, and so calmed down that fighting was no longer even in the cards.

Cynthia, Patty, Carrie Mae and many others, their lives all touched by the miracle of taking charge of their own thinking and allowing their health to rise up and show them a new and better way.

As Roger Mills says, "People's lives become what they think is possible."

Beyond the caring and the openness that initially drew them out, the residents learned about their great, unlimited resource of health within, and that they could recognize their own thinking that kept this health obscured. This combined realization proved so powerful that it would be impossible for them to see life in the same way. Further, they learned the path to their health: through a calm and quiet mind.

Although the ladies would not have expressed it this way, once they gained this understanding they did not really think about it much. It simply became a natural part of their day-to-day existence— so what was the big deal? Looking back became difficult to relate to.

It seemed almost as if they were looking back on people who no longer existed, people whom they could no longer find.

It would be foolish, however, to think that stumbling blocks weren't encountered along the way. Not everyone in the projects caught on. Especially at first and for some throughout, some residents such as Sandy were dead-set against what Mills was trying to do.

Thelma: I went through a lot after I went through the classes. It was the same tenants that called names on me and put down what Dr. Mills was doing and told lies on him. They had about two or three meetings, and I told them right in the meeting, "You're all lying. I didn't say this, and I didn't say that." But Dr. Mills would tell me, "You have to watch what you say around people. Talk less and you won't give them much to go on." And that's true. That's very true, because these people here take what you say and use it against you. He really taught me about that too, and that's why now I watch what I say to people, and it's good to be like that. But then, when those people saw that we were changing, it made a big difference. They would even go to him for counseling. The same ladies would go to him and get some advice about going into the drug program and said they were 100% behind him. Then they wanted to come to the classes. Most of them came around all right.

Chief Ivy: Some people are suspicious. They think you're building false hope by saying, "If you want to be something, you can be something." A lot of people don't buy into that because they think some people will never have the ability to do much more than they're doing. And Roger's gone in saying that in your mind, in your self, you have that ability. If you bring it out, train it, nurture it, then, as self-esteem builds, if you want to do it you're capable of doing it. And who can argue with that concept? Roger has shown that he has applied it, and implementation is everything.

Rosie: Most of the ladies that were doing nothing are working or going to school. The South Dade skills center sits directly behind Modello project. It had been there ever since Modello had been there. Not one person had actually participated in that program and finished. And when the big group came in with the media and stuff, they were, like, "We're going to get you all some transportation, we're going to give you all some child care, and you're all going to go to school." Well nobody still went to school! I mean, common sense would tell you with the skills center right behind them, if they wanted to go, they would go. But after people started to get involved and get motivated, *then* they started not only to go over to the skills center but to go to other places and to do different things.

Pam had been there from the beginning. Until she met Roger Mills she wouldn't have believed the changes possible.

Pam: Only twenty or so women had exposed themselves to Roger's Psychology of Mind approach to varying degrees. But those twenty involved themselves in the different programs like the P.T.A., which in turn had an impact on the community such as the drug dealers. But the impact spread further. Those twenty also had neighbors, and despite the fact that their neighbors weren't going or didn't want to have anything to do with Roger Mills, what would have normally been a neighborly dispute, where your kid did something to my kid, now they weren't reacting in their normal, volatile way. So it had a way of permeating the neighborhood. No matter that the majority was not involved. The atmosphere of the whole project changed. That's what makes it so hard to describe to people. There's a critical mass somewhere that, if you can affect a handful of people, it's like a domino effect. And that doesn't mean that Joe understands why he's not fighting with you as often as he used to. He may have no idea at all what the reason for that is. But one person, one Lisa, or one Rosie who was a real hothead, calming down in her life, can affect everyone in Rosie's path. She was no longer responding or reacting in a way that could bring things to a point where you'd have to call the police. And it included those of us who were working there. It was just a real steady state that started to exist over there.

It became clear, at least to this author, after talking with the ladies extensively, that their perspective would quite likely never shift back—and if it does it will be only temporary and chalked up to an extended low mood. This success lasts!

Rosie: Now I know that I don't beat myself in the head any more trying to make myself happy [laughter]. If I'm in a bad mood, I recognize my mood levels, and later on we can sit down and we can work it out. I feel I would like to go into other housing projects and talk to other women and just help people, especially women that have been abused by their boyfriends or their spouses. I feel like I have a lot to offer.

Cicely: It surely made a difference in my life. I look at myself and I say I came a long way, because I remember when I really didn't have time with my kids like I was supposed to. I didn't have the patience with them. And that's the main thing in this: it's love. You've got to have that deep love. You got to have that big deep love in your heart for those people, and if you've got that love, it's going to show. When you're working with people you can't take things personal, you've got to learn to forgive and love and go on and reach out for people. I've seen the drug problem there in our community. I've seen the families. I've seen the heads of household not doing anything with their life, having nothing positive about their life. I've seen the kids not going to school— running around everyday. The parents wouldn't even bother with their kids. So many of us had to reach out in the community, and it made a big difference. Now you hardly see any drugs. There's a few in there, but it came a long ways. The children are going to school everyday and they're making good grades. The parents or heads of the household, some are going to school, some have got jobs, and most everyone in the project is doing something positive with their lives. Because when we started in the community and let them know we cared and that we loved them and we let them know there is a better life for them, that they don't have to be in that negative state; that they can have a positive life.

Have faith, and your problems will work out for you. I've come through a lot of changes in my life. Everybody in the program changed a lot. All of them. It made us feel good about ourselves, and we were able to go out and work and make our own money instead of staying home on welfare. Our own money, that's something! That's what made us feel good too, going out there and helping people, and being there for them. If it weren't for Dr. Mills, I don't know where I'd be today. I don't know if I'd be here today.

Irene Edminster: When you raise your perception of the problem, the whole way you deal with it and the whole way you feel about it is different. I think it was an internal change. Our perception of what was going on in classrooms with these children changed, and that changed how we felt about it and how we dealt with it, and in turn you saw the children change. It changes you. But that philosophy, once you start owning it, becomes so much a part of you that you don't define it any more that way. You just have a growth within yourself. It made me a much more understanding and compassionate person. I think it gave me a much calmer stance in dealing with problems, because you began understanding that their whole perception of the problems is different from yours, and that there are multiple realities depending on who you are and how you perceive the situation. I found it very helpful.

Lisa: After I got the understanding, that, yes, you are going to have these problems, things are going to come up in your life that you're going to have to deal with, but you get to know that whatever's happened today is not going to ruin the rest of your life. Whatever happens today, so what? You go on with your life. Just because I had a bad day today doesn't mean tomorrow's going to be a bad day. That was one thing that I had to understand. Because when I got into my depression, it would just drag on and drag on, and I couldn't see another day without this happening. I figured this is the way it's going to be. Now if I have a bad day? Big deal. Tomorrow's better, and it doesn't linger and keep me in that depressing state. And like Doc would always say, it's so simple that you really can't explain to people how you come to this realization—because it *is* simple. Sometimes it's just too simple to explain to people what you caught on to. I didn't have to go through psychiatrists and all this, and hey, I'm fine! That's what you call mental health.

Thelma: After Dr. Mills and Rosie and some of the other ladies talked to me, and they stuck with me and showed me love, and they showed me that they was my friends, they just pulled me out of it, and made me a better parent than what I was, so I really appreciate them. They really would just hang right in there with me. And I just had to show them my appreciation because they were taking their time out with me. I didn't want what they were doing to just go in one ear and out the other ear, so I had to keep to it. A lot of people ask me, they say, "Well, did you go to a place to stop you from drinking?" I say "No." They say, "Well, how do you just stop?' But the way that they treated me, and they encouraged me, and the words that they would tell me and was teaching me—it just made me better.

Everything Dr. Mills said, he did it. If he said he would bring something as small as a penny, he would bring it. And he showed us so much love, and I watched him, and that's what really turned me around. I sat down and watch him and took in what he said. But then I didn't want his teaching to be in vain. I wanted him to see. I just didn't want to come out and tell him, I wanted to show him. And he saw it. Him and Pam and Lloyd and a few others saw it in me. They saw that I wasn't drinking. They saw my attitude, and they saw my spirit different. They saw a big change. Everybody saw that. We made one another proud of our group together. We got to talking about our problems, and it drew us closer together. We all care about the other because we're all in the same boat—and we all came out victorious.

Cynthia: Since I've been in the parenting class and have been like a leader in Homestead Gardens—I'm on the building and zoning board in Homestead, I'm the Vice President and treasurer for our Homestead Gardens P.T.A. and Tenant's Council, I'm on two C.A.A. [Community Action Agency] advisory boards—so now I thank Dr. Mills's program because that was the best thing that ever happened in my life. Because I can never say that I was ever a bad mother, I just didn't know when to use my common sense. I didn't know how to watch my kids to get in a state of mind where we could get along, where I was more like a friend instead of a monster that would bam on them all the time because I'm getting a call from a teacher. I just thank God for the class.

Lenny: All it takes is a second to look and feel good about yourself, to make you want to change. I don't want to look at someone like he's a bad person. All it took was a second to listen to what somebody told me to make that change in me. Because if you listen you'll understand—just look at what they're talking about. Before, we wouldn't have made it, because we didn't care.

* * *

What made this Health Realization approach work?

It would be easy to attribute the success in Modello and Homestead Gardens to the program structure—the leadership class, the parenting classes, the P.T.A. and Tenant's Council, the social work, the teacher training, the rap groups in the schools, the informal counseling, all the services offered. But the structure was not so unique. Many places have instituted similar program structures without the same effects. The structures were merely the vehicles through which to convey these understandings.

It would be easy to attribute the success to the community development process— hanging out to learn what the people wanted and helping them take the power to improve their conditions. Tom Petersen, Pam Gibson and Roger Mills were all very skilled community organizers. Yet, while the community empowerment process was indispensable for opening doors, and while it provided the glue that held the effort together, the real changes occurred within people's minds. The key difference was that these ladies learned something important about how they functioned psychologically which changed their outlook on life. Once they felt that their lives were worth something, they then wanted to change the conditions in which they lived.

It would be easy to attribute the success to Roger Mills. Yet he was anything but a charismatic leader that people would want to follow. He was merely the gentle conveyor of knowledge that people could use to change the way they thought about their lives. He was able to convey it because he lived it himself, because he had the foresight to hire staff that had the feeling. Then they naturally taught it to others in their own special ways.

At one point during the project the man in charge of resident services for the housing authority came down to Modello very excited about the results.

"We're going to do this in other housing projects! Lloyd, tell me what you did."

He quizzed Lloyd about the structure and process, the parenting groups, how often they met, how they organized the P.T.A.

Lloyd kept saying, "Look, it's not the structure. It's the feeling. It's the psychology. It's the understanding behind this that makes the difference."

"Yeah, yeah, yeah. Don't worry, I'll get my staff to do it. Just tell me what to do."

"Look, it's the training we got at the beginning," said Lloyd, trying to slow the man down. "It's what we learned for ourselves that changed us as human beings that we then shared with them."

The man left without understanding. That was the problem with trying to communicate what had happened. It was not easy for some people to comprehend. What they were saying seemed too simple; there had to be another hidden answer.

But nothing was hidden. The answer lay in simplicity itself.

Dr. Mills: The residents started to realize that what was keeping them down in life was their thoughts. See, they'd bought the con game. They'd bought the lie. They'd bought the rap that they're supposed to be poor and not be able to do any better—because they're Black, because they dropped out of school, because they started having children when they were thirteen, because they're in public housing and on welfare, because of whatever. They bought into that set of beliefs—but it's just a thought. *It's just a thought!* Everything is created and maintained via thought. That's the simplicity of it. And all they did was let go of that way of thinking, because they started to see it as beliefs programmed like a computer, as opposed to reality—not in a judgmental or guilty way or with any kind of negativity—just as a fact. If you put one crack in someone's "normal" way of thinking, what comes up in its place is common sense. That's all it is. It's a psychological vantage point. It's kind of like if you're lost in the forest and you can't find your way out, and suddenly someone lifts you up above the trees in a helicopter, and you say, "Oh I see the way out of the forest!" That's common sense. It's a higher ground that shows you the bigger picture and all the different variables that are impacting on your situation, and how to move those variables in the direction you want to go. And it's innate. Everybody has it. It's at the core of your psychological makeup. But it's something beyond that. It's the ability to see where everybody else is coming from, where they are getting stuck, and where you are.

It is so simple sometimes our minds can't comprehend it: *When people think differently about their lives, their lives change.*

The difficulty lies in helping people realize this fact. Health Realization / Psychology of Mind is in a continual evolutionary process of discovering how to better enable people to find their own way to their health.

If it still sounds too good to be true—that it is impossible to believe that such massive changes occurred in the people's lives—all one has to do is talk to anyone whose life has been touched by this approach. See the changes talking place in other housing projects and low income neighborhoods around the country where Health Realization has been put into effect, such as in the Mt. Hope housing project in the South Bronx, or in Coliseum Gardens in Oakland, or through the Glenwood-Lyndale Community Center in Minneapolis, or in its application to community policing in St. Paul, or throughout the social services agencies in Santa Clara County, California, or in many other places where Health Realization is beginning to be applied. No one has to try to convince anyone of anything. It is all there for anyone to see.

And it is only the beginning . . .

Dr. Mills: When George [Pransky] and I started out, we had no idea what was creating those changes out on Saltspring Island. That's the same thing people feel when they come to Modello or Homestead Gardens. They see the results, and you try to tell them what happened and they just get this confused look on their faces. They can't make the connection, because it's an intangible thing. It's almost a spiritual thing. What's happening is spiritual growth—via a beautiful feeling. That's the learning. The change didn't come from any specific structure or form of intervention. It came because a new feeling came into the community, a new level of consciousness. And as some parents picked it up it started to spread and spilled over into other people, and all of a sudden everybody was feeling a little better about themselves. Everybody was seeing ways to make their family environment a nicer place for their children. So the feeling changed. The level of understanding changed, and it changed in such a subtle way that a lot of times we didn't even realize it until after the fact. What happened there was truly magical and can't be explained.

"So if it's so simple," people ask, "why doesn't everyone pick this up and live this way?"

Dr. Mills: See, the problem people have in picking this up in general is that everybody has some psychological investment in their own separate realities, in their past experiences, in who they think they are, in what they think has gotten them to the point where they are now, in what we're calling "the ego." And honestly, the ego doesn't exist—it's an illusory thing too. Because it's just a self-image; it's just a bunch of thoughts. But that's the biggest barrier, because people are caught up in the importance of those thoughts and in the reality of that ego-created way of thinking that took them a lifetime to develop [laughs]. And no matter how negative it is, or how self destructive it is, they're invested in it. They think they have to hold on to it for their identity. See, people don't know their true identity. That's the problem! They think that ego-created reality is who they are, that it's their real identity and that's what they think their survival depends on. So they're going to hang on to it for dear life. But if they start to see what their true identity as a spiritual being is, as a beautiful, loving human being, as a wise person—that inner wisdom—they'd let go of that one so fast it would be unbelievable.

"How do you know that people are innately healthy?"

Dr. Mills: Look at young children. You don't see any one to two year olds with low self-esteem. In the research on "resiliency" they found that most of the kids who grow up in crazy environments or in dysfunctional families turn out okay—without interference. The majority turn out healthy. There's something in there that gets those kids through that particular experience. The researchers say there's something inside people called resiliency. But then they say, "How do we put it into kids?" And that's how they get off track. They don't see what is obvious to me in terms of their data—it's already there. They come through these terrible situations on their own without an intervention. Somehow they had it within them already. We're saying that what we found is that if you teach people that they have this natural resiliency and capacity for mental health inside them, when they get caught up in illusory process thinking, all they have to do is stop and see if they're taking those thoughts seriously. If you lose the feeling, it doesn't seem like you have it—it doesn't seem to me like I have it when I lose it—but that's the illusion at that time! It's the surface. Deep inside every human being is a loving, compassionate, wise, healthy, sane, motivated, responsible human being—every human being! Don't get caught in the surface. Because that's the illusion. *MIND* is always instantly available, as soon as we stop using our thoughts in that illusory way.

Central to the practice of Health Realization are three conditions that must be in place for its potential to have the best chance of being realized, to have a deep effect on another's life. The first is to become a mentally healthy, contented person oneself—to live in that feeling. Simply by living it, other people may appreciate what they see and want some of it for themselves.

Dr. Mills: You have to go within and find that deeper, nice feeling within yourself, and it can't be connected to anything outside. As soon as its connected to something outside, you're dependent again. You can't save anybody, honestly. The only person you can help is yourself. You can teach people how to help themselves, but it's like that old saying, "You can lead a horse to water"—but they have to drink. You can show people the way to mental health.

You can tell people in no uncertain terms how to get to mental health. There is a direct route, and you can tell people what it is. But if they don't listen, that's their free will. You've got to have infinite patience because you can't have any investment in them responding or changing. You accept people where they are. That's why we were so successful in public housing, because we just accepted people completely where they were. We just went in and were ourselves and treated them as if they were totally okay the way they were and didn't put any pressure on them to change. And if the people pick up that feeling then its easy for them to change.

The second condition is that people's mood levels have to be in a nice feeling to help them out of their negative state of mind. People can't hear anything when they're upset, so it is important to do whatever it takes to get that person in nicer state. Often it takes talking about anything but the problems at first—until they calm down enough and have a good enough rapport established for them to be able to hear.

> **Dr. Mills:** People have to pick up a feeling that there's something here that's nice, that's positive. That's why we spent so much time at Modello at the beginning just getting the feeling out there, just having fun with people, having parties, having field trips, going to the zoo, going to the beach, going to plays—because we wanted people to see that there's a nicer feeling available to them than what they were used to. So it's that feeling.

The third condition is to have listened beyond our own biases to people's underlying assumptions about life. For example, what would make someone think that child abuse is an okay thing to do? We want to listen to understand with a clear mind—until it occurs to us what is keeping them in their state and how we might reach them.

Only after these three conditions have been successfully realized do we "teach psychological facts"—teach the principles of how all people function mentally, as expressed throughout this book. And the path is always through a clear mind.

> **Dr. Mills:** That shows them the route to mental health. It is teaching basic principles of human functioning that are absolutely true—across culture, gender, socioeconomic lines, everything. It is teaching impersonal facts about their psychological functioning

in a way that points them toward a higher level of mental health—that every human being functions exactly the same way relative to *Mind, Thought, and Consciousness*. And you teach them the futility of looking into their past for the answers—that's where the problems came from, but the past doesn't hold any answers. The answers come now via the realization that the past now is only a thought—it's only a set of thoughts carried through time. Then, assess their ability to realize and use these psychological facts, to function on their own in a more responsible, independent way. They see things in a new way. They see that they weren't seeing things right. They see how these facts about their psychological functioning affect their lives day-to-day. If you start to understand these psychological facts you become your own best psychologist, because you learn from everything that happens. Every time you go down, or get into a fight with your spouse, later on you say, "Oh, I see what happened there," and you learn something—if you have the honesty to get off of your "position." And don't be afraid to tell stories, to give people hope.

Thus, the idea is to point people in the direction of three principles that, together, create our experience of life. *Mind*, the source, the life force, the intelligence behind life. *Thought*, the power to create (via mental activity). *Consciousness*, the power to experience. And we can only experience what our thoughts create. But since it would be too unrealistic to go into a community talking Mind, Consciousness and Thought, Roger Mills had to help them see the principles in action in their own lives by whatever means necessary, in hopes that they would pick it up.

So what makes the difference between those who do pick this up and those who don't?

Dr. Mills: I just think that they have to want something better. That's the only readiness. I just think that you have to want some change in your life. You have to want things to be nicer and then be caught in a moment of openness when your radar is not up and hope something gets through under that early warning system and hits home. I think people have to want their life to be nicer—want something nicer than what they have. And they have to want to be willing to do that without knowing what that's going to be like. A lot of people say they want change, but they're not willing to let go of a lot of their beliefs about life or about themselves or about their spouse or about how the world is—and that takes some courage. People are living that reality, and it seems real to them and right to them, and they've spent most of their life maintaining that point of view or that way of looking at things, maintaining that they're right and justifying it and finding evidence that it's true and that other people are wrong. People have to be willing to change their thinking. A lot of people want to change, but they don't want to change how they think [laughs]. They want a better marriage, but they don't want to stop seeing their spouse as that rotten s.o.b. that's the cause of all their problems. "Given that my spouse is a rotten s.o.b. that's causing all my problems, how can I make my marriage better? [laughs]. I think that people have to let go, to see that there's something about their thinking that has to shift. It's like Archie Bunker. If I had told Archie Bunker that his problems had something to do with his thinking—in the form of all his prejudices and all—he would think I was nuts. He would probably not be able to look at that at all. And I don't think people are willing to change unless they're willing to look at that.

So how would he work with Archie Bunker?

Dr. Mills: [laughs] Well, I'd do with him like I would do with anyone else. I would try to get rapport. I'd get to know him. I would hang out with him. I would try to feel comfortable with him on his terms, like I did at Modello. I had to get into their reality, and hang out with them in their world, and feel comfortable in their world, start to understand it, and see that it was innocent, and that people were doing the best they could being that way. Again, just drop hints every once in a while—and play hard to get. Have you ever noticed that when you're in somebody's face trying to convince them of something, they're harder to convince? And if you play hard to get then they come and they want it.

Even so, it is sometimes still hard to imagine that it could have such an impact.

Dr. Mills: When we first got the grant funded a lot of people said, "It will never work. Their circumstances are too strong against them. You can't raise people's self-esteem and well-being in that kind of setting—until you change the circumstances." But what happened is, once their self-esteem went up, their level of well-being, their level of common sense, then they wanted something better, and they saw the possibility of it, so they started to take charge of the circumstances. As soon as people started letting go of their attachment to their negative or alienated beliefs, their natural propensity to function in a healthy way came to the surface. The first year we started working with thirty or so families. When those people started to change, their buoyancy, their positive movement toward a higher state of mental health spilled over to other people, and the whole community started to rise. They've left that world where they're in danger and their kids are in danger. They've left that world! You just step out of that world. Life is levels of understanding within our very consciousness. And every time your level rises you walk into a whole new world.

And it is only the beginning . . .

Epilogue: The Hurricane

Andrew roared through the projects as if strapped to the front of a runaway train, racing out of control at 145 miles an hour. The fastest Nolan Ryan ever pitched a baseball was 103. Perspective.

As the raging wind blew down everything that wasn't nailed down and pried up everything that was, cutting a swath of devastation thirty miles wide and sixty miles deep, there, rising above the rubble, stark and dark against the oncoming dawn and pounding rain, stood the housing projects of poured solid concrete: Modello and Homestead Gardens.

Yet, even Modello couldn't withstand the next month of solid rain that came streaming through its weakened roofs and ceilings. As the water poured in, the people poured out, a ghost project left behind.

Walking carefully among the deserted, broken buildings it was hard to imagine that Modello was once a vital and thriving community, especially one that had undergone such massive change.

What had happened to the people?

* * *

Lisa had moved out of Modello nearly three years earlier to improve her life and give her children a better chance. She had found the strength to overcome. Then came Andrew.

It began around 2:15 that morning as a horrifying wind struck a heavy blow to the midsection of the house. Until that moment they didn't know if they'd be hit with its full force. No mistaking it now. The eye of the storm was closing in. They huddled together in the master bedroom—Lisa, her man, their twelve year old son and nine and five year old daughters. To try to protect them they covered the children with pillows and comforters. Where could they find shelter?

Lisa's eyes landed on their big walk-in closet, the only safe place in sight. Before she could direct everyone there, she realized she forgot something and hustled after it. The moment she stepped into the living room, BOOM!—the windows exploded into a million pieces. Lisa hit the floor, as she had so many times before in Modello gunfire. Glass whizzed by her head as if the whole front of the house had burst.

Over the wind's roar she yelled, "Get to the closet!".

Huddled in the closet they tried to ride it out, scared beyond belief. They heard objects breaking in the house. They heard water gushing and the roof peeling up. They had to find out what was going on.

"Whatever happens," Lisa said firmly to the kids, "don't come out!"

The search was futile. Chaos reigned. They could see nothing and had to scurry back to the closet, doing their best to settle in, so scared they didn't realize their feet were covered by two inches of water.

Her son yelped, "I smell salt water!"

Panic set in. Did this mean flooding from the ocean, usually seven miles away?

Huddled en masse they moved out of the closet, eyes darting about for a place to hide. Window shutters flapped and banged against the walls. Lisa tried to clear her head. She remembered the ladder to the attic, but wind seemed to blow through the house as if there were no walls. Water sprayed from the roof and ceiling. They squinted through the darkness, wind, and spray.

"Oh my God!"

They could see right through the ceiling to the roof, and part of the roof was gone. The attic was out! If the water rose higher there would be nowhere to climb.

So they ran to another room, but the room started shaking and glass started breaking. They ran to the bathroom, but jagged glass lay all over the floor. All over the house they darted, searching for safety. What about the utility room! It had no windows.

Try as they might they couldn't reach it! The whole front of the house—the large front windows—had completely blown out. Gone too were the sliding glass doors at the back end of the house. The storm was in their house!

As quickly as it started it calmed. Everything stopped. The eye looked down upon them. A reddish glow encircled all.

Feverishly they tried to nail back the boards. A feeble, rushed job. If they could only keep out some of that wind . . .

WHOOOOOOSHHH, BAMMMM!!! The wind suddenly roared back with such ferocity it ripped away their work in one second, laughing at them, smashing what was left of the back of the house, blasting through the glass sliding doors and hurling half their furniture into the back yard.

They couldn't make it to the utility room.

"BACK TO THE CLOSET!!!" No getting out now.

Sitting on the closet floor, they pushed their feet hard against the door and wrapped up the kids, shivering, dripping wet. Drained. They rode it out in the pitch blackness, listening as best they could to a portable radio. They had no flashlight batteries, for once everyone realized the storm might hit with full force people panicked and "the stores went wild." Because of the wind they couldn't light candles, so for hours upon hours they sat in the darkness. Nothing else could be done.

Into Lisa's mind popped the words, "Stay calm!" Intuitively she knew if she panicked the kids would panic too and maybe run out and get hurt. She needed to be calm so they would stick together and watch out for each other. Then the floor started shaking so badly they wondered whether an earthquake too had struck.

Lisa prayed to herself, "Dear God, let me make it, because if something happens to me, then all this will come down on top of the kids, and nobody will be able to get them out. Please God, let my children survive!"

Lisa knew she had to survive to save them, but she honestly didn't think she or anyone else would live to see daylight.

"If something does happen to me," she continued, "please let someone find my kids." They would go berserk.. She pictured them among all the clutter, with no one to watch over them. How would they survive?

Finally the wind died to normal storm-strength. Daylight. The closet door creaked open. They staggered out. Half their house was gone. Water everywhere. Everything ruined.

Lisa stared at the disaster in disbelief, then looked at her kids. They'd made it! After struggling all those years in Modello she had been so proud to live in this house. Now only half of it stood. Everything they owned had been wrecked. But they were alive! It was all that mattered.

They walked out onto what was left of the streets. Total devastation. Nothing recognizable. They couldn't fathom it. Nearly all the houses were half gone.

They honestly didn't think they would find any survivors. Lisa knocked on the door of one of her neighbors. No answer. She kept knocking. For five or six minutes she knocked without response. About to give up, someone appeared, completely shaken. At many houses it was the same. Everyone was so afraid, hiding in closets, under furniture, anywhere they could find—so panicked they didn't realize someone was trying to get to them. The storm seemed to break everything and everyone apart.

Lisa never thought about her newfound state of mind that had undoubtedly helped her through. It had kicked in automatically. People—other families—seemed to be falling apart around her. Lisa felt grateful that everyone was safe.

"There's no use in crying," she said to her children in a soft, gentle voice, conveying every ounce of her love ."There's no use in getting depressed, because if you do, that's not going to change anything."

Lisa had already learned that lesson. Before this storm her life had become so beautiful. This was just another stepping stone. Whenever she tried to accomplish anything in her life, something always reared its head saying, "No, no! You're not going to do this." But just as she'd learned to lick the rest, she wasn't going to let something like a monster storm or losing all her material possessions get in the way. She had life! She had her family. What could be more special than that? This was just one more stepping stone.

* * *

When the storm hit Cicely was in Perrine with her mother and the entire family—all fifteen of them stuffed into one bedroom. Miraculously, it was the only room in the house spared. In the living room, kitchen, other bedroom, and bathroom they could look up to the sky. Oddly, it seemed that in everyone's damaged home one room was spared.

As with her friend Lisa, after the storm Cicely went out to help others. She witnessed extreme hardship, so many lives damaged. People were taking it very hard. Many were saying, "There's no hope."

No one could blame them. After the storm it rained so much the roofs in the projects began to cave—everyone's furniture and clothing ruined. As Cicely said, "It was real rough there for a while."

Cicely told her people, "You got to keep on hanging in there, you know? When you're going through a hard, hard task, you just hang in there, and there's a blessing on the end."

Cicely's smile twinkled. She'd lost her teeth in the storm, but it didn't matter. Her warmth could have thawed glaciers. "When you're going through something that's hard," she repeated to everyone, "you just got to hang in there. There's a blessing on the end."

Cicely had already learned that lesson. Only a few short years ago her life had been about as hard as it could get, and she had overcome.

* * *

Thelma still lived in Modello in her ground-level apartment when the storm hit. The concrete walls had seemed pretty solid against the wind—until the roof blew off the upstairs apartment and rain began pouring in.

Soon they were standing in water to mid-thigh.

At 9:30 that morning she and her nine remaining kids scooted upstairs. Though the storm was over they were too scared to come out. Earlier, they thought it had ended and came out to see the sky lit up a spooky red. Then they'd been blasted "like you couldn't believe." Nobody had told her about any "eye."

They weren't about to take another chance. Around 11:00 they peeked out and saw others stumbling around outside. It must be safe to come out now.

As she walked onto her porch to witness the damage Thelma's jaw hung open. The entire roof—gone! Half the trailer park across the street now lay in twisted, mangled remains in the middle of Modello; the other half lay across what used to be a field but now looked more like ocean.

"Ooooh, I just can't believe it!" she said aloud to no one.

In a flash of fear her thoughts shifted to her oldest daughter who not long ago had moved into her own house a few blocks away. Thelma stumbled over the rubble in her path. When she saw her daughter's house, her heart sank to the depths of her soul. Nothing was left but the steps! Literally nothing was left standing in her whole house. Did she survive? Did she make it? How could she have?

But she did!

"The only thing I could find in there to hold on to was the couch," said her daughter. "I put that couch on top of me, and just held on for dear life. Mama, I was so scared!"

In disbelief Thelma stared at what was left of the couch. Her daughter had held onto that couch so tight she could see her hand print all the way through it. Thelma began to pray. She was in a state of shock.

The shock turned into a daze, and the days merged into weeks. For a week they went without water or anything cold to drink. The second week they somehow got some water and ice. But she had no way to cook food, so she dug two holes outside and got a little two-burner stove and a small gas tank to cook and heat water to bathe the kids.

FEMA arrived to inspect the house and about a week later sent Thelma a check for $2500. She was so grateful for FEMA! "If it wasn't for FEMA," she said, "I don't know what I would have done." Immediately she cashed it and picked up some bleach and a generator to start the washing machine. Her kids' clothes were stacked all the way to the ceiling. Most were ruined and couldn't be saved.

Still in a daze she trudged to the Red Cross where she received a voucher to buy clothes. With such a large family it didn't go very far.

She said to her kids, "The only thing we can get now is some coats, because it's going to be cold."

With the little that remained she bought some pants for her kids and sheets for the beds.

For a month she felt as if her spirit had left her. "I didn't know if I was going or coming." Thelma shut herself off from people. Andrew stole precious things from her that she'd had for years, since her oldest girl was born. It made her cry. Nothing could replace what Andrew took.

When she had to go out and saw the everyone's living conditions, it penetrated her heart.

Yet, little by little she began visiting and talking with her neighbors and slowly began to come back to herself.

"You know," she realized, "it's a blessing just by us being here, "because a lot of people, they died behind this. It's a big blessing that we're still alive."

After the storm it rained for an entire month. The Modello roofs had been destroyed and leaked so badly everyone had to be moved out. Thelma received two tiny trailers for her nine kids.

"For a moment there," she confided, "I had forgot about my psychology. I had put it aside. Then I had to go back and pick it back up. I realized that I needed it—for support for the kids mostly—because it really shook the kids up."

Gradually she began to remember what she had learned. "I had to ease that psychology on them." She knew she needed to take their minds off the disaster. So she picked up some videos from Blockbuster which miraculously hadn't been completely destroyed in the storm. She brought them to McDonalds—which was offering free food—where they ate and played on the little rides. Then she picked up some games and cards, and they watched more movies. They hung out together and tried to enjoy pleasant moments.

The rain stopped for only four days. Each time the rains came the kids would get scared and holler, "Here come Andrew! Here come Andrew!"

"That told me I had to go back and pick up my psychology," she said. She couldn't let her kids keep thinking this way. They thought the rain meant another huge storm.

"It's not any storm," she reassured them. "It's just rain."

She had to make them feel secure again.

Some weeks later, while taking her kids shopping, her seven year old said, "Momma?

"What?"

"I hate Andrew."

"What do you mean, baby? Why?"

"Because Andrew don't do nothing but just kills people. I hate Andrew!"

It suddenly struck Thelma that her little boy thought that Andrew was a man.

"Look, Andrew is a name. It's the name of it. Andrew is a wind, baby. And if you would have been in the way of that wind that night, Andrew would have taken you up along with it," she laughed. "Andrew is just a name, honey. Andrew is not a human being like we are."

"He's not no man?"

Thelma's heart went out to him. "No. Andrew is wind, baby—off the ocean."

Later, Thelma said, "So I got them back like that. It worked out all right. They're doing fine now."

* * *

Patty had just arrived back in Florida from a visit out of state when the storm hit. She hadn't yet reached her home in Leisure City where since leaving Modello she'd lived for two years. She hadn't time to prepare.

Not that it would have helped. They lost everything. All that remained of her house was the foundation.

Luckily, she'd left her children at her mother's, and they were all right. If they had stayed home no doubt they would have all been dead. Patty's father, on disability because his leg had been amputated, was living with them. It would have been a mess. Patty stood in the rubble, staring where his bedroom used to be. All the walls had blown down. Nobody could have survived.

Patty felt raped! Nothing she had learned about patience helped her now. It grabbed her and wouldn't let go.

But as the weeks wore on and she had time to reflect, she realized, "Thank God we weren't in there!" The shock began to dissipate.

She began to talk with her kids to help them understand. They could have been dead, and they weren't. That was a blessing. It would all get better.

Eventually it did. It took a couple of months before she felt like her old self again.

* * *

Rumor had it that Rosie's roof had fallen in the day after the storm and badly hurt her twelve year old son. Her old friends were worried about her.

Her friend, Jolene said that Rosie had told her, "I don't know how Psychology of Mind can help me with this."

Rosie then paused for a while and said, "Yes I do." she nodded. "Yes I do."

* * *

After the storm, compared with those who had not been touched by Psychology of Mind, these ladies were doing great.

Lisa: I see some that I thought were in a bad state before—they're blown away now. I look at myself, I look at Cicely and some of the other ladies, and we're still there. And people are saying, "How can you be so happy?" My house looks like a storage room, sure, but I'm, like, so what? I've got a roof over my head. My kids are being fed. One day maybe it'll get fixed up if we ever get the insurance straight. But other than that, I don't need this gorgeous, beautiful house to survive. I can survive just fine like this. But some people are just blown away. I know a lot of families in Modello that I knew that were already in a bad situation. I know, being in these little tiny, small trailers, it just has to be rough. I used to pass by these ladies and it was always, "Hi, Miss Lisa!"— always glad to see me, because even though I left Modello and I've been gone three years I'm still the same old Lisa. And now their heads are like this [bowed down], and you have to really go to them a couple of times and make some kind of funny wisecrack or something to get them going. I know it's got to be hard. And it's got to be terrible for the children.

But what I really saw when the hurricane came—you're in your daily routine and you think most people really don't care, but it was a shock to me when all these people volunteered, and they donated. It was unbelievable. Every time I received something I felt like just crying. It was absolutely beautiful. It really restored your faith in human nature, it really did, because you always read so many things in the newspaper. It was, like, all at once when the storm happened people just let all those other things go, and they were just there. It was absolutely amazing!

* * *

Hurricane Andrew, however, had changed Modello forever. It would never be the same. Until Modello could be repaired FEMA stuffed the residents into tiny, look-alike, sardine-like trailers, row upon row in a makeshift trailer park catycornered across from Modello. Many residents moved out. Others moved in. Even in the Homestead Gardens housing project, which emerged from the storm relatively unscathed, relatives and friends whose homes had been wrecked moved in and now shared the units. The dynamic changed. It would be impossible to know whether there would have been lasting impact beyond the four to five years it had already lasted.

The only thing one could do was trace the lives of the people—and the lives of the people who had been touched by Psychology of Mind/Health Realization continue to soar like eagles.

Notes and Bibliography

Note: The author initially had each reference cited within the text of the manuscript. Because of the type of book it is, the decision was made not to clutter the pages with innumerable footnotes. Instead, all sources used in this book are listed below in alphabetical order by author or taped interview. For the reader interested in more detailed reference information she or he may write to Jack Pransky, NEHRI, RR2, Pransky Rd., Cabot, VT 05647 to request the specific citation in question. Further, all direct quotes in the book—in fact all information in the book—came from either taped interviews with the sources of the quotes, or with someone who attributed the quote to the other person in the course of a dialogue—or they came from a videotape, report, newspaper or magazine article.

Taped, personal interviews held in December, 1992, December, 1993, and January 1996 with the following people:
Cicely (name changed)
Lenny (name changed)
Lisa (name changed)
Patty (name changed)
Ruby (name changed)
Thelma (name changed)
Lloyd Fields
Cynthia Stennis
Pam Gibson
Roger Mills
Judge Tom Petersen
Sam MacKinnon
Rita Shuford
Collen del Terzo
Irene Edminster
Maria Garcia
Janyce Waters
Police Chief Ivy
Police Officer Tom Cheney
Dr. Witty, School Principal

Resource and reference materials used for story background:

Asayesii, G.(1985, July 3). 1-Man Task Force Tackles Inner-City Woes: Novel effort seeks to help school kids. *The Miami Herald.*

Circuit Court of the Eleventh Judicial Circuit of Florida in and for the County of Dade (1984, July 17). Final report of the grand jury. Miami, FL.

Dade Schools and Neighborhoods Consortium Report (January, 1987). Looking Beyond the Schoolyard. Miami, Fl: Schools and Neighborhood Intervention Consortium, Joseph Caleb Center.

Due, T. (date unknown). Program Boosts Parent's Spirits. *The Miami Herald.*

Fernandez-Varela, F., Stokes, W.M., and Thomas, R. (1988, October 18). Bridges to the Future: A Neighborhood in Transition. United Way South Dade Action Committee and United Way Modello Task Force.

Informed Familes Parenting Series (videotape) (1991). Miami, Fl: Informed Families

May, P. (1987, June 21). New Market Offers New Hope for Modello housing project. *The Miami Herald.*

Mehalik, L. (1987, March 13). Project Residents Want to Stand on Their Own Feet. *South Dade News Leader.*

Mills, R.C. (1991). A New Understanding of Self: Affect, State of Mind, Self-Understanding, and Intrinsic Motivation. *Journal of experimental education.* 60: 67-81.

Mills, R.C. (1991). The Psychology of Mind Applied to Substance Abuse, Dropout, and Delinquency Prevention: Modello - Homestead Gardens Intervention Project. Paper presented to the Florida Alcohol and Drug Abuse Association Annual Conference, Orlando, FL.

Mills, R.C. (1988). The Modello Early Intervention Project: A Model for Prevention; A demonstration project based on Psychology of Mind. Presented at the Seventh Annual Conference on the Psychology of Mind. Miami, FL.

Mills, R.C. (undated). Applications of Psychological Approaches in Doing Community Development Work in Low-Income Communities: Community Psychology and Community Work. R.C. Mills & Associates.

Mills, R.C. (undated). Community Empowerment: Leadership and Collaboration. The keys to community and personal revitalization. R.C. MIlls & Associates

Mills, R.C. and Lesser, M. (undated). Some Facts about Our Moods and Our Children's Behavior (booklet). Miami-Dade Community College, South Campus.

Mills, R.C. (undated). What Are We Learning about Self and Intrinsic Motivation. R.C. Mills & Associates.

Mills, R.C., Dunham, R. & Alpert, G. (1988). Working with High-Risk in Prevention and Early Intervention Programs: Towards a Comprehensive Wellness Model. *Adolescence.* 23:643-660.

Modello Today Show and Modello Conference (videotape) (1990). Minneapolis, MN: Grant Booker Video Co.

Modello Early Intervention Program (videotape)(1991). Minneapolis, MN: Grant Booker Video Co.

Modello Early Intervention Program. Quarterly Progress Reports to Bureau of Criminal Justice Planning and Assistance (1988-1990)

Peck, N. Law, A. & Mills, R.C. (1987). Dropout Prevention: What We Have Learned. Eric Clearinghouse.

Reno, J. (1989, May 3). Letter to Dade County Manager, Metro Dade County and Assistant County Manager, Dade County HUD.

Rowe, S. (1990, May 10). Revolution from Within: With the Help of Determined Residents, South Dade's Housing Projects are Changing—for the Better. News Fi. *The Miami Herald.*

Stewart, Barbara (1987, October 4). Mission Implausible. *Florida Magazine. The Orlando Sentinel.*

Today Show. NBC (1990, April). Segment aired re: Modello/ Homestead Gardens Intervention Program.

Videotape (1990). Psychology of Mind Annual Conference. Minneapolis, MN (unpublished).

Viglucci, A. (1987, November 12). Reno Wants Task Force on Social Services. *Miami Herald.*

Other works cited in this book:

Bailey, J. (1990). *The Serenity Principle*. San Francisco: Harper & Row.

Banks, S. (1998). *The Missing Link*. Vancouver, BC: Lone Pine Publishers.

Carlson, R. (1997). *Don't Sweat the Small Stuff*. New York: Hyperion.

Carlson, R. and Bailey, J. (1997). *Slowing Down to the Speed of Life*. San Francisco: HarperCollins.

Kammeraad-Campbell, S. (1989). *Teacher: Dennis Littky's Fight for a Better School*. New York: Plume.

Mills, R.C. (1995). *Realizing Mental Health*. New York, NY: Sulzburger & Graham

Mills, R.C., Belvens, K., and Pransky, G. (1979). Toward a New Psychology. Unpublished manuscript.

Nelsen, J.(1986). *Understanding: Eliminating Stress and Finding Serenity in Life and Relationships*. Rocklin, CA: Prima

Pransky, J. (1991). *Prevention: The Critical Need*. Cabot, VT: NEHRI Publications. (Formerly published Springfield, MO: Burrell Foundation and Burlington, VT: Paradigm Press.)

Pransky, G. (1998). *The Renaissance of Psychology*. New York: Sulzberger & Graham.

Pransky, G. (1990). *The Relationship Handbook* (formerly called, Divorce is Not the Answer).Blue Ridge Summit, PA: TAB Books.

Suarez, R., Mills, R.C., & Stewart, D. (1987). *Sanity, Insanity, and Common Sense*. New York: Fawcett Columbine.

Another recommended book:

Pransky, J. (1998). *Parenting from the Heart*. Cabot, VT: NEHRI Publications.

For additional resources on Health Realization/ Psychology of Mind, visit the Psychology of Mind Resource Center Web Site at *www.psychologyofmind.com* or call 1-800-481-7639 in the U.S. or 61 8 9274-8877 in Australia.

Other Books by Jack Pransky ⟶

Other Books by Jack Pransky

PREVENTION: THE CRITICAL NEED

This groundbreaking book is the first to translate prevention research into practical application for practitioners in the field. It defines the wide-ranging, still young field of prevention and explores the factors that contribute to and mediate a host of problem behaviors such as substance abuse, violence, child abuse and neglect, delinquency, teenage pregnancy, teenage suicide, mental-emotional problems, welfare dependency. It presents a clear framework in easy-to-understand terms that delineates research-based programs and elements that constitute effective prevention practice—from prenatal care to early childhood education to parent education to school improvement to youth development to community change to work-based prevention and much more. The book presents extensive interviews with top preventionists, including Dr. George Albee and Ben Cohen of Ben & Jerry's Ice Cream. Some other topics covered are community development, planning for desired results, practical evaluation, marketing prevention, prevention policy development, spirituality as prevention, and more. This book has also been used as a textbook in many colleges and universities. It is "resiliency" in action.

"Jack Pransky . . . has produced a monumental book, not only in size, but in content. I commend it to anyone who is genuinely concerned about doing something effective about preventing social problems and mental disorders in this country . . . This book will establish him among the stars of public health and primary prevention."

George Albee, Ph.D.

"Jack Pransky . . . has compiled for the first time a valuable description of prevention work in all its diversity . . . Prevention: The Critical Need deserves to be widely read."

William A. Lofquist, Development Associates

Burrell Foundation/Paradigm Press (1991).
Now in its third printing through NEHRI Publications.

PARENTING FROM THE HEART

Just when you thought you'd heard it all, here is a new and different, refreshing approach to parenting that makes it a pleasure to raise children. Parenting from the Heart cuts through to the essence of parenting to focus on what lies behind parenting techniques so parents won't have to rely on them. This is the Health Realization approach to parenting. It is a warm, easy-to-understand, down-to-earth, simple but effective approach that prevents problems in young people and builds resilience. Yet it presents the opposite of most other parenting books and courses where parents are expected to put a host of techniques into practice and know the "right" thing to do in any given situation. Instead, this book points parents to their own hearts and common sense. Topic include: living in an environment of love and positive feelings; innate health and common sense; we are what we think; states of mind/moods; what problem behavior is; disengagement ~ tapping into common sense to guide interactions; deep listening; teaching kids what they need to learn; and setting limits and discipline. A must resource for any complete parenting bookshelf.

"Jack Pransky demonstrates clearly how every parent can access the wisdom and perspective needed to raise healthy, happy, and even wise children—a true breakthrough in the field of parenting . . ."

Roger C. Mills, Ph.D. author, *Realizing Mental Health*

Foreword by H. Stephen Glenn, author of *Raising Self-Reliant Children in a Self-Indulgent World, Developing Capable People,* and coauthor of *Positive Discipline A-Z*

How to Order:

Copies may be ordered from NEHRI Publications, NorthEast Health Realization Institute, RR 2 Pransky Rd, Cabot, VT 05647 ~ 802-563-2730. Quantity discounts are available.

For information on lectures, seminars, workshops, courses or trainings with Jack Pransky, call (802) 563-2730.

Jack Pransky is Director of the Northeast Health Realization Institute. He authored the books, *Parenting from the Heart* (1997) and *Prevention: The Critical Need* (1991), which received critical acclaim for its down-to-earth, practical approach to prevention. He also co-authored the Espaler* Prevention/Health Realization Curriculum for middle school students (in press). Pransky has worked in the field of prevention since 1968 in a wide variety of capacities and now provides consultation and training throughout the U.S. and beyond. He is also co-founder/director of the nonprofit consulting organization, Prevention Unlimited which created the Spirituality of Prevention Conference. Jack now specializes in applying Health Realization to prevention and resiliency.

---

* = relapse in reverse